IDENTITY,
PERSONAL IDENTITY,
AND THE SELF

IDENTITY,
PERSONAL IDENTITY,
AND THE SELF

JOHN PERRY

Hackett Publishing Company, Inc.
Indianapolis/Cambridge

06 05 04 03 02   1 2 3 4 5 6 7

For further information, please address:

Hackett Publishing Company, Inc.
P. O. Box 44937
Indianapolis, Indiana 46244–0937

www.hackettpublishing.com

Cover and interior design by Abigail Coyle

Library of Congress Cataloging-in-Publication Data

Perry, John, 1943–
        Identity, personal identity, and the self / John Perry.
            p. cm.
        Includes bibliographical references and index.
        ISBN 0-87220-521-5 (cloth) — ISBN 0-87220-520-7 (paper)
            1. Philosophical anthropology.   2. Identity (Philosophical
concept)   3. Self (Philosophy)   I. Title.

    BD450 .P46216 2002
    128—dc21
                                                            2001051551

The paper used in this publication meets the minimum requirements of
American National Standard for Information Sciences—Permanence of
Paper for Printed Library Materials, ANSI Z39.48–1984.

Contents

Introduction

A man once called an economics department in which a friend of mine worked and asked exactly how one went about receiving a Nobel Prize. My friend replied that one first has to do something of significance; had the caller done that? "I've made a great discovery" was the answer. "*It's just paper!*" The caller, it turned out, was standing outside of a bar in a pay phone booth, fondling a twenty-dollar bill, rubbing it with his fingers, and staring at it in amazement and shock. "It's just paper," he repeated. "It's not worth a damn thing. Everyone just *thinks* that it is."

The man had indeed made a great discovery, but unfortunately he had been anticipated by a number of others, so a Nobel Prize was not in his future. He had made the discovery that paper money is intrinsically worthless, just paper. It is only the fact that people accept it in trade that allows it to function as if it were worth anything.

The man had made the first step on the way to a pinnacle of a triad that represents the vaguely Hegelian structure of many philosophical problems. First there is the thesis: the set of prereflective but often deeply held assumptions people have about important things, such as knowledge, identity, personal identity, freedom—and money. Then there is the antithesis: the doctrine that because some of these assumptions are false or at least groundless, we do not have the important thing. There is no knowledge, because nothing meets the prereflective standard; there is no identity, because things change; there is no personal identity, because there is no soul; and there is no freedom, because all is determined. And money is worthless, for even the purest gold is only of use as money because people accept it as such.

Did our would-be Nobel Laureate just chuck his twenties in the nearest dumpster? If he did, he was surely back looking for them when he sobered up—probably sooner than that. On his return to the dumpster, he would have taken the third step in our Hegelian triad; he would have reached the synthesis: perhaps the value of money is a bit of a fraud on us all; maybe it is intrinsically worthless; and so forth. But still, it is damn useful—definitely worth having. There is nothing around that's better for buying things, that's for sure. And, come to think of it, what else could it mean to be worth something?

There is something about practical things that knocks us off our philosophical high horses. Perhaps Heraclitus really thought he couldn't step in the same river twice. Perhaps he even received tenure for that contribution to philosophy. But suppose some other ancient had claimed to have as much right as Heraclitus did to an ox Heraclitus had bought, on the grounds that since the animal had changed, it wasn't the same one he had bought and so was up for grabs. Heraclitus would have quickly come up with some ersatz, watered-down version of identity of practical value for dealing with property rights, oxen, lyres, vineyards, and the like. And then he might have wondered if that watered-down vulgar sense of identity might be a considerably more valuable concept than a pure and philosophical sort of identity that nothing has.

The more abstract and philosophical the issue, the longer we seem to stay astride of our high horses, and even more so when the cherished beliefs intersect with religious creeds and cultural values that shape our lives. Personal identity is a concept more central than any that can be imagined. The philosopher John Locke set in motion a process of accumulating insights, however, that has made the tumble all but inevitable for the student of personal identity. It seems appropriate to personal identity, the relation each of us has with our earlier selves and later selves-to-be, that it consist in some perfectly clear, sharply bounded, nonconventional, and intrinsic relationship. We seem to ourselves to be of basic and important things, and the identity of basic and important things should not be matters for the conventions of language and the vagaries of commerce or even the Supreme Court to decide. Who I am, whether I am the same as a person who did something in the past, ought to be clear, given the facts. And it ought not to depend on distant things, and it ought not to depend on things that have no relevance to whether I deserve reward or punishment for the act in question. And the nature of this personal identity ought to give me a clear, distinct, compelling, and special reason to act on behalf of the person I will be, a different sort of reason than I have to act on behalf of others—not necessarily stronger or better but completely different.

Personal identity does not meet this high standard. Perhaps a few drinks might be relied on to get us from thesis to antithesis, but since Locke this sense is usually provoked by "puzzle cases"—cases in which the issue of personal identity is not clear, and repeated theoretical attempts to make it clear all seem to reveal that the deciding issues will not be intrinsic in any sense of that vague but profound philosophical notion.

Between the time, in the late sixties, when the first of these essays appeared and the present time, early in the new century, when the last were written, a sort of stern prohibition movement against puzzle cases was mounted by Kathleen Wilkes (1988). Wilkes makes a persuasive case that the method can be abused and that there are plenty of interesting things to think about that come up with real people. Still, if one thinks of puzzle cases in philosophy as tools for knocking concepts off their high horses, rather than as some kind of attempt to do science without experiment, they can be quite useful. Philosophical puzzle cases are an instance of the simplest and most powerful of our methods of inquiry, the method of differences, applied to the most interesting of human problems. The method can be abused, as can food, sleep, drink, and sex. As in those cases, even when abused it has its rewards.[1]

These puzzle cases provoke in us a sense of disappointment; personal identity doesn't seem capable of resting on so august, eternal, and clear principles as would seem appropriate. The antithesis is not a pretty place. To deny the reality of or the importance of our identity seems self-defeating at best, psychotic at worst.

It is important, then, to reach the summit, the synthesis, a philosophical point of view that allows us to keep our sense of identity, and to appreciate its importance without being wedded to a picture of it that is false or incoherent. How do we get there?

I think of these essays as a record of a fight to reach the synthesis, to get some sort of philosophical grip on the disappointingly contingent,

---

[1] See Unger (1990) for a defense of the method and interesting applications of it, including what strikes me as a rewarding if wearing overuse of the method; Unger puts demands on his own sense of identity in the light of elaborate puzzle cases to the point of engaging in self-abuse. For another thoughtful defense of thought-experiments, see Cohnitz, forthcoming.

extrinsic, conditioned, vague, and ultimately somewhat unprincipled nature of my own identity and everyone else's. I'm hoping for something a step beyond Hume's recommended method, in similar circumstances, of sloth and indifference.

The first step is to become clear about the nature of identity. That is the topic of the first section of this book. The first two papers deal with one of many important phenomena that Peter Geach was largely responsible for bringing to the attention of philosophers. I call this phenomenon the *relativity of individuation;* I distinguish the phenomenon from Geach's account of or explanation for it, which he called the *relativity of identity.* In these essays, I reject Geach's relativity-of-identity thesis and suggest a different account of the relativity of individuation. On my account it is not that there are different kinds of identity, but that there are different ways of putting phenomena into packages that count as things, that account for the relativity of questions of identity to the sorts of things being considered. The positive part of this account was used in the third essay, "Can the Self Divide?" to deal with the case of fission, when one thing or person splits into two. The puzzling case in question involved persons, so this essay might also fit into the next section. But I think the crucial issues involve identity, so I have included it in the first section. The fourth essay was written for this volume, or perhaps I should say was finished for this volume, since some of the ideas go back to my dissertation of 1968, and many expand on points made or suggested in "Can the Self Divide?" It presents my view in a systematic way and develops some new ideas.

The second section of the book contains papers on personal identity. My view is basically sympathetic to the Lockean idea of analyzing personal identity in terms of memory. In essay 5 I argue that this leads us away from a "logical construction" theory of the self towards a causal theory of personal identity and an "inferred entity" theory of the self. Essay 6 is a critique of Williams's critique of the memory theory in his "The Self and the Future" and elsewhere; essay 8 is a survey of the important versions of and critiques of the memory theory from Locke to Shoemaker and Parfit.

The older essays in sections I and II were once intended to serve as the basis for a coherent book on personal identity. During my sabbatical in 1975–76, I tried to write such a book but failed. I did some work on identity and personal identity. Essays 5 and 7 are based on sections of this book. My *Dialogue on Personal Identity and Immortality* was also written during that year. But in working on the intended book I became bogged down in problems connected with self-knowledge. The main problem was that I didn't know the first thing about self-knowledge—what I meant when I used the word "I" to express it. I published two papers on this topic: "Frege on Demonstratives" and "The Problem of the Essential Indexical." Various issues and ideas in the philosophy of mind and language connected with these efforts dominated my philosophical work for the next fifteen years, in what time remained during long stints as chair of the Department of Philosophy and then as director of the Center for the Study of Language and Information at Stanford University. Most of the substantial papers written during this period are collected in *The Problem of the Essential Indexical* (2000). I think the results of these investigations are extremely relevant to a number of philosophical problems, including consciousness (see *Knowledge, Possibility, and Consciousness* [2001a]) and personal identity.

I think I am now beginning to understand how all of this fits together. This book attempts to give a bit of renewed life to some old papers that I think will still be rewarding for students to study; to explain those ideas in them a bit more clearly, and in some cases to reinterpret some of my own arguments and results more plausibly; and, finally, in the last three essays, to explore the connection between the problems of identity and personal identity and the issues of indexicality and reflexivity in thought and language that I have been exploring since work on the personal identity book was broken off.

I record debts to a number of people in footnotes to the essays; they are all still deeply felt. I benefited a great deal from working with Bill Uzgalis on his dissertation about Locke, and have had many good conversations with him over the years about identity and what philosophers have thought about it, and have always learned something. Daniel Cohnitz read the penultimate draft; he caught a number of errors and made helpful suggestions. Deborah Wilkes of Hackett Publishing encouraged me to assemble the old papers and work on some new ones for this volume, and was encouraging every step of the way. Abigail Coyle was very helpful, encouraging, and patient.

Below is a list of the reprinted essays with their original place of publication. I am grateful to the editors and publishers of the various journals and books for permission to reprint the essays.

Essay 1, "The Same *F*," was originally published in *The Philosophical Review* 79, no. 2 (1970): 181–200.

Essay 2, "Relative Identity and Relative Number," was originally published in *The Canadian Journal of Philosophy* 7, no. 1 (1978): 1–14.

Essay 3, "Can the Self Divide?" was originally published in *The Journal of Philosophy* 69, no. 16 (7 September 1972): 463–88.

Essay 4, "The Two Faces of Identity," was written for this volume.

Essay 5, "Personal Identity, Memory, and the Problem of Circularity," was originally published in *Personal Identity,* edited by John Perry. Berkeley: University of California Press, 1975, pp. 135–55.

Essay 6, "Williams on the Self and the Future," is a reworked version of a review of Bernard Williams's *Problems of the Self,* which appeared in *The Journal of Philosophy* 73, no. 13 (1976): 416–28.

Essay 7, "Personal Identity and the Concept of a Person," originally appeared in *Contemporary Philosophy: A New Survey,* volume 4, *Philosophy of Mind,* edited by Gottorm Floistad. The Hague: Martinus Nijhoff, 1983, pp. 11–43. It has been revised.

Essay 8, "The Importance of Being Identical," was originally published in *The Identity of Persons,* edited by Amélie Rorty. Berkeley: University of California Press, 1976, pp. 67–90.

Essay 9, "Action, Information and Persons," was written for this volume. A couple of paragraphs were lifted from Perry (1994); I had to change "Quayle" to "Dick Cheney" and change the reference of "Bush" from George to George W.

Essay 10, "The Self, Self-Knowledge, and Self-Notions," was written for this volume but borrows heavily from Perry (1990,1998).

Essay 11, "The Sense of Identity," was written for this volume.

I. IDENTITY

1

The Same *F*

In several places Peter Geach has put forward the view that "it makes no sense to judge whether *x* and *y* are the 'same' . . . unless we add or understand some general term—the same *F*" (1962, p. 39). In this paper I discuss just what Geach's view comes to; I argue that there are no convincing reasons for adopting it and quite strong reasons for rejecting it.

I agree with criticisms of Geach made by David Wiggins in his book, *Identity and Spatio-Temporal Continuity* (1967), some of which are repeated here. I hope, however, to shed more light than he has on the motivations for Geach's view and to state somewhat more systematically an opposing one. This is possible in part because of an article by Geach on this topic which has appeared since Wiggins's book (Geach 1969a).

1. Geach versus Frege

Geach generally develops his view of identity in conscious opposition to Frege; he emphasizes that his view is the result of noticing an important fact that he thinks Frege missed:

> I am arguing for the thesis that identity is relative. When one says "*x* is identical with *y*" this, I hold, is an incomplete expression; it is short for "*x* is the same *A* as *y*" where "*A*" represents some count noun understood from the context of utterance—or else, it is just a vague expression of some half-formed thought. Frege emphasized that "*x* is one" is an incomplete way of saying "*x* is one *A*, a single *A*," or else has no clear sense; since the connection of the concepts one and identity

"The Same *F*" was originally published in *The Philosophical Review* 79, no. 2 (1970): 181–200. Reprinted by permission.

come out just as much in the German "ein und dasselbe" as in the English "one and the same," it has always surprised me that Frege did not similarly maintain the parallel doctrine of relativized identity, which I have just briefly stated. (1969, p. 3)

I maintain it makes no sense to judge whether x and y are "the same" or whether x remains "the same" unless we add or understand some general term—the same F. That in accordance with which we thus judge as to the identity, I call a criterion of identity; . . . Frege sees clearly that "one" cannot significantly stand as a predicate of objects unless it is (at least understood as) attached to a general term; I am surprised he did not see that this holds for the closely allied expression "the same." (1962, p. 39)

Frege has clearly explained that the predication of "one endowed with wisdom" . . . does not split up into predications of "one" and "endowed with wisdom." . . . It is surprising that Frege should on the contrary have constantly assumed that "x is the same A as y" does split up into "x is an A (and y is an A)" and "x is the same . . . y." We have already by implication rejected this analysis. (1962, pp. 151–52)

We can best see what Geach's view of identity amounts to, and what considerations might weigh in favor of it, by seeing just how he disagrees with Frege. What does Geach mean by denying that, for example, "being the same horse as" "splits up" into "being the same as" and "being a horse?" We can better understand the disagreement if we first list the points on which Frege and Geach might agree.

First, I think that Frege could agree with Geach that an utterance of the grammatical form "x and y are the same" might not have a clear truth value and that this situation might be remedied by adding a general term after the word "same."[1] For instance, the utterance "What I bathed in yesterday and what I bathed in today are the same" might not have a clear truth value in a certain situation, although "What I bathed in yesterday and what I bathed in today are the same river" or "What I bathed in yesterday and what I bathed in today are the same water" do have clear truth values. And Frege would further agree, I believe, that the truth values of the last two statements might

---

[1] I base my remarks about what Frege could say and would say on his general view of these matters as expressed in various writings and not on any specific discussion of this problem. My general view about identity owes much to Frege's remarks in his *Grundlagen der Arithmetik* (1884/1960), sec. 62 ff., and those expressed by W.V. Quine in *From a Logical Point of View* (1963), pp. 65 ff.

differ: it might be true that I bathed in the same river on both days but false that I bathed in the same water.

Second, I think Frege could agree that in adding the general term after the word "same," one could be said to convey a criterion of identity and that the original utterance is deficient in that no criterion of identity is conveyed.

And, finally, I think Frege might agree with reservations in saying that in supplying a general term and conveying a criterion of identity, one is making clear which relation is asserted to hold between the referents of the statement. Frege must admit that the truth values "*x* and *y* are the same *F*" and "*x* and *y* are the same *G*" may differ. For instance, "Cassius Clay and Muhammad Ali are the same man" is true, but "Cassius Clay and Muhammad Ali are the same number" is not true. This shows that "being the same man as" and "being the same number as" are not extensionally equivalent and therefore do not express the same relation. But, having admitted this, Frege might add that, in an important sense, one relation is asserted in both cases. And this is where Frege and Geach disagree. To see how the relations might be said to be the same in each statement after all, let us compare a case Frege might regard as analogous.

Consider "being a left-handed brother of" and "being a red-haired brother of." These quite obviously express different relations, for they are not extensionally equivalent. But these relations differ in a way that leaves them intimately connected. "Being a left-handed brother of" clearly splits up into "being a brother of" and "being left-handed." To say that Jim is a left-handed brother of Mike is to say no more or less than that Jim is a brother of Mike and Jim is left-handed. And the same thing is true of "being a red-haired brother of." The two relations involved do not differ, we might say, in being two different kinds of brotherhood, left-handed and red-haired. The job of the words "red-haired" and "left-handed" is not to tell us what kind of brotherhood is being asserted. Rather, they assert something about the first referent in addition to the relation asserted. In such a case, it is very natural to say that the relations are in a sense the same, for the words "left-handed brother of" and "red-haired brother of" express a conjunction of two conditions, only one of which is relational. And that condition which is relational is the same in both cases—namely, being a brother of. One important consequence of this is that it follows from "*x* is a left-handed brother of *y*" and "*x* is red-haired" that "*x* is a red-haired brother of *y*." We can express this by saying that "is a red-haired brother of" and "is a left-handed brother of" express restrictions of the relation "being a brother of" to, respectively, the domains of the left-handed and the red-haired.

Now compare with this the difference between the relations expressed by "being a better golfer than" and "being a better swimmer than." These are different relations. But they do not differ in the way those just examined differ. "Being a better golfer than" does not break up into "being better than" and "being a golfer." There is no such thing as just being better than. This is the reason that it does not follow from "x is a better golfer than y" and "x is a swimmer" that "x is a better swimmer than y."

Frege's position is that "being the same F as," like "being a red-haired brother of," splits up into a general relation and an assertion about the referent; it breaks up into "being the same as" and "being an F."[2] This is what Geach denies. He thinks that "being the same F as," like "being a better golfer than," does not split up. Just as there is no such thing as being just "better than," Geach says that "there is no such thing as being just 'the same'" (Geach 1957, p. 69).

This, then, is the difference of opinion between Frege and Geach. Geach's succinct statement of his view is, "[I]t makes no sense to judge whether x and y are 'the same' . . . unless we add or understand some general term—the same F." (1962, p. 39) But this disguises the real nature of the dispute. Frege would not deny, and I will not deny, that in significant judgments of identity a general term that conveys a criterion of identity will be implicitly or explicitly available. I shall not try to refute Geach by producing a case of being the same that is not a case of being the same F for some general term "F." That is not the issue. The issue is the role of the general term and the criterion of identity that it conveys.

The view I advocate, and which I believe to be Frege's, is that the role of the general term is to identify the referents—not to identify the "kind of identity" asserted. According to this view, x and y cannot be the same F but different G's; if x and y are the same F, then the relation of identity obtains between x and y, and any statement that denies this is false. In particular, no denial of identity of the form "x and y are different G's" can be true. Frege cannot allow the possibility

---

[2] It should be pointed out that Frege would not regard this equivalence as a helpful analysis of "being the same F." See the remarks cited in note 2.

that x and y are the same F but different G's.[3] But, on Geach's view, there is no objection to such a case. On his view, just as it does not follow that Jones is a better golfer than Smith from the fact that he is a better swimmer than Smith and is a golfer, so too it does not follow that x is the same G as y from the fact that x is the same F as y and is a G. Thus Geach says,

> On my own view of identity I could not object in principle to different A's being one and the same B . . . as different official personages may be one and the same man. (1962, p. 157)

If we can find an example in which x and y are the same F but x and y are different G's, we shall have to admit Geach is right in rejecting Frege's view, just as if there were cases of people who are left-handed and brothers but not left-handed brothers, we should have to give up the view that "being a left-handed brother" splits up into "being left-handed" and "being a brother."

Before considering some examples that seem to be of this form, I would like to point out an interesting consequence of Geach's view. Geach's view differs from Frege's in allowing the possibility of a true statement of the form "x and y are the same F but x and y are different G's." But if we can find a counterexample of this form, we shall have to give up more than Frege's view. We shall have to give up some principles about identity that seem very plausible.

If we are going to view a statement of the form "x is the same F as y" as asserting some relation expressed by "is the same F as" of the referents of "x" and "y," then this relation should behave, on Frege's view, as a restriction of the general relation of identity to a specific

---

[3] This may seem inconsistent with the view I attributed to Frege with respect to the bathing example. The river I bathed in yesterday and the river I bathed in today are water, and they are the same. Shouldn't it follow that they are the same water? Well, in the sense in which the rivers are water, they are the same water and were the same water yesterday—although the river I bathed in today is not the water the river I bathed in yesterday was. Two confusions need to be avoided. First, the statement in question, that the river I bathed in yesterday and the river I bathed in today are the same water, is not an identity statement (see discussion). Second, the truth of this statement in no way conflicts with the falsity of "The water I bathed in yesterday and the water I bathed in today are the same," which, on one interpretation, is what "What I bathed in yesterday and what I bathed in today are the same water" amounts to in the example in question.

kind of object. As such, it should share some of the properties ordinarily attributed to identity: transitivity, symmetry, and substitutivity. Reflexivity is lost: every object need not be the same F as itself, for all objects are not F's. But these relations should be at least weakly reflective: any object that is the same F as some object must be the same F as itself. But any counterexample to Frege will also be a counterexample to some of these principles. Consider any such counterexample. It is in the form of a conjunction. The second conjunct says that x and y are different G's. If we make the substitution in this conjunct that the first conjunct licenses us to make, the result is "x and x are different G's." To accept this result is to deny that the relation expressed by "the same G" is even weakly reflexive, which requires either that such relations are not transitive or not symmetrical. To deny the substitution is to deny that these relations confer substitutivity. If we accept Geach's view, we shall have to abandon some traditional and rather plausible logical doctrines.

2. A Counterexample?

In "Identity," a recent article from which some of the earlier quotations were drawn, Geach has explained his views at greater length than before. At first glance, the views expressed in that article may seem difficult to reconcile with those I have just attributed to him; it is a difficult article. Although Geach says that "at first sight" his own view seems to conflict with "classical identity theory"—the view that identity is a reflexive relation that confers substitutivity—he never points out in so many words that it will have to be abandoned if his theory of identity is correct. Nevertheless, the view Geach expounds does turn out to be, when carefully examined, just the view I have attributed to him and does have the consequences I said it has.

Geach's view is best understood, I think, by looking first at his examples and then considering the rather involved argument and doctrine those examples are supposed to illustrate. These examples, as interpreted by Geach, are of just the sort we found required to refute Frege's view.

Consider the following list of words:

A. Bull
B. Bull
C. Cow

How many words are on the list? It has often been pointed out that such a question is ambiguous; the right answer might be "two" or it might be "three." One explanation of this ambiguity is that the answer depends on what kind of object we are counting, word types or word tokens; there are three word tokens but only two word types on the list. But this is not the way Geach looks at the matter. According to him, there are not two kinds of objects to be counted, but two different ways of counting the same objects. And the reason there are two ways of counting the objects is that there are two different "criteria of relative identity." The number of words on the list depends on whether *A* and *B* are counted as one and the same word; they are counted the same according to the criteria of relative identity expressed by "word type," but not according to the one expressed by "word token." Geach's claim is then that the conjunction

(1) *A* is the same word type as *B*, but *A* and *B* are different word tokens.

is true. And this conjunction seems to be just the sort of counterexample required to prove Frege wrong.

The rather involved and difficult doctrine that precedes such alleged counterexamples as this in Geach's article seems to me best viewed as an attempt to undermine some distinctions implicit in fairly obvious objections to such examples. I will now state those objections and in the next section explain how Geach seeks to undermine them.

First, in order to be of the form "*x* and *y* are the same *F*, but *x* and *y* are different *G*'s," the referring expressions in the example that correspond to "*x*" and "*y*" will have to refer to the same objects in the first and second conjuncts. The sameness of expression is not sufficient. If it were, the true statement "John Adams was the father of John Adams" would be of the form "*x* was the father of *x*" and a counterexample to a principle of genealogy. It seems a plausible criticism of Geach's proposed counterexample that it fails for just this reason; in the first conjunct of (1) "*A*" and "*B*" refer to word types, in the second to word tokens. Indeed, the role of the general terms "word token" and "word type" is just to tell us to what objects—the types or the tokens—those expressions do refer.

One might reply to this objection by saying that the fact expressed by (1) could as well have been expressed by

(2) *A* and *B* are different word tokens but the same word type.

In (2) the expressions "*A*" and "*B*" appear only once; it might be claimed that it becomes very dubious, in virtue of this single appearance, to claim that four references to three referents take place within (2).

But there is a second criticism. Even if the occurrences of "*A*" and "*B*" are interpreted as referring to the same objects in both conjuncts of (1), or as not being multiply referential in (2), it is still far from clear that either (1) or (2) is a good counterexample. There is a further requirement. It is not sufficient for a statement to be what Frege, or most other philosophers, would call an identity statement that it contain the word "same" or be of the verbal form "*x* and *y* are the same *F*." For example, "Sarah and Jimmy are members of the same family" is not an identity statement; no one would suppose its truth required that everything true of Sarah be true of Jimmy. Nor are "The couch and the chair are the same color" or "Tommy is the same age as Jimmy" identity statements. These statements are of course closely related to identity statements; the first two, for example, are equivalent to "The family of Jimmy is identical to the family of Sarah" and "The color of the couch is identical to the color of the chair." But as they are, they are not identity statements: the relation of identity is not asserted to obtain between the subjects of the statements—Jimmy and Sarah, the couch and the chair. Yet it is clearly a further requirement of a counterexample to Frege that both conjuncts be identity statements in the relevant sense. That is, the conjunct that says "*x* and *y* are the same *F*'s" must be an assertion of identity, and the conjunct that says "*x* and *y* are different *G*'s" must be a denial of identity. For example, no one should suppose that "The couch and the chair are the same color but different pieces of furniture" would be a good counterexample to Frege.

It seems clear to me that if we assume that "*A*" and "*B*" refer to word tokens throughout (1), then the first conjunct of (1) is not an assertion of identity, but merely an assertion that *A* and *B* are similar in a certain respect or have some property in common; they are both tokens of the same type, they have the same shape—they are "equiform." Note that this conjunct could be more naturally expressed "*A* and *B* are of the same type" or "*A* and *B* are tokens of the same type." In this way the conjunct resembles the statement "The couch and the chair are the same color," which could more naturally be put "The couch and the chair have the same color" or "The couch and the chair are of the same color." But identity statements are not more naturally expressed in such ways; we feel no temptation to say that Lyndon Johnson and LBJ are of the same man or have the same man.

Thus Geach's counterexample seems open to the following objections. If "*A*" and "*B*" refer to the same objects throughout (1), the first conjunct of (1) is not an identity statement, and the counterexample fails. If both conjuncts are identity statements in the required sense, "*A*" and "*B*" must refer to word types in the first conjunct and word tokens in the second, and the counterexample fails.

3. Must We Ever Choose Identity?

We find in "Identity" a rather abstract line of arguments which, if correct, will show the criticism I have just made of Geach's counterexample to be based on untenable or at least unnecessary notions: the notion of word types as a kind of object different from word tokens and the notion of a statement of identity ("absolute" identity) as opposed to a resemblance or common property statement ("relative" identity). The only distinction needed, according to Geach, is between different kinds of "relative" identity:[4] being-the-same-word-type and being-the-same-word-token.

To understand Geach's argument, we must first notice a rather interesting point. A great many propositions are about particular things. For instance, the proposition "The pen I am writing with is blue" is about a particular object—the pen in my hand—which is referred to by the subject term. An assertion of the proposition can be looked upon as asserting of that pen that it has a certain property—being blue—which is expressed by the predicate. Now, part of understanding an utterance that expresses such a proposition is understanding under what conditions the proposition expressed would be true.

---

[4] It is important to see that statements of "relative" identity are not what I have called "identity statements" at all, but what I would prefer to call "statements of resemblance" or "common property statements." The statements on p. 7, for example, are what Geach calls statements of relative identity. Relative identity should not be confused with restricted identity (see p. 4). On my view, a restricted identity statement can be reworded, without changing referents, as a clear identity statement: to say "Leningrad and Stalingrad are the same city" is just to say "The city of Leningrad is identical with the city of Stalingrad." This is not true of statements of relative identity—and that is why they are not identity statements.

The interesting point to which I wish to call attention is just that this element in, or requirement of understanding, the utterance does not generally require knowing which object the subject term of the proposition refers to and exactly what the predicate asserts of it.

A simple example will establish this. Consider the sentence "*Pa*" in the language *L*. I inform you that the utterance "*Pa*" is true if and only if the word in the box stands for a much misunderstood notion.

Identity

You understand the English; you now know the truth conditions of "*Pa*." But my explanation has not determined the referent of "*a*" or the condition expressed by "*P__*." Even if we take the English sentence

The word in the box stands for a much misunderstood notion.

as a translation of "*Pa*," nothing has been said about which parts of the English sentence correspond to which parts of "*Pa*." Different translations of the elements seem equally allowable:

   a: the word in the box
  P__: __ stands for a much misunderstood notion
   a: the box
  P__: the word in __ stands for a much misunderstood notion

It is possible, in certain easily imagined cases, to know the truth conditions of a great many sentences of some such language without being clear about the proper interpretations of their parts. Suppose "*Pa*" is true if and only if the type of which the word in the box is a token is often misspelled. On the basis of this information, two interpretations of "*P__*" and "*a*" seem allowable:

   a: the type of which the word in the box is a token
  P__: __ is often misspelled
   a: the word in the box
  P__: is a token of a type that is often misspelled

We might be told the truth conditions of a great many sentences containing "$P\_$" and "a" and still be in the dark as to their proper interpretation. For example, we might be told that "Fa" is true if and only if the type of the token in the box is often capitalized, that "Pc" is true if and only if the first word on the author's copy of this page is often misspelled, and so forth. This additional information about further sentences would not resolve the problem of interpretation.

The relation between the referring expressions "the token in the box" and "the type of the token in the box" is that the latter refers to an object which is identified by means of a reference to the object identified by the former. Thus, "the type of the token in the circle" identifies the same type as "the type of the token in the box"—although the tokens are different.

Identity

Suppose we were told that "Pb" were true if and only if the type of the token in the circle were often misspelled. Then, clearly, "Pb" is equivalent to "Pa." But is "a" identical with "b"? This is just the question of the proper interpretation. If "$P\_$" means "$\_$ is often misspelled," then "a" and "b" refer to the same word type. If "$P\_$" means "$\_$ is a token of a type that is often misspelled," then "a" and "b" refer to different word tokens (of the same type).

To show that a is not identical with b, it would be necessary only to establish that a has some property b lacks; if a and b are identical, they must share their properties. Suppose there is some predicate "$S\_$" in L such that "Sa" has a different truth value than "Sb." Clearly, we could conclude that a is not identical with b, that a and b are different tokens, not one and the same type.

Suppose we are told that "$R(a,b)$" is true if only and only if the token in the circle and the token in the box are tokens of the same type.

> a: the type of the token in the box
> b: the type of the token in the circle
> $R(\_, \_)$: $\_$ and $\_$ are identical

a: the token in the box

b: the token in the circle

$R(\_\_, \_\_)$: $\_\_$ and $\_\_$ are equiform

Which should we choose? Well, if we choose the first interpretation, then everything true of a will have to be true of b. So if there is some predicate "$S\_\_$" in L such that the truth values of "$S(a)$" and "$S(b)$" are different, the second interpretation would have to be chosen. If not, it would seem that we would be free to choose the first.

Suppose, however, there are no such predicates. Would that fact be sufficient justification for interpreting "$R(\_\_, \_\_)$" as "is identical with"? In a sense, it would not force us to do so. Even if there were no predicate like "$S\_\_$" in L, it still might be that "$R(\_\_, \_\_)$" does not mean identity. It might be just accidental that there are no such predicates; perhaps the speakers of L have not yet noticed any properties that distinguish word tokens or think them unworthy of expression in their language.

To have the formal properties required to express identity, an expression "$R(\_\_, \_\_)$" in L need satisfy only the following two conditions:[5] (i) for any referring expression a in L, "Ra,a" is true; (ii) for any referring expressions a and b, and any predicate ϕ in L, if "Ra,b" is true, "ϕa" and "ϕb" are materially equivalent. The force of the last paragraph is that these necessary conditions for expressing identity are not logically sufficient. "$R(\_\_, \_\_)$" might satisfy these conditions and not express identity—but just the kind of similarity (or relative identity) appropriate to the objects in the domain of L.

Now let us make a rough distinction between an object of a kind K and an occurrence of a kind K. An occurrence of a kind K is an object which, although is not itself a K, is the sort of object, or one sort of object, which would ordinarily be employed in ostensively identifying a K. For example, a word token is an occurrence of a word type because we ostensively identify word types by pointing to a word token and saying "the type of which that is a token" or even "that type." Surfaces or physical objects are occurrences of colors, because we ostensively identify colors by pointing at surfaces and saying "the color of that" or "that color."

---

[5] Double quotes occasionally function as quasi-quotes. I am ignoring problems of nonextensional contexts.

Our choice in interpreting "*R(a,b)*" is just this: to interpret "*a*" and "*b*" as references to word types and "*R(__, __)*" as "is identical with" or to interpret "*a*" and "*b*" as reference to occurrences of word types (which is to say, as references to word tokens) and "*R(__, __)*" as expressing one kind of what Geach calls "relative identity"—namely, "is equiform with."

Geach's argument, as I understand it, is this. We might very well have a reason to choose the second interpretation—for example, that there is in *L* a predicate "*S__*" such that "*Sa & ~Sb*" is true. Moreover, even if we do not have such a predicate in *L,* we might choose to add one in the future and should not close this option ("limit our ideology"). But no circumstances are conceivable in which we are forced to choose the first interpretation. We are always theoretically free to take the second. Moreover, there is a general reason for not choosing the first: in doing so, we multiply the entities to which we allow references (types now, as well as tokens) and thereby "pullulate our ontology."[6] But then there is never any reason to interpret a predicate in *L* as expressing identity, rather than some form of relative identity, and never any good reason to interpret the references in *L* to be to things which have occurrences, rather than to occurrences themselves. But then are not the very notions of identity, and of a reference to such an object, suspect? And, if this is so, are we not justified in waiving the criticisms made of the counterexample to Frege in section 2 of this essay, since those criticisms are completely based on these notions?

4. In Defense of Identity

The charges that the interpretation of "*R(__, __)*" as "is identical with" would restrict ideology while pullulating the universe are completely unfounded.

Consider the language *L+*, which contains all of the sentences of *L* plus sentences composed of the predicate "*K(__, __)*" and the referring expressions of *L*. The sentences of *L+* which are also sentences of *L* have the same truth conditions in *L+* as in *L*. "*K(a,b)*" is true if and only if the word token on page 10 is more legible than the word token on page 11. Then clearly, "*R(__, __)*" does not express identity

---

[6] In the original essay, I misquoted Geach as having said "pollute" rather than "pullulate," to spawn.

in $L+$. "$R(a,b)$" is true, but "$K(a,b)$" and "$K(a,a)$" are not materially equivalent, or so we shall suppose.

Now, all of this does not in the least show that "$R(\_\_, \_\_)$" does not express identity in L. The facts that "$R(\_\_, \_\_)$" does not express identity in $L+$ and that the symbols used in L and $L+$ are largely the same, and that the truth conditions of the shared sentences are the same in each, do not entail that the shared expressions have the same interpretation.

If, however, we think of L and $L+$ as successive states of the same language, actually employed by humans, then the evidence that "$R(\_\_, \_\_)$" does not confer substitutivity in $L+$ is grounds for thinking it is only an accident that it did in L—the earlier state; perhaps no one had conceptualized the relation being more legible than, or any other property capable of distinguishing tokens. This seems to be Geach's view: As our language grows, what now has the formal properties ascribed by the classical view to identity (what is an "I-predicable" in Geach's terminology) may cease to have them. To pick out any one stage of the language and say that those expressions that are I-predicables at that point must always be, are somehow necessarily, in virtue of their meaning, I-predicables is to "freeze" the language—to prohibit it from growing in certain directions.

This argument is confused. Suppose we interpret "$R(\_\_, \_\_)$" as expressing identity and take L to have as its domain word types. We are in no way blocked from adding the predicate "is more legible than" to L. It would be a futile gesture unless some names for word tokens were also added, but there is also no objection to doing that. In that case we have not $L+$, but $L++$—L plus "$K(\_\_, \_\_)$" plus some names for word tokens. Nothing in L prevents us from taking "$R(\_\_, \_\_)$" as expressing identity; in so doing we do not block the development of L to $L++$.

What about the claim that interpreting "$R(\_\_, \_\_)$" as expressing identity will "indecently pullulate our ontology"? To make this point, Geach introduces another example; a look at it will indicate the sorts of confusion that underlie this charge.

As I remarked years ago when criticizing Quine, there is a certain set of predicables that are true of men but do not discriminate between two men of the same surname. If the ideology of a theory T is restricted to such predicables, the ontology of T calls into being a universe of androids (as science fiction fans say) who differ from men in just this respect, that two different ones cannot share the same surname. I call these androids surmen; a surman is in many ways very much like a man, e.g., he has brains in his skull and a heart in his breast and guts in his belly. The universe now shows itself as a baroque Meinongian structure, which hardly suits Quine's expressed preference for desert landscapes. (1969a, p. 10)

Here we have a language fragment whose predicates are such that all the same predicates apply to me, my father, my brother, and the rest of the Perrys, and the same is true of the Smiths and Joneses, and so forth. If the words in this language fragment corresponded to English, then there would be nothing to stop us, says Geach, from interpreting "has the same last name" as expressing identity; this would be an *I*-predicable in the rump language. Then, he suggests, the names in the language fragment will have to be reinterpreted as names of surmen, which are queer and objectionable entities.

But, as far as I can see, nothing more objectionable than families would emerge from this reinterpretation. I cannot see why Geach thinks it should require androids. The entity that has all the persons with a certain last name as occurrences (parts or members) is clearly something like a family and not anything like an android. Moreover, this example is not analogous to the theoretical descriptions Geach gives in his abstract arguments; here we go from the richer language to the leaner; it is not clear how the predicates (such as "has guts in his belly") are to be reinterpreted in such a case, and Geach gives us no directions.

It seems to me that any cogency that attaches to Geach's claim of indecent pullulation can be traced to a confusion of his position with some sort of nominalism. Geach's position seems to presuppose nominalism: the thesis that, in our terminology, only occurrences are ultimately real. But it amounts to far more. The nominalist would claim that "being of the same type" is analyzable in terms of "equiformity" and that references to types are in some sense eliminable; Geach seems to claim that they are not only eliminable, but never occur in the first place.

The disadvantages of interpreting a predicate such as "$R(\_\_, \_\_)$" as identity are thus illusory; are there any advantages?

The most obvious is that if we interpret "$R(\_\_, \_\_)$" as "equiform" even though there are no predicates in L that discriminate between tokens, then we seem to be granting that the speakers of L refer to a kind of object, tokens, between which they have no means of distinguishing. But if tokens cannot be individuated in L, is it really reasonable to suppose that the users of L are actually talking about tokens but have just not bothered to express in the language any of the ways they use to tell them apart?

This point does not have its full weight with the example of L. L, a language with a restricted subject matter of the sort dealt with only by those with access to a richer language, presents itself as an artificial language. It clearly might be reasonable for someone to stipulate that the referring expressions in some artificial language he is discussing should be construed as referring to tokens even if they could be construed as referring to types; he might, for example, want to compare L with wider languages such as L+, and this might be more conveniently done if L is so construed.

But suppose an anthropologist should have the following worry. He arrives at a coherent and plausible translation scheme for a certain out-of-the-way language. In this scheme a certain predicate, "$R(\_\_, \_\_)$," is translated "$\_\_$ is identical with $\_\_$." In the thousands of conversations he has recorded and studied, he has found no cases in which natives would deny that an object had the relation expressed by this predicate to itself; he has found that, in every case, once natives find objects have this relation, they are willing to infer that what is true of one is true of the other. In a murder trial, the prosecution tries to prove, and the defense to disprove, that this relation obtains between the defendant and the murderer. But our anthropologist is a Geachian. He worries, Does "$R(\_\_, \_\_)$" really express identity? Do they really talk about people, or only stages of people? This is absurd. Some internally consistent theory about the natives' beliefs and linguistic practices could be formulated that casts this sort of metaphysical doubt on any entry in the anthropologist's dictionary. He need not have any special worries about identity; in the situation described, there is no real room for doubt.

With regard to one's own language, it seems clear that we can pick out predicates—for example, "is one and the same as"—which, in some sense I shall not here try to analyze, owe their logical properties (transitivity, symmetry, and so forth) to their meaning and could not lose them merely by virtue of additions to the ideology of the language or to changes in the state of the nonlinguistic world. Such predicates express the concept of identity.

Thus, as far as I can see, Geach has no effective arguments against the dilemma posed in section 2 for any counterexample to Frege. Until some counterexample is put forward to which those objections do not apply, we have no reason to reject this part of Frege's account of identity. In the next section, I shall examine an example of the required form which may seem more powerful than the one discussed thus far.

5. Same Clay, Different Statue

Suppose Smith offered Jones $5,000 for a clay statue of George Washington. Jones delivers a statue of Warren Harding he has since molded from the same clay and demands payment, saying, "That's the same thing you bought last week."

It is the same piece of clay but a different statue. It seems, then, that we can form the awkward but true conjunction

> This is the same piece of clay as the one you bought last week, but this is a different statue from the one you bought last week.

What are we to say of this sentence (see Wiggins; 1967, pp. 8ff.)?

Following the criticisms of such counterexamples outlined in section 2, we could either say that "this" and "the one you bought last week" refer to pieces of clay in the first conjunct and statues in the second or that one or the other of the conjuncts does not assert or deny identity.

To maintain the first criticism, we must claim that "this statue" and "this clay" would not in this situation refer to one and the same object, that the clay and the statue are not identical. This view seems paradoxical to some, but I think it can be reasonably defended. There are things true of the one not true of the other (for example, the piece of clay was bought in Egypt in 1956, but not the statue), and the piece of clay may remain with us long after the statue is destroyed. There is clearly a rather intimate relation between the two; I would argue that this relation is that the current "stage" of the piece of clay and the current "stage" of the statue are identical. We might well reserve the phrase "are the same thing" for this relation, while using "identical," "are the same object," "are the same entity," and so forth for the notion whose logical properties were formulated by Leibniz and Frege. But the point I wish to insist on at present is simply that there is nothing paradoxical about maintaining that the clay and the statue are not identical and a great deal that is problematical about maintaining the opposite.

If all the references are to the statue, then "being the same piece of clay" simply amounts to "being made of the same piece of clay" and does not express identity. If all the references are to the clay, then "__ is a different statue from __" should be construed as meaning "__ is a different statue than __ was," which amounts to "__ is formed into a statue that is not identical with the statue __ was formed into."

Having these alternative unobjectionable analyses of the apparent counterexample does not constitute an *embarras de richesses*. The speaker's intention to refer to the clay or the statues, or the clay in one conjunct and the statues in the other, might be revealed by later turns in the conversation. But he need not have any such intentions, just as when I say "This is brown" with a gesture toward my desk, I need not have decided whether I am referring to the desk or its color.

6. Conclusion

Let me then summarize my position. (1) In identity statements such as "This is the same river as that," the general term plays the same role as it does in "This river is the same as that river"; it identifies the referents and not the "kind of identity" being asserted. (2) Apparent counterexamples to the equivalence of "x and y are the same F" and "x and y are F's, and are the same" of the form "x is the same F as y, but x and y are different G's" err either because (i) they have the grammatical, but not the logical, form of a counterexample, since the referring expressions do not have the same referents in both conjuncts, or (ii) one of the conjuncts does not assert or deny identity, but one of the other relations often expressed by phrases of the form "is the same F as." (3) Geach's criticisms of the distinctions implicit in (i) and (ii) are unfounded.[7]

[7] I am grateful to a number of persons for commenting on earlier versions of this paper; I would particularly like to thank Keith Donnellan and Wilfrid Hodges.

2

Relative Identity and Relative Number

1. Introduction

Geach has claimed that Frege had an insight about number which should have led him to the doctrine of relative identity:

> I maintain it makes no sense to judge whether x and y are "the same" or whether x remains "the same" unless we add or understand some general term—the same F. That in accordance with which we thus judge as to the identity, I call a criterion of identity. . . . Frege sees clearly that "one" cannot significantly stand as a predicate of objects unless it is (at least understood as) attached to a general term; I am surprised he did not see that this holds for the closely allied expression, "the same." (Geach 1962, p. 39)
>
> Frege has clearly explained that the predication of "one endowed with wisdom" . . . does not split up into predications of "one" and "endowed with wisdom." . . . It is surprising that Frege should on the contrary have constantly assumed that "x is the same A as y" does split up into "x is an A" and "x is the same as . . . y." We have already by implication rejected this analysis. (pp. 151–52)

Here is the relevant passage from Frege, including his footnote:

> If it were correct to take "one man" in the same way as "wise man," we should expect to be able to use "one" also as a grammatical predicate, and to be able to say "Solon was one" just as much as "Solon was wise." It is true that "Solon was one" can actually occur, but not in a way to make it intelligible on its own in isolation. It may, for example, mean "Solon was a wise man," if "wise man" can be supplied from the context. In isolation, however, it seems that "one" cannot be a predi-

"Relative Identity and Relative Number" was originally published in *The Canadian Journal of Philosophy* 7, no. 1 (1978): 1–14. Reprinted by permission.

cate.* [*Usages do occur which appear to contradict this but if we look more closely we shall find that some general term has to be supplied, or else that "one" is not being used as a number word—that what is intended to assert is the character (not of being unique, but of being unitary).] This is even clearer if we take the plural. Whereas we can combine "Solon was wise" and "Thales was wise" into "Solon and Thales were wise," we cannot say "Solon and Thales were one." But it is hard to see why this should be impossible, if "one" were a property both of Solon and of Thales in the same way the "wise" is. (1884/1960, p. 40)[1]

Another passage, which it will be helpful to have before us, is this one:

[A] colour such as blue belongs to a surface independently of any choice of ours. . . . The Number 1, on the other hand, or 100 or any other Number, cannot be said to belong to the pile of playing cards in its own right, but at most belong to it in view of the way we have chosen to regard it and even then not in such a way that we can simply assign the Number to it as a predicate. (p. 29)

I have defended Frege's failure to adopt the doctrine of relative identity in essay 1.[2] But I did not there defend the consistency of his doctrine of number and his treatment of identity. I wish to do so here.

---

[1] The *Grundlagen* (1884/1960), from which Geach's quotes and these quotes are drawn, was not Frege's major work and not his last word on the issues here discussed. When I speak of "Frege's views," I mean only his views in the *Grundlagen*.

[2] See also Wiggins (1967), Nelson (1970), and Feldman (1969). Geach replies to Feldman (1969b), and seems to include other critics in *Logic Matters* (1972). In correspondence, Geach has informed me that my criticisms are based on misunderstandings and not worth replying to in print. I am unconvinced, however, of any misunderstandings relevant to my criticisms of relative identity. I did, as Jack McIntosh has observed, take Geach to say "pollute" at one point where he said "pullulate." An excellent discussion of Geach's views on identity and related matters appears in Dummett (1973), chap. 16. On the whole, Dummett does an excellent job separating the insightful from the implausible in Geach's writings on these issues. However, Dummett and also W. V. Quine (1973) maintain that something like Geach's doctrine of relative identity is true "as long as the sides of the identity sentence are demonstrative pronouns" (Quine, p. 59; see Dummett, pp. 570–95). It is true that such sentences, and many others not involving demonstratives, are in some

2. What Is Relative Identity?

First, however, we must remind ourselves what the doctrine of relative identity is and is not.

The doctrine of relative identity includes the claims that (i) "*x* is the same *A* as *y*" does not "split up" into predications of "*x* is an *A* (and *y* is an *A*)" and "*x* is the same as *y*"; (ii) there are, or could be, cases of "*x* is the same *A* as *y*, but *x* and *y* are different *B*'s," where *A* and *B* are count nouns (Geach 1962, pp. 151–52); (iii) there is no such thing as being just "the same" (Geach 1962, p. 157; Geach 1972, p. 249). I take (i) to be the central claim, with which Frege clearly disagreed, (ii) is evidence for it, and (iii) a consequence of it.

The doctrine of relative identity can easily be mistaken for more plausible doctrines, with which there is no evidence that Frege would disagree and which do not support claims (i), (ii), and (iii).

A. The doctrine that singular terms are count-noun laden. The function of singular terms is to identify entities, and it's plausible to suppose that such identification requires an understanding of what kind of entity is being identified. If I extend my finger towards a building and say, "That is what Jones donated to the university," you may under-

---

sense incomplete or deficient and can be completed by inserting an appropriate general I-term after the word "same." (See "The Same *F,* p. 3ff., and sec. 2 in this essay.) But the problem is not, as Dummett supposes, that in such sentences "it is correct to say, with Geach, that 'the same' is a fragmentary expression" (p. 570). For, surely the indeterminateness of "This is the same as that" (said, e.g., by Heraclitus' wife rather slowly, with two pointings towards the Cayster) has the same source as the indeterminateness of "This was here yesterday" (said in similar circumstances), in which the allegedly fragmentary expression does not occur. The information required, in both cases, to make good the indeterminancy is which objects are referred to, not what kind of identity is predicated. (If we suppose, with Quine, that we are at a stage of language at which experience has not yet been clumped into objects, it is surely not the kind of identity that is in question. No identity, we might say, without entity. [Even if we don't say that, as I argue we shouldn't in the next essay, the issue seems to be how we individuate, not what kind of identity.]) In both cases, inserting the appropriate general term after the demonstrative will suffice. In spite of Wiggins' admirable analysis of a wide variety of examples, I believe he is also not completely clear about this; his treatment seems to involve retaining different kinds of identity while not allowing the possibility of "same *F,* different *G*'s" emphasized by Geach. See Shoemaker (1970b) and Perry (1970b).

stand me to be making a cutting remark when my motive is laudatory. You take me to be referring to a brick, where I meant the whole building. The problem is with the singular term; if I had said "this building," I would have succeeded in identifying what I was talking about. This plausible doctrine does not support, but under-cuts, the doctrine of relative identity. We might have thought this latter doctrine was supported by an example such as the following: Heraclitus points at successive moments toward the Cayster, saying "This isn't the same as that." If we think "this" and "that" are singular terms in good order, we might think a good explanation of the inde-terminate nature of what he's saying is that we don't know whether he has in mind river identity (in which case he's wrong) or collec-tion-of-molecules identity (in which case he's right). And this might lead us to think that "This is the same river as that, but this and that are different collections of water molecules" is good support for claim (ii) or relative identity and hence for claim (i). But the singular terms are incomplete; the problem is not that we don't know "what kind of identity" is in question, but that we don't know whether Heraclitus is making a silly remark about a river or a substantial point about collections of water molecules.

B. The doctrine that everything belongs to some kind or another. This is perhaps a denial of one version of the doctrine of "bare particulars." Given any statement of the form "x and y are the same," there will be a true "completion" of it of the form "x and y are the same A." Given the last doctrine, the completion may, of course, be redundant. These two doctrines guarantee that in such statements of identity there will be explicitly or implicitly understood some count noun or sortal. The plausibility of these doctrines does not add to the plausibility of the doctrine of relative identity, but subtracts from it, for they provide a less drastic explanation for the facts cited as evidence for that doctrine.

C. The doctrine of the diversity of criteria of identity. In judging that the man I saw last week is the one before me now, I do not use the same criteria I use in judging that the same battleship that was docked at Long Beach last Friday is still docked here now or in judging that the number of 49er fans in my living room is the same as the number of people in my living room.

But what are criteria of identity? As Geach has observed, the word "criteria" obscures an important distinction between the kinds of evi-dence usually employed in making identity judgments of a certain kind and the conditions of identity. For example, it's good evidence that the ship docked there last Friday is the same as the one there now, that the registration number on the hull is the same. But sameness of registration number is neither necessary nor sufficient for ship identity. Presumably something such as spatiotemporal continuity, which would seldom be directly observed by even the crew over a weeklong period, is necessary and sufficient.

But on either understanding of "criterion of identity," it seems clear that the criteria of identity are relative to the kind of item in question. If we confuse our criteria of identity, in either sense, with the relation of identity, the doctrine of relative identity will follow straightaway. But this is a mistake.

3. Frege on Criteria of Identity

Frege was well aware of the fact that different kinds of objects have different criteria of identity. When he is trying to give a criterion of identity for numbers (in the second sense), he pauses and fixes the criterion of identity for directions as an example. The criterion of identity for directions is parallelness; for numbers it is equinumerosity (Frege 1884/1960, p. 79).[3] But parallelness and equinumerosity are not, so to speak, on the same level as identity. Parallelness is a relation between lines, equinumerosity a relation between concepts. In each case, when we give the criteria for the identity of A's, we are not saying what relation A's must be in to be identical, but saying what relation some other sorts of entities (lines or concepts, in these cases) must be in to be instances of the same A. Equinumerosity and parallelness are not two kinds of identity, one for directions and one for numbers.

When Frege observes that

a is parallel to b

comes to the same thing as

the direction of a is identical with the direction of b

his point is to explain the meaning of "the direction of __." This needs explanation, he argues, for we have no intuition of directions,

---

[3] Frege's word for the "possibility of correlating one to one the objects which fall under the one concept with those which fall under the other" is *gleichzahlig,* which Austin translated as "equal"; I prefer "equinumerous."

although we do have intuitions of straight lines and parallel lines. We understand already the concept of identity, for "in universal substitutability all the laws of identity are contained" (Frege, 1884/1960, p. 79). Thus only directions remain to be understood, and the above equivalence almost succeeds:

> We carve up the content in a way different from the original way, and this yields us a new concept. (Frege 1884/1960, p. 75)[4]

Frege's general conception of a criterion of identity seems to me to be sound and susceptible to generalization beyond the abstract sorts of entities with which he was wont to deal.

For any kind of object A, we can ask: (i) How do A's manifest themselves? What entities play the role for A's that straight lines play for directions? We can call this the class of A-occurrences. (ii) What relation plays the role for A's that parallelness plays for directions? That is, what relation obtains between A-occurrences of the same A? Such a generalization of Frege's schema might allow for different occurrence relations, as well as different "criteria of identity," for objects of different kinds or categories.

This scheme needs much working out, no doubt. But it has at least one merit. It allows us to appreciate the diversity and importance of criteria of identity while distinguishing this from the doctrine of relative identity.

4. Frege on Number

Now let us turn to Frege's view about number to see whether it should have led him to the doctrine of relative identity.

The remarks in the second quote from Frege at the beginning of this paper occur as he is exploring the suggestion that number is "on a level with colour and shape . . . a property of things." Frege objects:

> [I]f I place a pile of playing cards in [someone's] hands with the words: Find the Number of these, this does not tell him whether I wish to know the number of cards, or of complete packs of cards, or even say

---

[4] I say "almost," for Frege finds a difficulty: we haven't yet explained why England, for example, is not a direction. He solves this problem by defining "the direction of line a" as the extension of the concept "parallel to line a."

of honour cards at skat. . . . I must add some further word—cards, or packs, or honours. (1884/1960, p. 28)

So far, then, Frege has denied that number is a property of a pile of cards in the way that being blue might be a property of the pile. At this point, he might adopt what I shall call the doctrine of relative numbers: "having the number two" is not a single property. There is no such thing as having the number two simpliciter. There are just a bunch of relative number properties: having the pack number two, having the card number two, having the honors-at-skat number two, and so forth. Once we see this, we are free to allow that the pile, after all, has the number properties. It has the pack number two and the card number one hundred four. It does not, however, have the pack number one hundred four or the card number two. There is no number it both has and has not and no problem. The doctrine of relative numbers would be a reasonable stablemate for the doctrine of relative identity. To say that x is identical with y is to say that x and y are one. So the need to ask, "which kind of identity?" pressed by the doctrine of relative identity, is merely a special case of the need to ask "what kind of number?" pressed by the doctrine of relative numbers.[5] It

---

[5] William Alston and Jonathan Bennett (1984) claim that I am right in disapproving of Geach's doctrine of relative identity and right in thinking that what I call the doctrine of relative numbers accords with relative identity. But they think I am wrong in supposing that the doctrine of relative numbers is significantly different from Frege's own doctrine. They think Frege's treatment of cardinality implies Geach's doctrine of relative identity, and they think both Frege and Geach are wrong.

Patricia Blanchette (1999) agrees with Alston and Bennett that Frege's treatment of cardinality and the doctrine of relative numbers are not significantly different. But she thinks neither of them implies Geach's doctrine of relative identity. So she agrees with me in rejecting Geach's doctrine of relative identity and accepting Frege's treatment of cardinality. But she thinks I am wrong to suppose that the doctrine of relative numbers amounts to pretty much the same as Geach's relative identity. I think Blanchette is right.

Blanchette says,

[The doctrine of relative numbers] is indeed a harmless variant of Frege's view. We can define the first in terms of the second, as follows: Say that a pile P has the relative cardinality 'n-Fs' iff P is comprised of objects falling under the concept F, and the concept F-in-pile-P numbers (in Frege's original sense) n. (p. 217)

seems clear that Frege did not adopt anything like the doctrine of relative numbers. Rather than multiplying the kinds of numbers attributed to the pile, he rejects the idea that the pile has a number at all. In the quote just given, the following remark was omitted:

> To have given him the pile in his hands is not yet to have given him completely the object he is to investigate. (p. 28)

A little later he says, "an object to which I can ascribe different numbers with equal right is not really what has a number" (p. 29). In remarks quoted at the beginning of this paper, Frege seems to allow a sense in which numbers belong to the pile:

> The number 1 . . . cannot be said to belong to the pile of playing cards in its own right, but at most to belong to it in view of the way we have chosen to regard it. . . . But this sense is pretty weak and even then not

---

Let's call the doctrine of relative numbers, so defined, RN. Blanchette holds, contrary Alston and Bennett, that RN is inconsistent with Geach's doctrine:

> RN is the doctrine that a given pile has different 'relative cardinalities' in the sense that it can be divided into parts in different ways; Geach's doctrine is that a given pile has different 'relative cardinalities' because even given a particular way of dividing it into parts, these parts are only 'relatively' identical or non-identical with one another. (p. 217)

So far so good. It seems clear to me, however, that RN does not have the consequence that "There is no such thing as having the number two simpliciter," which was a key step in what I called "the doctrine of relative numbers." All that follows from RN is that piles have only relative numbers, not that there is no such thing as having numbers simpliciter. Piles do not have numbers simpliciter because they are not the right kinds of things to have numbers. Concepts are the sorts of things that have numbers. RN gives us no reason not to introduce the property of having the number two simpliciter, as long as we are careful to note that it is a property of the concept *decks in the pile* and not a property of the pile. So either Blanchette misunderstood me, or I misdescribed the doctrine I was after. I'm afraid the second choice is more plausible.

RN is a doctrine of well-behaved relative numbers, similar to the view that some philosophers have of well-behaved relative identities. Identity is relative, because what is involved in being the same statue, for example, isn't what is involved in being the same clay: some kind of object must be involved in order to make an identity judgment. But there are no objects *a* and *b* that are identical relative to one kind of identity, but distinct relative to

in such a way that we can simply assign the number to it as a predicate. (p. 29)

If number is not a property of the pile, what is it a property of?

A considerable portion of the *Foundations of Arithmetic* is occupied with that question. The solution comes in section 46:

> [T]he content of a statement of number is an assertion about a concept. If I say "Venus has 0 moons" . . . a property is assigned to the concept "moon of Venus," namely that of including nothing under it. If I say "the King's carriage is drawn by four horses," then I assign the number four to the concept "horse that draws the King's carriage." (1884/1960, p. 59)

This explains why we must "add some further word—cards, or packs, or honours" before the question "Find the number of these" tells the recipient of the card pile what we want to know. These additional words don't tell him what kind of numbers are involved

---

another. If you think that happens, you are simply not clear about what objects you are talking about. On such a view, there seems to be no obstacle to introducing identity simpliciter.

I intended for doctrine of relative numbers to be a wilder doctrine than these and have the consequence that there is no such thing as having the number two simpliciter. However, the doctrine I go on to describe doesn't seem to have the consequence, and seems pretty much to accord with RN. I didn't identify the doctrine I had in mind, and Blanchette is right about the one I identified.

It seems to me that there is a doctrine that one could arrive at by being deflected from the Fregean path, in the way his pile example suggests one might be deflected. The doctrine I had in mind could not be summarized as Blanchette summarizes it, but if anything in the opposite way: something like a pile can be divided into parts in different ways in the sense that one can use different relative numbers to number a pile. This is a somewhat incoherent view, because I was attempting to find a doctrine about numbers that could serve as a stablemate for the doctrine of relative identity, which I regard as somewhat incoherent. The view I went on to describe, however, is not this incoherent wild view, but simply RN.

I agree enthusiastically with Blanchette, then, on substantive points of philosophy and Frege-interpretation, and somewhat less enthusiastically agree with her claim that the doctrine of relative numbers, as I described it, is more like Frege than Geach. (Added 2002)

but which concept is being asked about. Thus when I say, as perhaps a philosopher might, pointing at a pile of cards,

(1) The number of these is two.

I might have in mind either the true statement

(2) The number two belongs to the concept *packs contained in this pile.*

or the false

(3) The number two belongs to the concept *cards contained in this pile.*

The difference between (2) and (3) is not the kind of numbers involved. The number two that belongs to the first concept is just the number two that doesn't belong to the second. The difference lies in the concepts to which that number is asserted to belong.

It is, then, incorrect to say that "Frege sees that 'one' cannot significantly stand as a predicate of objects unless it is (or at least understood as) attached to a general term" (Geach 1962, p. 39). "One" is, according to Frege, not a predicate in any case, but the name of an object, the number one (1884/1960, pp. 67ff.). What gets predicated is "having the number one." And the general term (e.g., "card" or "pack") functions to identify the concept which is asserted to have the number. As Frege puts it:

> Several examples given earlier gave the false impression that different numbers may belong to the same thing. This is to be explained that we were there taking objects to be what has number. As soon as we restore possession to the rightful owner, the concept, numbers reveal themselves as no less mutually exclusive in their own sphere than colours are in theirs. (1884/1960, p. 61)

5. A Tension in Frege's Account?

But, still, if Frege held that having the number one is a property of concepts, shouldn't he have held this too of identity, given the intimate relation between identity and oneness? So isn't something awry with his account of identity?

The intimate relation between identity and oneness is illustrated by the fact that (4) and (5) come to the same thing.

(4) Flora and Bossie are the same.

(5) The number one belongs to the concept *is Flora or is Bossie.*

To obtain the identity predicate from (4), one would erase "Flora" and "Bossie," yielding (6):

(6) [ ] and ( ) are the same.

The same operation with (5) gives us (7):

(7) The number one belongs to the concept *is [ ] or is ( ).*

The fact that (6) and (7) are predicated of cows and not concepts in no way threatens Frege's claim that (8) is predicated of concepts:

(8) The number one belongs to { }.

The relation between the property of having the number one and the relation of identity is still intimate enough: the property of having the number one will belong to any nonempty concept all of whose instances are identical.

Statements (4) and (5), of course, might fail to express a complete thought. Suppose, for example, a rancher in the habit of naming both his herds and his cows points in the direction of the same cow, but different herds, on successive days (the cow having changed pastures), saying, "That's Bossie" the first day and "That's Flora" the second. Then we might not know whether (4) and (5) said something true about a cow with two names or something false about herds. This might be cleared up by addition of the count noun "cow":

(9) Flora and Bossie are the same cow.

(10) The number one belongs to the concept *cow that is Bossie or Flora.*

In the case of (9), the addition of "cow" would clear things up by telling us what we are talking about. In (10) it would answer the question Of which concept is having the number one predicated? In a sense, (4) and (5) are incomplete for the same reason. We do not know of which concept having the number one is predicated in (5) because we don't know to what objects "Bossie" and "Flora" refer. The power of the word "cow" to clear up these questions requires no explanation by the doctrines of relative number and relative identity.

Thus I claim that Frege's views about number and identity in *Foundations of Arithmetic* are consistent. A question remains, however. For it is not at all clear that either of these views are consistent with the passage Geach actually cited, which I have not yet discussed.

6. A Troublesome Passage

In this passage Frege says that if "one man" should be taken as analogous to "wise man," "one" should be a grammatical predicate. The suggestion seems to be that it is not. Although "Solon was one" actually does occur, it, unlike "Solon was wise," is not "intelligible on its own in isolation." It might mean "Solon was a wise man." The point Frege is making is supposed to be clinched by observing that "we cannot say Solon and Thales were one."

Frege might mean to be making a point about identity and individuation here. He might be supposing, with regard to "Thales" and "Solon," that they are ambiguous in the way we imagined "Flora and Bossie" to be, that in addition to being names of different men, they are used as names of the same herd or pack of men or man-fusion or man-aggregate or committee. His point would then be that without a general term, such as "man," which tells us what we are talking about, we haven't said anything determinate. If this is what Frege is saying, this passage is consistent with, and supports, his views about number and identity. But I really don't think Frege has anything like this in mind. If he had, he would probably have said so or at least used an example, such as the pack-of-cards example, more appropriate to the point.

In the section in which this passage occurs, Frege is arguing against a view, which he finds in Euclid and Schroeder, that units are a certain kind of thing, those things with the property expressed by "is." In addition to his earlier arguments against the view that number is a property of things, Frege adds this one:

> It must strike us immediately as remarkable that every single thing should possess this property. It would be incomprehensible why we should still ascribe it expressly to a thing at all. It is only in virtue of the possibility of something not being wise that it makes sense to say "Solon is wise." The content of a concept diminishes as its extension increases; if its extension becomes all-embracing, its content must vanish altogether. It is not easy to imagine how language could have come to

invent a word for a property which could not be of the slightest use for adding to the description of any object whatsoever. (1884/1960, p. 40)

The passage in question occurs immediately after this.

If we ask ourselves what Frege could be saying in the passage in question, which would support and is required by this argument, we are led to the following interpretation. "Solon is one" has a use only when there is a non-all-embracing concept in the background, for example, as an answer to the question "Were there any wise men in those days?" It does not tell us some property of Solon's expressed by "is one," for "is one" is only grammatically, and not logically, a predicate. It tells us how many, or at least how many, things have the background property, that is, how many things fall under a certain concept. On Schroeder's view, since both Solon and Thales are units, it should follow that "Solon and Thales are one." But this does not follow, for it is not true.

Frege clearly thinks that if someone were to say "Solon was one" or "Solon and Thales were two," it's appropriate to ask "One what?" or "Two what?" In this way, these statements are similar to "This is the same as that" (same statue or same lump of clay?) or "There are two of these on the page" (two types or two tokens?). But on this interpretation, the resemblance would be misleading. For the "One what?" question is not a request for a criterion of identity, to tell us what is being talked about (or in Geach's view, what kind of identity is involved), but rather a request for a non-all-embracing concept relative to which the claim will be of some interest.

Interpreted this way, Frege has said everything he needs to say about Schroeder and has said nothing inconsistent, or even particularly relevant to, his views on number and identity.

But, unfortunately, this doesn't seem to be what he is saying either. For he does not say that although "is one" can be a grammatical predicate, grammar is misleading here; he seems to say it just can't be a grammatical predicate. And he does not simply say that such sentences as

(11) Solon is one.

(12) Solon and Thales are two.

are, in the absence of a non-all-embracing background concept, useless, but that they are unintelligible. And he does not simply say that (12) is false, but that it's something "we cannot say."

What he does actually say seems to me inconsistent with his view of number, false, and unmotivated.

Consider

(13) Thales and Solon are two wise men.

Statement (13) seems like it should be acceptable to Frege. But (13) seems to be an attribution of a number to something. On Frege's view, it would have to be a concept that has the number two. Which concept is it? Two is not the number of wise men (or if it is, [13] doesn't tell us so). Two is the number that belongs to the concept *is Solon or is Thales*. But then (13) must amount to

(14) Solon and Thales are wise men, and the number two belongs to *is Solon or is Thales*.

But if this makes sense, its second conjunct should make sense:

(15) The number two belongs to *is Solon or is Thales*.

But if (13) is the ordinary way of expressing the thought better expressed by (14), shouldn't the ordinary way of expressing the thought better expressed by (15) be (12)? But Frege seems to think that (12), except as an incomplete version of (13), is unintelligible. So Frege's view of number seems to lead to the conclusion that (12), however useless, is perfectly intelligible, while in the passage in question he denies this.

He seems wrong to deny it. It's dubious that (12) is even useless much less unintelligible. If someone thought that "Thales" was Solon's pseudonym, (12) would seem an acceptable way to tell him otherwise. It certainly seems to make sense. The utility of (11) seems less secure. But we might want to deny, say, "Ellery Queen is one," given that Ellery Queen's novels are coauthored. If so, "Agatha Christie is one" then seems true and useful. It seems to make perfectly good sense, and Frege's view of number seems to show us the sense it makes.

It's hard to see why Frege should have said things that aren't required for his argument, aren't true, and aren't consistent with the account of number, which is his main accomplishment in the *Foundation of Arithmetic*. Perhaps he really was thinking about identity and individuation. Or perhaps he got careless.

Has Frege, then, clearly explained something in this passage, which, had he followed it through, would have led him to the doctrine of relative identity?

I don't think so, because I don't think Frege explains in this passage anything clearly at all.

7. Conclusion

To sum up: The account of number Frege puts forward in the *Foundation of Arithmetic* is compatible with the account of identity he gives there. And he does not put forward the doctrine of relative number, which seems a natural extension of the doctrine of relative identity.

On the other hand he does say, in the passage Geach actually cites, something incompatible with the view about number he later develops.

3

Can the Self Divide?[1]

Brown, Jones, and Smith enter the hospital for brain rejuvenations. In a brain rejuvenation, one's brain is removed, its circuitry is analyzed by a fabulous machine, and a new brain is put back in one's skull, just like the old one in all relevant respects but built of healthier gray matter. After a brain rejuvenation one feels better, and may think and remember more clearly, but the memories and beliefs are not changed in content. Their brains are removed and placed on the brain cart. The nurse accidentally overturns the cart; the brains of Brown and Smith are ruined. To conceal his tragic blunder, the nurse puts Jones's brain through the fabulous machine three times and delivers the duplicates back to the operating room. Two of these are put in the skulls that formerly belonged to Brown and Smith. Jones's old heart has failed and, for a time, he is taken for dead.

In a few hours, however, two individuals wake up, each claiming to be Jones, each happy to be finally rid of his headaches but somewhat upset at the drastic changes that seem to have taken place in his body. We shall call these persons "Smith-Jones" and "Brown-Jones." The question is, Who are they?[2]

"Can the Self Divide?" was originally published in *The Journal of Philosophy* 69 no. 16 (7 September 1972): 463–88. Reprinted by permission.

[1] I am heavily indebted to many persons for comments on earlier versions of this paper, especially David Lewis, John Vickers, David Kaplan, John Bennett, Richard Rodewald, Sydney Shoemaker, and Jaegwon Kim.

[2] I first heard this case described by Sydney Shoemaker in a seminar. Shoemaker discusses a body-transplant case in his book *Self-Knowledge and Self-Identity* (1963). Body transplants may some day be medically as well as logically possible. See the remarks of Christian Barnard quoted in *Newsweek*, 23 December 1968, p. 46.

1. A Problem for the Mentalist?

One thing is clear: they are not each other. Smith-Jones is lying down; Brown-Jones is sitting up. Brown-Jones is thinking of his nurse; Smith-Jones is thinking of Jones's companion (they both think of the nurse while being nursed, the companion otherwise, but right now the nurse is in Brown-Jones's room). So all sorts of things are true of the one but not true of the other. Perhaps we could sort these things out in some way consistent with the single-person hypothesis: a certain person is sitting-in-room-102-and-lying-in-room-104, etc. But there is no motivation for such maneuvering, for there is no unity of consciousness. Brown-Jones cannot tell by introspection what Smith-Jones is seeing, thinking, wishing, etc., and vice-versa.

Smith-Jones and Brown-Jones each claim to be Jones. Certain philosophers—John Locke,[3] Anthony Quinton,[4] and H. P. Grice,[5] to mention just three—hold theories of personal identity that seem to commit them to agreeing with both Smith-Jones and Brown-Jones.

---

[3] Locke discusses personal identity in chap. 17 of book 2 of his *Essay Concerning Human Understanding* (1694). He says at one point, "as far as this consciousness can be extended backwards to any past action or thought, so far reaches the identity of that person" (p. 39).

[4] In "The Soul" (1962), Quinton argues that persons are "'fundamentally" souls, a soul being a series of mental states. Roughly, two soul-phases belong to the same soul if they are "connected by a continuous character and memory path" (p. 59). (Quinton gives a more precise account of this relation.)

[5] Grice gives his analysis in "Personal Identity" (1941) in terms of the notion of a "total temporary state," which is composed of "'all the experiences any one person is having at a given time" (p. 86). Grice's analysis (pp. 87–88) is equivalent to the following. Let Sxy be the relation between total temporary states:

> x contains an experience such that, given certain conditions, y would contain a memory of it.

Then two total temporary states belong to the same person if and only if they are both members of a set closed under the relation Sxy v. Syx. This analysis gives the result that both Smith-Jones and Brown-Jones would have had all of Jones's experiences. Unfortunately, it also gives the result that Smith-Jones and Brown-Jones are one. It could be amended to avoid this unfortunate result by requiring (as Grice's preliminary analyses seem to) that no two members of the set in question occur at the same time.

They analyze the identity of persons in terms of memory or "continuity of consciousness," or memory and potential memory. Each would surely want to say in a simpler case of apparent bodily transfer (such a case as we would have if either only Smith-Jones or only Brown-Jones survived) that the resultant person is who he remembers being. These analyses, when applied to the case at hand, give us the result that both Smith-Jones and Brown-Jones were Jones. Each did all the things Jones did. They used to be the same person.

My intuitions agree. I do want to say of this case that Brown-Jones and Smith-Jones did all the things they seem to remember doing, that they both were Jones and so were one another.

But certain philosophers maintain that it is at least almost as clear that we should not say that Smith-Jones and Brown-Jones are who they claim to be, as that we should not say that they are a single person—the former, in fact, following directly from the latter. And, according to these philosophers, what Locke, Grice, and Quinton are committed to saying simply shows that their theories of personal identity are wrong. For, consider this. We agreed that (1) was clearly true:

(1) Smith-Jones is not the same person as Brown-Jones.

But the claims of Smith-Jones and Brown-Jones, and the results of applying the analyses of personal identity mentioned, seem to come to (2) and (3):

(2) Smith-Jones is the same person as Jones.
(3) Brown-Jones is the same person as Jones.

But from (2) and (3), by the symmetry and transitivity of identity, we obtain (4):

(4) Smith-Jones is the same person as Brown-Jones.

Thus (2) and (3) lead us to (4), which is known to be false as surely as (1) is known to be true. The theories of personal identity that led us there must then be wrong (adapted from Williams 1957/1973, p. 8ff.; see also Flew 1951, p. 67).

In this paper, I defend the theories of personal identity in question against this argument. I shall not say anything about the respective merits of Grice's and Quinton's analyses, or others for which this case appears to pose a problem, being content to defend these various plausible analyses against this particular argument. I shall refer to such analyses as "mentalist analyses of personal identity" and shall speak of a defender of such as "the mentalist." Of course, there are analyses of personal identity that might be called "mentalist" besides Quinton's and Grice's, and some of these do not commit us to saying, of this case, that Brown-Jones and Smith-Jones used to be Jones.[6] They seem to me to be wrong for that reason. I agree with Quinton that mentalist analyses of personal identity need not be incompatible with behaviorist or materialist theories of mind; the problems of mind and body and personal identity, though related, should not be conflated.

2. Idea for a Solution

To defend the mentalist, we need to become clearer about the nature of a philosophical theory of personal identity and about the nature of the objection being considered.

Let me begin with a simpler problem, that of table identity. Suppose Alf has a limited understanding of what we mean by "table." If we point to a certain part of a given table and ask him what color the table is at that spot, he will give the correct answer. Thus, if we point first to one leg of a brown table and ask, "Is this table brown here?" and then to another spot on the same table and ask the same question, Alf will answer "yes" both times. But if we then ask him, "Is there a single table that is brown here and also brown here?" (pointing successively

---

[6] One such is that developed by Sydney Shoemaker (1970a). Shoemaker would deny that either Brown-Jones or Smith-Jones was Jones (see p. 278n). At least part of Shoemaker's motivation for denying this is his belief that it involves "'modifying the usual account of the logical features of identity" (p. 279n). That I deny; this paper is my argument for that denial. Shoemaker's analysis builds into every claim of the form "This is the person who did A" the negative-existential claim that no one else in the entire universe has the criterial relation to the doer of A, and this seems implausible to me. Shoemaker (1970b) argues that this objection [which was made by David Wiggins (1967)] does not apply if the criterial relation requires a causal chain, for "it can be established without a survey of the entire universe whether some other person's memories are connected . . . by the same sort of causal chain" (p. 543). But it's not the difficulty of the survey that is the point. Rather, it is that the question whether Smith-Jones brushed his teeth before the operation shouldn't depend on whether Brown-Jones lives or dies.

to the same legs we pointed to before), he will shrug his shoulders. What does Alf lack? He does not know what counts as a single table. We might want to express this by saying, "Alf doesn't know what relation must obtain between this table and that table (pointing twice to the same table) for them to be the same." But this is wrong, for Alf might know quite well that the relation in question is identity. His problem is with the concept of a table, not with the concept of identity. Alf doesn't know what relation must obtain between a number of table parts for there to be a single table of which they all are parts. The rest of us do know what that relation is, although of course articulating it in a nontrivial way would be a philosophical exercise of some difficulty. I shall call the relation that obtains between two table parts, if and only if there is a table of which they are both parts, the spatial unity relation for tables. When Alf learns what counts as a single table, he learns to recognize when this relation obtains.

Now take a somewhat different case. Suppose Alf can now very well say whether this table part and that table part are parts of a single table. But suppose we point to a table and ask him, "Is that table brown?" He answers, "Yes." We then move the table to a different room, paint it green, and ask, "Is that table green?" He gives the right answer in both cases. We then ask him, "Is there a single table that was brown and now is green?" Alf shrugs his shoulders and cannot answer.

Alf still lacks mastery of the concept of a table. He doesn't know what counts as a single table, or the same table, through time. Again, he knows what relation the table that was brown must have to the table that is green for the right answer to the question to be "yes." The relation, of course, is identity.

But Alf does not know what relation must obtain between temporal parts of a table for them to be temporal parts of a single table. It may be objected to this that we have no notion of a temporal part of a table; what I glance at when I glance at a table is a whole table and not just a part of it. But we do have the notion of the history of an object—a sequence of events in which it is, in some sense, a main participant. When we glance at a table, we see the whole table, but we witness only a portion of its history. Alf's problem, then, is that he doesn't know what relation must obtain between two portions of table histories for them to be portions of the history of a single table. And now we can simply introduce the notion of a temporal part by saying that a is a temporal part of b if and only if a is a part (in the ordinary sense) of the history of b. Alf doesn't know what relation must obtain between two temporal parts of a table for them to be temporal parts of a single table. This relation I call the temporal-unity relation for tables. To analyze it in a nontrivial way is the problem of table identity.

Notice that I am not merely imagining Alf to be in a poor position to reidentify tables he hasn't seen for a while. It's not just that he's unclear about what would be good evidence for table identity. Rather, he's unclear about what this state of affairs amounts to.

Now we all know, in a sense, what the temporal-unity relation for persons is. But the philosophical problem is, I take it, to articulate this knowledge in some nontrivial way, to say what the relation is that obtains between temporal parts (or, as I shall call them, person-stages) of a single person. This relation is what Grice and Quinton give explicit analyses of and what Locke suggests an analysis of.[7]

It is extremely important not to confuse the unity relation for an object with the relation of identity. Of course the two are connected in an important way. If a and b are (temporal or spatial) parts of an object of certain kind K, and R_K is the (temporal or spatial) unity relation for K's, then, if the K of which a is a part is identical with the K of which b is a part, a must have R_K to b. But, nevertheless, R_K is not the relation of identity and must not be confused with it.

The logical properties of identity are well known: identity is necessarily transitive, symmetrical, and reflexive. Now our example shows that the relations suggested by some philosophers as an analysis of the temporal-unity relation for persons are not transitive.[8]

---

[7] For Quinton (1962) the relation would be the relation of indirect continuity, with the understanding that each soul-phase is indirectly continuous with itself. For Grice (1941) as amended in note 5, it is the relation of comembership in an appropriate set closed under *Sky* v. *Syx*. In both cases, the analysis is stated in a format not precisely like the one I have suggested; Quinton talks about soul-phases and Grice about total temporary states, rather than person-stages. I shall not attempt to discuss the comparative merits of these approaches; the points I make in this paper could be made in the terminology of either Grice or Quinton.

[8] Richard M. Gale (1969) argues persuasively that (as I would put it) the temporal-unity relation for human bodies is not logically transitive either, and so Williams's objection is not a good argument in favor of a bodily continuity analysis of personal identity. I tend to agree, but this does not solve the problem of the dividing self; it merely enlarges the number of philosophers who should be bothered by it.

For, let *j* be a person-stage of Jones that occurs before the operation, and let *b-j* and *s-j* be temporal parts of Brown-Jones and Smith-Jones, respectively, that occur after the operation, and let R be the relation suggested by Quinton or Grice. Then *j* has R to *b-j*, and *s-j* has R to *j*. But *s-j* does not have R to *b-j*. Now, if we confuse identity with the unity relation, it will seem clear that R is an incorrect analysis. Once we have made the distinction, however, it seems a legitimate question whether R must necessarily be transitive.

The answer, however, may still seem quite obvious. A simple argument seems to show that, since identity is a necessarily transitive relation, so too with any unity relation. Suppose *a*, *b*, and *c* are K-parts and R_K the unity relation for K's. Then, if we have a counterinstance to the transitivity of R_K,

a has R_K to *b*

b has R_K to *c*

not-(*a* has R_K to *c*)

it seems to follow that

The K of which *a* is a part is identical with the K of which *b* is a part.

The K of which *b* is a part is identical with the K of which *c* is a part.

Not-(the K of which *a* is a part is identical with the K of which *c* is a part).

But since this consequence is absurd, so must be the supposition.

This argument is, however, mistaken. To shed some initial doubt on the dogma that a unity relation must be transitive, consider the following case. Suppose there to be Siamese twins joined at the thumb. Now consider the three thumbs, *a*, *b*, and *c* (*b* is the shared thumb). There is a single body of which both *a* and *b* are thumbs. That is, the (spatial) unity relation for human bodies holds between *a* and *b*. And, similarly, there is a single human body of which both *b* and *c* are parts. But there is not a single human body of which both *a* and *c* are parts. So, if R_B is the spatial-unity relation for human bodies, *a* has R_B to *b*, *b* has R_B to *c*, but not-(*a* has R_B to *c*). Thus the spatial-unity relation for human bodies is not transitive.

Why does this not lead to a breakdown of the transitivity of identity? The reason is simple and instructive. It seems that we should be able to infer

The body of which *a* is a part is identical with the body of which *b* is a part.

The body of which *b* is a part is identical with the body of which *c* is a part.

Not-(the body of which *a* is a part is identical with the body of which *c* is a part).

which violates the transitivity of identity (given its symmetry).

But, given the case in question, the referring expression "the body of which *b* is a part" is, of course, improper. There is no unique body of which *b* is a part. Thus, given any reasonable theory of definite descriptions, the first two sentences of our inconsistent triad are not true, and the transitivity of identity is saved.

This point contains the essential insight that seems to me to lead to a satisfactory reply to the objection in question. But, as we shall see, its application to the more complicated case of identity through time is not a simple and straightforward matter.

3. The Branch Language

To apply the point made in section 2 of this essay to the case of the apparently dividing self, the mentalist might argue as follows. The objection is based on my alleged commitment to (1), (2), and (3):

(1) Smith-Jones is not the same person as Brown-Jones.

(2) Smith-Jones is the same person as Jones.

(3) Brown-Jones is the same person as Jones.

I seem to be committed to these because I analyze personal identity in terms of a relation, *R,* which does obtain between the person-stages *j* and *b-j* and the person-stages *j* and *s-j.* But, in fact, this does not commit me to (2) and (3). These sentences contain a proper name, "Jones." But this proper name turns out, contrary to what everyone thought, never to have been assigned to a person at all. The person-stages of Jones (as we say) that occurred before the operation were stages of both Smith-Jones and Brown-Jones. Thus any attempt to name a person by identifying one of these stages would have miscarried: although we had identified a single person-stage, we would not have identified a single person and so would not be in a position to assign the name. Thus (2) and (3) turn out on my analysis to be untrue. I can say that both Smith-Jones and Brown-Jones did all the things done (as we say) by Jones; they did the things they remember doing. But there is no single person Jones they both were. And there was no single person doing the things they did, just as no one person would have pushed a button if that button were pushed by the shared thumb of the Siamese twins mentioned in the last section. Thus, although my analysis of the relation that holds between person-stages when they are stages of a single person is not logically transitive, this does not commit me to the absurd denial of the transitivity of identity.

Before considering the merits of this response, I must make a methodological digression. The mentalist's problem is that he seems to be committed to an inconsistent set of sentences. But sentences can be judged inconsistent only in the framework of a theory about their truth conditions. The sentences in question state that persons had in the past or will in the future have certain properties. Any solution to the mentalist's problem will then be a theory about the truth conditions of such sentences which shows either that the particular sentences in question are consistent or that the mentalist is not committed to them.

The method I shall use to analyze alternatives is to state the truth conditions of sentences about past and future properties of persons in terms of statements about the properties of person-stages and the temporal-unity relation for persons, which I shall refer to as "R." It turns out that, even if we agree upon the analysis of the unity relation and upon the properties of the various person-stages in our example, there are still alternatives as to the account we give of a person having a property at a time. It is my intention to consider these alternatives and to argue that one of them solves the mentalist's problem.

I need first to explain, however, under what conditions a person-stage has a property. To do this, I must first distinguish between basic and nonbasic properties. A person's basic properties, at any time, are those properties which he has in virtue of events that occur at that time. His nonbasic properties are those which he has wholly or partly in virtue of events that occur at other times. If a person is now in room 100 but in a few minutes will be in room 102, then he has both the properties *being in room 100* and *being about to be in room 102*. The first is basic, the second nonbasic.

Let P designate a basic property. Then a person-stage x, which occurs at time t, satisfies the conditions for having P if and only if every person of which x is a stage satisfies the conditions for having P at t. Alternatively, x has P if and only if "This person has P," uttered while pointing to x, is true.

This method of assigning properties to person-stages does not presuppose a prior understanding of personal identity—of what a person is. The conditions under which an ostensively identified person has a basic property may be known or stated without knowing or stating the conditions under which a person will have or has had that property. This is the point that was made in the discussion of Alf and table identity. Alf knew that every table before him was green, although he did not know whether the table that was brown a moment before was before him and did not even know under what conditions that would be true.

Without the distinction between basic and nonbasic properties, the method of assigning properties to person-stages would be circular. In order to assign a nonbasic property to a person at a given time, one would have to know under what circumstances certain things happened to *that same person* at other times.

I assume that the nonbasic properties that a person has at a given time are a function of the basic properties he has at that and other times. Having made this assumption, I feel free to ignore nonbasic properties in the sequel. The project is to examine accounts of the truth conditions of sentences of the form "N has F at t," where "N" names a person, "F" designates a basic property, and "t" designates a time.

The defense suggested in this section amounts to one theory of this sort. It asserts that we speak what I shall call the *branch language*. Let us say that a set of person-stages is a *branch* if and only if all the members of the set have R to one another and no stage that has R to all the members of the set is not a member. Given a mentalist analysis of R, all the person-stages thought to be of Jones plus all the post-operative stages of Smith-Jones form a branch, and all the person-stages thought to be of Jones plus all the post-operative stages of Brown-Jones form another. The set containing all the person-stages in both of these branches is not itself a branch. The view suggested is that the history of a person forms a branch; there is a one-to-one correspondence between persons and branches, the branch of each person containing just his person-stages. To say that a person has a certain property at a certain time is just to say that there is a person-stage belonging to that person's branch which occurs at that time and has that property. The view needn't be that persons are branches, but for the sake of simplicity we shall suppose that that identification is made.

Now suppose that persons acquire names in the following way. Names are assigned to person-stages—say, at baptism. The name names the person (branch) of which that person-stage is a member. A sentence

N has F at t

is true if and only if *the* branch named by N, that is, *the* branch containing the person-stage to which N is assigned, contains a person-stage that occurs at t and has property F. If there is no such branch—as there would not be if the person-stage to which N is assigned is a member of two branches—the sentence is false. A sentence of the form

N is identical with M

is true if and only if the branch containing the person-stage to which N is assigned is identical with the branch containing the person-stage to which M is assigned. If there is no unique branch for N or M, the sentence is false. The language for which this sketch is correct is the branch language. In the earlier response, the mentalist was supposing that English is the branch language.[9] What are the merits of this view? Is our concept of a person the concept embodied in the branch language? I think not. The mentalist, in adopting this solution, would be leaving the ordinary person far behind; for the ordinary person is not willing to admit that there was not a single person, Jones, before the operation, doing all the things Smith-Jones and Brown-Jones seem to remember doing. Metaphysical considerations also seem to weigh against this view. Consider the possible world just like the world

---

[9] I have not, of course, given anything like a complete account of the branch language, nor do I of the person-stage language or the lifetime language, which are described later, but I believe I have said enough to make the solution advanced in this paper to the problem at hand clear.

Schematic letters such as N, F, and t are used in displayed sentences as metalinguistic variables for the appropriate classes of object-language expressions; such displayed sentences should be regarded as in quasi-quotation. Elsewhere, these same letters are sometimes used as object-language variables for the appropriate entities; thus I say "the property F" and "the time t," rather than "the property expressed by F" and "the time designated by t."

described in section 1 of this essay, except that Jones dies the day before the operation. In that possible world there is a single person Jones before the operation, even according to the branch language. But before Jones's death there is, by hypothesis, no difference between that possible world and the world described in section 1. Whatever the merits of this last argument, it seems clear that we are reluctant to abandon the principle that each person-stage identifies a person, so that if we assign a name to a person-stage, we cannot but have named a person.

Nevertheless, I think this response suggests a more promising line. The next three sections are devoted to its development.

4. Another Strategy

Can the mentalist use the impropriety of "Jones" to save himself from self-contradiction without giving up the view that Jones was a single person before the operation? It seems that he might if he can give sense to the view that "Jones" was proper before the operation but improper after. He could then reject (2) and (3)

(2) Smith-Jones is the same person as Jones.

(3) Brown-Jones is the same person as Jones.

on ground of the impropriety of "Jones," but assert nevertheless (2') and (3'):

(2') Before the operation, Smith-Jones was Jones.

(3') Before the operation, Brown-Jones was Jones.

Both (2') and (3') answer the reasonable question "Which of the persons who existed before the operation were these two persons?" They were both the person Jones. (2') and (3') do not lead directly to the objectionable (4):

(4) Smith-Jones is the same person as Brown-Jones.

They lead only to

(4') Before the operation, Smith-Jones was the same person as Brown-Jones.

But can the mentalist assert (2') and (3') and (4'), without contradicting himself, given his commitment to (1)?

(1)   Smith-Jones is not the same person as Brown-Jones.

At first sight, the prospects for this seem slim. A variety of arguments can be given to show that (1), (2'), and (3') lead, along with certain other things the mentalist wants to say, as surely to self-contradiction as do (1), (2), and (3). The essential reasoning behind any of these arguments will be something like this. Both (2') and (3') say that Smith-Jones and Brown-Jones were the same person before the operation. That means that, uttered before the operation, (4) would have expressed a truth: [10]

(4)   Smith-Jones is the same person as Brown-Jones.

(Of course, only someone who knew what was going to happen would have bothered to say it.) But from (4) it would follow that everything that was true of Smith-Jones was true of Brown-Jones. But now suppose that after the operation Smith-Jones is in room 102 and Brown-Jones in room 104. Then the mentalist surely wants to say that (5) and (6) expressed truths before the operation:

(5)   After the operation, Smith-Jones will be in room 102.
(6)   Not-(after the operation Brown-Jones will be in room 102).

But then something, namely, the open sentence "After the operation, __ will be in room 102" was true of Smith-Jones but not true of Brown-Jones. So (4) cannot have been true.

In the rest of this section, I discuss the moves the mentalist must make if he is to evade this argument; these moves are in fact simply consequences of the view that "Jones" can be proper at one time, improper at another. In the next two sections, I consider whether the mentalist can give an account of what a person is—that is, an alternative to the branch language—that justifies making these moves.

---

[10] I take it that sentences express propositions at times, and some sentences express different propositions at different times. When I say a sentence is true at a time or true when uttered at a time, I mean that the proposition the sentence would express at that time is true.

First let us consider what we should say in a case the mentalist might find similar. The definite description "the senator from California" is occasionally proper, although usually it is not. Suppose Murphy resigns as senator Saturday and Tunney is not sworn in as his successor until Tuesday. In the interim, "the senator from California" is proper and denotes Cranston. Now, if on Monday we wanted to say of the unique person who is then the senator from California that he will be in Washington Tuesday, we might try (7):

(7)   The senator from California will be in Washington on Tuesday.

This we could distinguish from (8):

(8)   Tuesday the senator from California will be in Washington.

Statement (7), we might say, requires a person to uniquely fit the description on Monday and be in Washington on Tuesday; (8) requires that a person both uniquely fit the description and be in Washington on Tuesday. This would not be a report of ordinary usage, but a pardonable regimentation thereof. Statement (7) is true, (8) false. Thus on Monday we could not infer from the truth, then, of (9)

(9)   Tuesday Cranston will be in Washington.

and of (10)

(10)   Not-(Tuesday the senator from California will be in Washington).

to the falsity of (11):

(11)   Cranston is the senator from California.

That is, we could not at any time infer from (9) and (10) the falsity of (12):

(12)   Monday Cranston was the senator from California.

The point is that temporal adverbs have two roles. In initial position, they state that the sentence that follows is true at the time indicated. With (12) we can express at any time the proposition that we express Monday with (11). Within the predicate, the temporal adverb indicates at what time the subject has the property expressed by the predicate. When the time at which the sentence is true is the time of utterance, no initial adverb is needed; when the time at which the property predicated is to be possessed is the same as the time indicated by the initial adverb, or lack of it, no adverb is called for in the predicate.

The fact that "the senator from California" can be proper at one time, improper at another is of course just a special case of the more general fact that "the senator from California" may denote different objects when used at different times or in the scope of different temporal adverbs in initial position. Similarly, if we can show that it makes sense for a proper name to be proper at one time, improper at another, that will be a special case of the more general fact that such names may name different entities at different times or when in the scope of different temporal adverbs in initial position. If so, the argument

(5) After the operation, Smith-Jones will be in room 102.

(6) Not-(after the operation, Brown-Jones will be in room 102).

and, therefore,

(13) Not-(Smith-Jones is the same person as Brown-Jones).

is fallacious. The names "Smith-Jones" and "Brown-Jones" do not occur in (13) in the scope of the temporal operator "After the operation" as they do in (5) and (6). So they cannot be assumed to name the same entities, and (5) and (6) cannot be seen as establishing that something true of one of the entities named in (13) is not true of the other. All that can be inferred is

(14) After the operation, Smith-Jones is not Brown-Jones.

But the mentalist readily admits this; in fact, he insists upon it.

I believe that by distinguishing between (2) and (3) and (2') and (3') and distinguishing between the two roles of temporal adverbs, the mentalist can say everything he needs and wants to say about the case in section 1 without self-contradiction. The latter maneuver blocks the arguments that derive a contradiction from (1), (2'), and (3').

This defense, however, will not be very powerful until we have said more about the relationship between temporal adverbs in initial position and names. It's fairly clear why "the senator from California" denotes differently in (8) and (12). Intuitively, the temporal adverb completes the definite description; it tells us when the property in question, being a senator from California, is to have been possessed by the denotation. But it is not clear why a temporal adverb is needed to "complete" the name "Jones" nor how exactly this works.

In the next two sections I sketch two alternative accounts of our language, each of which provides an explanation of the way in which temporal adverbs and names function and each of which assigns, to the sentences in question, truth conditions that do not lead the mentalist to inconsistency. The first account I reject; the second, I argue, is essentially correct.

5. The Person-Stage Language

In discussing the notion of "strict identity," J. J.C. Smart once remarked:

> When . . . I say the successful general is the same person as the small boy who stole the apples I mean *only that* the successful general I see before me is a time slice of the same four-dimensional object of which the small boy stealing apples is an earlier time slice. (1959, p. 37)[11]

The intuition behind the branch language was that persons are enduring objects in some way composed of person-stages; although we may always identify one or more person-stages in ostensively identifying a person, the words "this person" denote not the person-stage occurring at the time, but the larger whole of which he is in some sense a part. But Smart's remarks suggest a radically different theory: we really refer, each time we use a personal name, to a particular person-stage. Persons are just person-stages and not the "four-dimensional" objects these compose. When I say, "the person you danced with last night is the person sitting on the sofa," the "is" does not express identity, but simply the relation *R*. The sentence says that this relation obtains between two distinct persons, the-girl-you-danced-with-last-night and the-girl-sitting-on-the-sofa. If we use "is" to express identity, the girl you danced with last night is not the

---

[11] To attribute to Smart exactly the theory embodied in the person-stage language as I develop it would be unfair; he remarks that he is permitting himself to "speak loosely."

girl sitting on the sofa. But in such contexts we would use "is" not in this way, but just to express R. In that sense, the one girl is the other. We might object to this theory by pointing out that we say, for instance, that the girl you danced with last night is now on the sofa. How could she be doing anything now if she was no more than a person-stage who barely survived the night with you? Here the person-stage theorist can respond that "the girl I danced with last night is sitting on the sofa" can be understood as an abbreviated version of "the girl I danced with last night is someone sitting on the sofa," where "is" again just expresses the relation R. Thus the sentence says that a certain dancing person-stage has the relation R to a certain sitting person-stage. We might object further that a single name, "Hilda," names both girls and names are presumed to stand for single objects. But the person-stage theorist denies the presumption. "Hilda" is systematically ambiguous; it names different persons at different times, so it is ambiguous, but the persons it names share the name by virtue of having the relation R to a certain person(-stage), say, Hilda-being-baptized, and so the name is systematically and coherently used in such a way that we are easily misled into supposing that it names a single entity.

Thus we can sketch the person-stage language. As with the branch language, each name is assigned to a person-stage. Now, however, instead of supposing that the name then names the branch of which that person-stage is a member, we suppose that it ambiguously names all the person-stages that have R to the assigned stage. But the ambiguity is systematic. At any given time of utterance or within the scope of any temporal adverb, the name will name only those person-stages which occur at the time of utterance or at the time indicated by the temporal adverb and have R to the assigned stage. If and only if there is exactly one such person-stage at a given time, the name is *proper at that time*.

A sentence of the form

N has F at t

uttered at time t' is true if and only if the person-stage named by N at t' has R to some person-stage that occurs at t and has F. A sentence of the form

N is identical with M

is true at t' if and only if the person-stage named by N at t' is identical with the person-stage named by M at t'. A sentence with an initial temporal adverb,

At t', N has F at t

or

At t', N is identical with M

is true if and only if the sentence following the adverb is true when uttered at the time indicated by the adverb.

Thus consider (15) and (16):

(15) Jones will be in room 102 after the operation.
(16) After the operation, Jones will be in room 102.

The first is true, before the operation, if and only if (15TC) is true:

(15TC) The person(-stage) named by "Jones" before the operation has R to some person(-stage) which occurs after the operation and is in room 102.

(We are assuming that "before the operation" and "after the operation" pick out definite times.) The second is true if and only if (16TC) is true:

(16TC) The person(-stage) named by "Jones" after the operation is in room 102.

Given our example, (15) is true, (16) false, for, "the person(-stage) named by 'Jones' after the operation" is improper—that is, "Jones" is improper after the operation—there being two person-stages at that time, s-j and b-j, which have R to Jones-being-baptized.

If we speak the person-stage language, the mentalist is in good shape. The three sentences which the mentalist claims to express truths before the operation, but which seemed to lead him into contradiction, are clearly consistent:

(4) Smith-Jones is the same person as Brown-Jones.
(5) After the operation, Smith-Jones will be in room 102.
(6) Not-(after the operation, Brown-Jones will be in room 102).

Sentence (4) is true if and only if the person-stage named before the operation by "Smith-Jones" is the person-stage named before the operation by "Brown-Jones"; all that can be inferred from (5) and (6) is that the person-stage named after the operation by "Smith-Jones" is not the person-stage named after the operation by "Brown-Jones."

On this theory, it seems that (17)–(20) are all true before the operation:

(17) Jones will be in room 102 after the operation.

(18) Jones will be in room 104 after the operation.

(19) Jones will not be in room 102 after the operation.

(20) Jones will not be in room 104 after the operation.

This means only that (19) and (20) must be carefully distinguished from the negations of (17) and (18), which are false. Sentence (19) is true if and only if the person-stage named by "Jones" has R to some person-stage that occurs after the operation and is not in room 102. So (19) is compatible with (17). This complication arises from the complicated nature of the facts, given the example in section 1 and so is hardly an objection to the person-stage language.

Similarly, the person-stage language must distinguish (21)

(21) Jones will be in room 102 after the operation, and Jones will be in room 104 after the operation.

from (22):

(22) Jones will be in room 102 and room 104 after the operation.

Statement (21) requires that the person-stage named before the operation by "Jones" have R to some person-stage occurring after the operation who is in room 102 and also have R to some person-stage occurring after the operation who is in room 104. But (22) requires that Jones have R to a single person-stage occurring after the operation who is in both room 102 and room 104. There is no such person-stage, so (22) is false.

The person-stage language allows the mentalist to say just what he wants about the example of section 1. Nevertheless, I think it would be a serious mistake to suppose that English is the person-stage language—that our notion of a person is just that of a person-stage.

The person-stage language and the branch language represent two very different ways of looking at the function of sortal terms such as "person." According to the branch language, when we say, "This person will have F at t," the word "person" is a part of the referential apparatus of the sentence. Together with the demonstrative, it identifies a certain enduring object, which has property F at time t. Such analyses of sortals I call *subject* analyses.

The person-stage language suggests what I shall call an adverb analysis of the function of a sortal. In the sentence "This person will have F at t," we are to think of the word "this" as identifying the subject of the sentence—a person-stage—and the remainder of the sentence as telling how, in what manner, that person-stage will have F at t. To be, as we might put it, personally F at t is not to be a person(-stage) that has F at t, but to have R, the relation of personal identity (now opposed to "strict identity," rather than a restriction of it to the domain of persons) to some person(-stage) that has F at t. Being personally F at t is like being married to a janitor; it's not being the janitor, but having a certain intimate relation to someone who is.

The adverb analysis of sortals is radically mistaken. The apparatus that must come with it—that "is the same as" does not mean "is the *same* as," that the little boy stealing apples is strictly speaking not identical with the general before me—seems to be, however consistently it may work out in the end, the progeny of confusion. Usually the confusion takes this line: we think that the general before us is big, but the little boy was small; if they were identical—*strictly identical*—everything true of the one would be true of the other. So they are not strictly identical. Nevertheless, we say that the general is just the same person as the little boy, so "is the same person as" must not mean strict identity. This is all confusion. There is nothing true of the general that is not true of the little boy. They were both small, and neither was a general at that time. The general and the little boy both had the property of being small; neither has it now. If we pick a temporal perspective and stick to it, not ignoring tenses, there is no difficulty. If we choose a timeless perspective, we must build dates into the properties we ascribe. We shall find that both the general and the small boy have the property of (say) "being small in 1920." Only if we ignore both tenses and dates do we get into trouble, and that is mere carelessness.[12]

---

[12] For discussions of the relation between identity and the unity relation (as I have called it) or gen-identity (as Carnap calls a similar notion), see Gottlob Frege (1884/1960), sec. 62ff.; Rudolf Carnap (1958), chap. G; and W. V. Quine (1953), pp. 65ff. For a criticism of the Frege view, see Peter Geach (1967). I discuss Geach's views in essay 1.

It seems, therefore, a mistake for the mentalist to take refuge in the view that we speak the person-stage language.

6. The Lifetime Language

The mentalist cannot take refuge in the theory that English is the branch language, for it allows what cannot be: that before the operation, in talking to Jones, we were not, in a perfectly clear sense, talking to a single person. It violates our linguistic intuitions—what we want to say about our example.

He cannot take refuge in the person-stage language, for it denies what clearly is true: that when I say of someone that he will do such and such, I mean that he will do it. The events in my future are events that will happen to me, and not merely events that will happen to someone else of the same name. The theory that English is the person-stage language violates our semantic intuitions; it gives an unduly complicated account of our language.

Is there any middle ground? Well, what entity is there that meets these two conditions: (i) there is, in a perfectly clear sense, just one of these entities identified by an ostension to Jones before the operation; (ii) everything that is in Jones's future (that is, everything that will happen to Smith-Jones or Brown-Jones) happens to a person-stage belonging to this entity? Clearly, one entity that meets these requirements is the Y-shaped structure composed of the branches of both Smith-Jones and Brown-Jones. I shall call any set of person-stages that meets the following condition a lifetime: there is some member in the set such that all and only members of the set have R to that person-stage. The Y-shaped structure, although not a branch, is a lifetime, for all person-stages in it have R to j, the preoperative stage of Jones. But the two branches that compose the Y-shaped structure are also each lifetimes.

At first sight the suggestion that persons are lifetimes seems quite unpromising, leaving the mentalist worse off than the hypothesis that persons are branches. For the preoperative stages of Jones belong to three lifetimes: the Y-shaped structure and each of its branches. If it was implausible to suppose that Jones was two persons all along, surely it is more implausible by at least a half to suppose that he was three.

But notice that each person-stage does identify a unique lifetime—the lifetime containing all person-stages that have R to it. Thus the principle that when we have identified a person-stage, we have identified a person, violation of which made the branch language seem implausible, is not violated by the lifetime language.

Let us say that a person-stage *determines* the lifetime it identifies in the way just described—the lifetime containing all person-stages with R to it. This is not the *only* way that a person-stage may identify a lifetime. There is another, and the different ways *may*, in bizarre circumstances, lead to different results. Notice that although each person-stage *determines* one and only one lifetime, it may be a member of several. The preoperative stage of Jones, *j*, *determines* the Y-shaped lifetime. But, in addition, it is a member of both branches of the Y, and each of the branches is also a lifetime. Neither of these is *determined* by *j*, but they both *contain j*.

Now, at any given time *t*, only a certain number of lifetimes will be *determinable*, in the sense that they are determined by some person-stage occurring at that time. Before the operation, neither of the branches are determinable in this sense: there is no person-stage occurring which has R to all and only their members. The Y-shaped lifetime is similarly not determinable *after* the operation.

Consider the person-stage *b-j*—a post operative stage of Brown-Jones. This *b-j determines* a lifetime, one of the branches of the Y-shaped lifetime, the *b-j branch*. Before the operation, the *b-j* branch is not determinable. Nevertheless, there *is* a lifetime determinable before the operation that contains *b-j*. There is, in fact, one and only one such lifetime—the Y-shaped lifetime. Thus *b-j* can be used to identify the Y-shaped lifetime: it is the unique lifetime, determinable before the operation, that contains *b-j*.

For any time *t* and any person-stage s, we can speak of the *lifetime identified by* s *at t*. This description will denote the unique lifetime determinable at *t* which contains s, if there is such; otherwise, it is improper. In normal circumstances, *if* there is a lifetime *identified by s at t*, it will just be the lifetime *determined by s*. But, in bizarre circumstances, such as those at issue in this paper, this identity will not hold. The lifetime identified by *b-j* before the operation is not the lifetime determined by *b-j*, but the lifetime determined by *j*. In normal circumstances, if s is contained in any lifetime determinable at *t*, the lifetime determined by s will be determinable at *t*. But in bizarre cases this will not be so: the lifetime determined by s is not determinable after the operation, but *j* is contained in a lifetime determinable at that time—as a matter of fact, in two, for both the *s-j* branch and the *b-j* branch are lifetimes.

Given these notions, we can sketch an account of a final and I think satisfactory refuge for the mentalist, the theory that English is a *lifetime language*. The lifetime language embodies a subject analysis of sortals. A person has a property F at t if and only if his lifetime contains a person-stage that occurs at t and has F. But the lifetime language also retains a systematic ambiguity of personal names reminiscent of the person-stage language. Indeed, it assigns exactly the same truth conditions to the relevant sentences as does the person-stage language. The lifetime language justifies the line of defense drawn in section 4 of this essay.

Again we assume that names are directly assigned to person-stages. Where u is the person-stage to which N is assigned, the lifetime determined by u is the *primary referent* of N. But N will also have a number of *secondary referents,* which probably will but may not be identical with its primary referent. The *secondary referent of* N *at time* t is the lifetime identified by u at t. If u does not identify a lifetime at t—if there is no unique person-stage at t with R to u—then N has no secondary referent at t, and N is *improper* at t. Thus, in the ordinary case, the secondary referents of N and its primary referent will be one. But in unusual cases they will not.

A sentence of the form

N has F at t

uttered at time t' is true if and only if the secondary referent of N at t' contains a person-stage that occurs at t and has F. A sentence of the form

N is identical with M

is true at t' if and only if the secondary referent of N at t' is identical with the secondary referent of M at t'. A sentence with an initial temporal adverb,

at t', N has F at t

or

at t' N is identical with M

is true if and only if the sentence following the temporal adverb is true when uttered at the time indicated by the temporal adverb.

Thus consider:

(15) Jones will be in room 102 after the operation.

(16) After the operation, Jones will be in room 102.

Sentence (15) is true before the operation if and only if (15TC') is true:

(15TC') The secondary referent of "Jones" before the operation contains a person-stage that occurs after the operation and is in room 102.

Sentence (16) is true if and only if (16TC') is true:

(16TC') The secondary referent of "Jones" after the operation is in room 102.

Sentence (15) is true, (16) false, for "Jones" has no secondary referent after the operation.

The sentences (4), (5), and (6), to the truth of which before the operation the mentalist is committed,

(4) Smith-Jones is the same person as Brown-Jones.

(5) After the operation, Smith-Jones will be in room 102.

(6) Not-(after the operation, Brown-Jones will be in room 102).

are consistent. Sentence (4) is true if and only if the secondary referents of "Brown-Jones" and "Smith-Jones" before the operation are one; all that can be inferred from (5) and (6) is that the secondary referents of "Brown-Jones" and "Smith-Jones" after the operation are distinct.

As before, (17)–(20)

(17) Jones will be in room 102 after the operation.

(18) Jones will be in room 104 after the operation.

(19) Jones will not be in room 102 after the operation.

(20) Jones will not be in room 104 after the operation.

all come out true before the operation. Again we must distinguish the negations of (17) and (18), which are false, from (19) and (20). Sentence (19) is true if and only if the secondary referent of "Jones" before the operation contains a person-stage that occurs after the operation and is not in room 102.

As before, we must distinguish (21) from (22):

(21) Jones will be in room 102 after the operation, and Jones will be in room 104 after the operation.

(22) Jones will be in room 102 and room 104 after the operation.

Sentence (21) requires that the secondary referent of "Jones" before the operation contains a person-stage occurring after the operation which is in room 102 and contains a person-stage occurring after the operation which is in room 104. Sentence (21) is true. But (22) requires that the secondary referent of "Jones" before the operation contains a single person-stage occurring after the operation which is both in room 102 and in room 104. Sentence (22) is false.

Now what is the answer to the fair question, "How many persons were there in Jones's room (room 100) before the operation?"?

On the one hand, "one" seems to be the correct answer, for there was only a single person, Jones, in the room. On the other hand, Smith-Jones and Brown-Jones were both there, so "two" seems like the correct answer. But, after all, three lifetimes (the Smith-Jones branch, the Brown-Jones branch, and the Y-shaped structure) contain the person-stage in room 100, so the answer would appear to be "three."

All three answers are correct—but they are answers to different, and distinguishable, questions. Consider open sentences of the form

x has F at t

A person satisfies such an open sentence *at a time*. Person z satisfies the given open sentence at time t' if and only if z is identifiable at t' and contains a person-stage that occurs at t and has F. The open sentence

x is in room 100 before the operation

is satisfied by exactly one person before the operation; so the answer to the question "How many persons are in room 100?" asked before the operation (and to the question "Before the operation, how many persons were in room 100?" asked at any time) is "one." After the operation, two distinct persons satisfy the open sentence; so the answer to the question asked at that time (and to the question "After the operation, how many persons were in room 100 before the operation?" asked at any time) is "two." There is no one time at which the correct answer to the question "How many persons were in room 100 before the operation?" is "three." But the lifetime language will have to allow us to make assertions such as

At some time, Brown-Jones was in room 100 before the operation.

which will be true just in case there is some time *t* such that

At *t*, Brown-Jones was in room 100 before the operation.

is true. The open sentence

At some time, *x* was in room 100 before the operation.

will be satisfied by person *z* if and only if *z* is identifiable at some time and contains a person-stage occurring before the operation in room 100. This open sentence is satisfied by three persons, and so the answer to "At any time, how many persons were in room 100 before the operation?" is "three."

Can these three persons be identified within the lifetime language? Not simply by the names "Smith-Jones," "Brown-Jones," and "Jones," for these identify persons only in conjunction with temporal adverbs or times of utterance. Not by definite descriptions of the form

the *x*, such that *x* has *F* at *t*

for these too may denote different persons at different times or in the scope of different temporal adverbs. We can identify them, however, by use of definite descriptions built up from more complicated open sentences. A definite description of the form

the *x*, such that at *t'*, *x* has *F* at *t*

denotes the person, if any, who is determinable at *t'* and contains a person-stage that occurs at *t* and has *F*. And it denotes this person at any time. Thus, the three characters in our story may be identified as

the person *x*, such that, before the operation, *x* was in room 100 before the operation

the person x, such that, after the operation, x was in room 102 after
the operation

the person x, such that, after the operation, x was in room 104 after
the operation.

These three persons are distinct and never were identical—and nothing I have said denies that, nor do (2') and (3').

What of fusions? In a convincing case of person fusion, in which a single person-stage has R to two simultaneous but distinct antecedent person-stages, I would argue that we should say the survivor was both of his precursors and had done everything each of them had done. The lifetime language gives this result. In cases of combined fusion and fission that I have considered, the lifetime language seems to remain adequate.

Thus the suggestion that persons are lifetimes (or at any rate entities correlated one-to-one with lifetimes) proves satisfactory. In any normal case, the lifetimes are just branches. This explains our propensity for making inferences valid in the branch language but not quite valid in the lifetime language, as when we infer that tomorrow Smith will be in Dubuque from the fact that Smith will be in Dubuque tomorrow. Further, the lifetime language, like the person-stage language but unlike the branch language, allows us to assign names to persons with confidence, without fear that future events will present us with the choice of contradicting ourselves or deeming many statements that seemed to be true false because of unforeseen improprieties. Whenever we isolate a person-stage, we have isolated a person, namely, the person (lifetime) determined by that person-stage. Finally, the lifetime language, like the branch language but unlike the person-stage language, allows us to mean by our words what we think we mean, to wit, identity by "is the same as" and so forth. It embodies a subject analysis of sortals. The lifetime language, then—or, more precisely, the theory that English is a lifetime language—satisfies both our linguistic and our semantic intuitions. Moreover, it has a certain naturalness. Who is Jones? The person who did all the things in Jones's past and will do all the things in his future. Jones's future includes both Brown-Jones's and Smith-Jones's, for it is true of Jones that he will do all the things they do. This is what the mentalist wants to say, and the lifetime language allows him to say it.

As was pointed out, the lifetime language and the person-stage language do not differ in the truth conditions assigned to sentences but do differ in the assignment of entities to the parts of the sentence. In both we have a rather elaborate system of identification. At each time, an entity is identified by a person-stage u or a name N assigned to it. In the person-stage language, the entity is the unique person-stage occurring at that time with R to u. In the lifetime language, the entity is the unique lifetime determinable at that time and containing u. The difference is that in the lifetime language, the entities identified by u at any two times when it identifies anything at all will very probably be the same; in the person-stage language, they will certainly be different. To the extent that there is no branching, the lifetime language is more economical than the person-stage language in having fewer entities in its domain of discourse.

7. Conclusion

In speaking of a case of a dividing self, Jonathan Bennett has remarked, "[T]he fission of a mind, if it could happen, would involve the concept of identity in the same way (whatever that is) as the fission of an ameba" (1967, p. 112).

This remark seems to me to conceal a mistake. It may be that if selves divided as often as cells or amebas divide, we would develop a concept for dealing with the phenomena our concept of a person now deals with that resembles, in matters of individuation and identification, the concept of a cell or an ameba. In a language embodying such a concept, it would apparently be correct to say that Jones died, and two new "persons" were born, at the time of the operation (see Carnap 1958, chap. G).[13] Whether we would develop such a concept is, I suppose, a matter for speculative linguistics. It might be rational for us to do so in those circumstances. That is a difficult philosophical question, difficult in part because of the importance of memory in questions about persons. I have not dealt with either of these questions directly, although what I have said may have some relevance to them. I have dealt with the question whether the mentalist account of the concept we have can survive an objection based on what appears to be logically possible. I claim it can. Whether the concept itself could survive, would survive, or should survive, if that

---

[13] See Carnap, op. cit., chap. H.

logical possibility became commonplace in actuality, is another question.[14]

Our "choice" of a language reflects certain pervasive empirical facts, and the transitivity of R is one such. A tribe that spoke the person-stage language might rationally, for the sake of economy, decide to adopt the lifetime language if empirical facts were such (as they are) that in doing so they would, for all practical purposes, be speaking the branch language. But if dividing (or fusing) selves were commonplace, not only in the minds of the philosopher members of the tribe but in reality, there would be little to recommend the lifetime language over the person-stage language. The comparative economy of the lifetime language is an empirical matter. How often selves would have to divide before its retention became more trouble than it was worth is a matter on which I shall not speculate.

Given the nature of our world, the lifetime language shares the advantages of both the branch language and the person-stage language. Insofar as R remains transitive, the lifetime language gives us the same economy as the branch language. But should there be counterinstances to the transitivity of R, the branch language would let us down. If we spoke it, we would have to check deep into the past and future to assign a name with confidence. We would have, as it were, no spot check for identity. We could not assume that we could tell whether A and B were identical merely by isolating them (him) at a particular time and conducting an examination. Here the lifetime language shares the advantages of the person-stage language. In the person-stage language one cannot go wrong in assigning names; if you have isolated a person-stage, you have isolated a person. The same is true of the lifetime language, for every person-stage determines a lifetime.

The evidence that the lifetime language is a correct approximation of that portion of English in which the mentalist describes the case with which we began is (i) R (some mentalist analysis of the relation between person-stages that are stages of a single person) seems to give

---

[14] Derek Parfit (1971) argues that a single instance of self-division is more than our ordinary concept of a person can handle. This I have, in effect, argued against. Parfit argues interestingly that consideration of such cases, and other even more bizarre possibilities, leads us to see that our concept of a person is unimportant and should perhaps be replaced with other "'ways of thinking." I would rather say our concept of a person is important in large part because our world does not realize such possibilities.

the correct analysis of personal identity; (ii) the case described in section 1 is conceivable; (iii) speakers of English without an overdeveloped fear of self-contradiction are perfectly willing to describe this case by (1), (2'), and (3') and unwilling to swallow the story that there were two persons all along; and (iv) a subject analysis of sortals is more natural and economical than an adverb analysis. At one point Arthur Prior was willing to abandon the transitivity of identity itself in order to preserve the point of view of (i) through (iv).[15] I believe the solution I have outlined is much less drastic. If we want the economy of the branch language and the nominal security of the person-stage language, we should speak the lifetime language. Is it so surprising that we do?

---

[15] Prior discussed this problem in two places. In "Opposite Number" (1957) he advocated abandoning the principle that "P" and "n-moments ago it was true that n-moments from then, P" are logically equivalent. In "Time, Existence, and Identity" (1966), he pointed out the inadequacy of his earlier suggestion and suggested abandoning the transitivity of identity. I hope the reader will agree without extended argument that a less drastic solution than this is desirable. My solution has some resemblance to one suggested but summarily rejected by Prior in "Opposite Number," p. 199.

4

The Two Faces of Identity

In this essay I offer an account of what we are looking for when we ask for the identity conditions of some category of things. The account is a development of those sketched in "The Same *F*" and "Can the Self Divide?" but goes importantly beyond them in several ways. Towards the end of this essay, I come back to the issue of dividing selves, reconsider the conclusion in "Can the Self Divide?" and decide I still think it is right.

The discussion of conditions of identity is often provoked by a puzzling case. It will be helpful to have one to refer to. In my *Dialogue on Personal Identity and Immortality,* I consider the fictional case of Julia North and Mary Frances Beaudine. In her novel *Who is Julia?,* Barbara Harris supposes that Julia is run over by a streetcar in saving the life of Mary Frances's child. Mary Frances has a massive stroke as a result of witnessing this. Thanks to postmodern medical science, we end up with someone I'll call Mary-Julia with Julia's intact brain and Mary Frances's intact body.

1. How Can Identity Conditions Be a Problem?

That A is the same person as B seems just to require that A and B are persons and that A is identical to B. That is, the relation of personal identity seems to be merely the restriction to the domain of persons of the relation of identity. And so it seems the problem of personal identity should break neatly into halves: what is required for A to be a person? And, what is required for A to be identical to B? And then it seems that the second half must already be solved. For there are, in logic texts, straightforward and relatively unproblematic accounts of

---

"The Two Faces of Identity" was written for this volume.

identity; identity theory is one of the least controversial areas of knowledge a philosopher is likely to need.

Yet it is not the first but the second half that gives us difficulty. Mary-Julia has Julia's brain and Mary Frances's body. We are sure of the personhood of all of the characters in our puzzle: Mary-Julia, Mary Frances, and Julia. No one denies the identity of Mary-Julia with Mary Frances or with Julia on the grounds that one or both is not a person, but, say, a machine or mannequin. It is the question of identity that perplexes.

It is not only personal identity, but identity of many kinds that gives rise to philosophical problems. Can the river stay the same when the water is constantly changing? Is the rebuilt church the same as the one that stood in the same place, serving the same congregation and called by the same name? In these cases the problem does not seem to be saying which things are and which things are not rivers or churches, but saying when rivers or churches are identical.

My goal in this essay is to say what it is we are wondering about when we wonder about the identity conditions of a kind of object. That is, what problem is left over when the clear and uncontroversial account of identity offered by logic texts has been digested? What is the relation between this single clear relation called "identity" and the diversity of problematic relations we use in making judgment about the identity of persons, rivers, churches, baseball games, and everything else?

2. The Logical Properties of Identity

Virtually every logic book contains a section on identity, stating the properties of this relation in a clear, concise, and unequivocal manner. Identity is *strongly reflexive:* every object is identical with itself. It is *symmetrical:* if A is identical with B, B is identical with A. It is *transitive:* if A is identical with B and B with C, then A is identical with C. All of these properties are obvious or even trivial when the central idea of identity is grasped: if A and B are identical, then there is just *one* thing that is both A and B. "A" and "B" are two terms that stand for *it.* For example, from transitivity and reflexivity one can prove that if A is identical with B and B with C, then C is identical with A. But this is obvious: when we go, by identity, from A to B, B to C, and back to A, we are in fact going nowhere; since we do not move, we need not return.

A further property of identity is embodied in the principle of the indiscernibility of the identical: if A and B are identical, then they have all properties in common. This principle, like the other properties of identity, seems obvious and uncontroversial once we grasp the connection between *identity* and oneness. If A and B were identical but had different properties, one thing would both have and not have those properties. And that cannot be. The indiscernibility of identicals is as clear, and should be as uncontroversial, as the principle that an object cannot both have and not have a certain property.

3. Is Identity Identity?

If identity is so clear and trivial, how can personal identity be so murky and important?

One possibility is that this clear notion of identity is not the usual notion of identity at all, or perhaps only one of a number of usual notions of identity, many of which share neither its clarity or its triviality.

We find many philosophers expressing variations on this idea. J. J. C. Smart, for example, once distinguished what he calls "two senses" of "is identical with." In "7 is identical with the smallest prime number greater than 5," we employ the strict sense, presumably what I have called pure identity.

> When on the other hand I say that the successful general is the same person as the small boy who stole the apples I mean *only that* the successful general I see before me is a time slice of the same four-dimensional object of which the small boy stealing the apples is an earlier time slice (Smart 1959, p. 37).

We would ordinarily say, in the circumstance Smart describes, that the general was the very person, the very same person, who stole the apples. So Smart's conception is that personal identity is not the same sort of identity we have with numbers and, further, that it is not, strictly speaking, identity. We should not simply assume, for example, that the relation the general has to the small boy has the properties identity theory requires of pure identity. And it is clear that Smart thought that, generally, when matters of continuity through space and time are relevant, we are not dealing with pure or strict identity.

Why should Smart have thought this? There can be no disagreement about the claim that "identity" and "same" can be used to express other relations than pure identity. Identical twins, for example, would not be twins if purely identical; here "identical" means roughly "exactly similar in appearance."

If the old general and the young thief are discernible, if they do not have all properties in common, they cannot be purely identical. While Smart does not say that they are discernible, this may be his reason for denying pure identity. At any rate, this is a common enough reaction to this sort of case to merit discussion.

"The boy is young and the general is not. So they are discernible and not identical." This is bad reasoning. Although the general is old, he was young; although the boy was young, he is now old. Both the general and the boy were once young and now are old. There is no clash of properties, no discernibility, and no reason to abandon pure identity.

We can treat properties in various ways, and unless we make sure to alter our conception of the principle of the indiscernibility of the identical accordingly, we will run into problems of the sort just encountered. Consider:

Mike ran to work Saturday, May 23, 1973.

Is this true because Mike has the property of having run to work Saturday, May 23, 1973? Or is it true because Mike had, that Saturday, the property of running to work? Let us say that *running to work Saturday, May 23, 1973* is a permanent property. If one has it ever, one has it always. *Running to work,* on the other hand, is a temporary property. One has it on the way to work but loses it once one gets there. If we choose to think in terms of temporary properties, which is natural in our tensed language, we must phrase the principle of the indiscernibility of identicals accordingly:

If A and B are identical, A has (had, or will have) at *t* just those properties B has (had, or will have) at *t*.

It will not generally be true, even if A is B, that A had all the properties B has or A has all the properties B had or A has all the properties B will have. But it will also not be true that A has all the properties A had or will have. When I finish this essay, I will no longer have a property I once had, of not having finished it yet. Things change, and they can remain identical, in the sense of being one and the same thing, while doing so.

This is a simple point, but there seems to be built into the human psyche a disastrous pair of natural tendencies: to think in terms of temporary properties and yet to regard the tense as an irrelevancy in the natural rendering of the indiscernibility of the identical. A cruel trilemma is thus posed: give up the principle, give up change, or suppose the identity of persons and chairs and rocks and rivers is not pure identity. But the trilemma is false. There is no reason of discernibility to deny the pure identity of the general and the boy.

4. The Circle of Predication and Individuation

So, personal identity requires indiscernibility, and there should be no objection to thinking of it as a restriction of identity to the domain of persons.

But why, then, should there be a problem of personal identity? If we have a complete account of identity, what more need be said about personal identity?

Consider Julia, Mary Frances, and Mary-Julia, the survivor of the transplant operation. The question is, who is this survivor? Mary Frances, Julia, or neither of them? By application of the indiscernibility of the identical, we know that if the survivor is Mary Frances, the survivor and Mary Frances will have all properties in common. Does this help us to decide? If we are not careful, it may seem to: Mary Frances didn't know French, the survivor does, so the survivor and Mary Frances are discernible and hence not identical. But this argument involves just the mistake exposed in section 2 of this essay. Mary Frances couldn't speak French before the operation. The survivor can speak French after the operation. This information doesn't discern. We would need to establish that the survivor could speak French before the operation or Mary Frances couldn't after the operation. But then we would have to know just what is in doubt. The question of whether the survivor could speak French before the operation is just the question of who she is. If she is Julia, then she could; if she is Mary Frances, then she couldn't, and her French speaking is a recently acquired trait gained through acquisition of what used to be someone else's brain. Only misapplied is the indiscernibility of the identical of any help in resolving the case. The principle really just guarantees that an identity puzzle will also be an indiscernibility puzzle.

The reason indiscernibility doesn't help is not that it is unconnected with personal identity, but because the connection is too close. For the survivor to have known French before the operation is just for the survivor to be identical with someone who, before the operation, knew French. To establish the one fact is to establish the other. Our understanding of what it is for a person to have had a property in the past is not separable from our understanding of what it is for a person to be identical with someone in the past.

We have, in effect, suggested, and rejected, a format for explaining the identity conditions for a certain kind of object, *Ks*. The suggested format was this:

> *x* and *y* are the same *K* iff *x* and *y* are *K*'s and *x* and *y* have all properties in common

The problem with this format isn't that the statements generated from it by replacing "*K*" with various kind terms aren't true; they are true. The problem is that we couldn't *explain* identity in this way, for the right side could not be understood unless we understood, for any property of *K*'s whatsoever, what it is for a *K* to have that property. And, unless *K*-identity is already understood, we don't have that understanding.

Now this suggests a more general problem. If we wish to explain or analyze what it is for this *K* and that *K* to stand in a certain relation, the natural way to do it seems to explain it in terms of the relations and properties that are necessary and sufficient for this relation to hold. That is, the natural way to do it is to talk about *K*'s. But understanding such talk requires understanding references to *K*'s, and predication about *K*'s, that is, understanding what it is for *K*'s to have the properties and stand in the relations used in the explanation. But, it seems, understanding predication about *K*'s presupposes an understanding of *K*-individuation, the identity conditions of *K*'s. It looks like we are faced with a circle, *the circle of predication and individuation*. To break the circle, it would be necessary to find *some* properties of *K*'s, and relations between *K*'s, which can be understood independently of individuation. The explanation could proceed, without circularity, in terms of this restricted set of relations and properties. If we review what we have said so far, it will seem that this strategy should work.

5. Identity's Two Faces

Identity seems to have two faces. On the one hand, it is a universal notion; any entity, of any kind, of any category, a snail or a number, is identical with itself. This can be said a priori. Whatever object you care to mention, even if I know nothing special about it, I can be sure that it is self-identical.

On the other hand, there seems to be a family of empirical relations that we call "identity," the determination of which may take careful and painstaking investigation. That the sun is always the same and is not new every day was, Frege noted, one of the most fertile of astronomical discoveries. It couldn't be determined a priori. That the man on the defendant's chair is the bank robber would be impossible for the jury to determine without careful attention to the evidence. And the relation between the man and the robber, about which the jury must deliberate, seems to have little to do with the relation that, say, the number of pencils on my desk has with the number of fingers on my hand or that the war raging in the Pacific in 1945 had to the one raging in Poland in 1939. We seem to have various relations for various kinds of objects that pass as identity and cannot be judged a priori.

We seem to have arrived at the following picture. For each kind of object K, there is a relation which is necessary and sufficient for K-identity. This relation is not identity, nor even generally equivalent to it, but it is equivalent in the restricted case of K's. Such a relation we can call the condition of K-identity.

Spatiotemporal continuity, for example, has often been suggested as the condition of identity for material objects, or at least for most types of material objects. Let's assume this suggestion is correct for the time being. Still, it is not the condition for baseball team identity, for baseball teams can undergo shifts from city to city at the stroke of a pen without in any sense passing through intervening places. Admittedly, the A's passed through Kansas City on their way from Philadelphia to Oakland, but the Giants moved from New York to San Francisco without passing through the Midwest at all. So the relation of spatiotemporal continuity, while it may be the condition of identity for rocks and trees, is not the condition of identity for baseball teams. It is even more clearly not the condition of identity for numbers, for numbers can't even stand in this relation.

Now, on this picture, an account of the identity conditions for a kind of objects K should look like this:

Where R is the condition of K-identity, x is the same K as y iff x and y are K's and x has R to y

Of course, R need not be a simple relation or one that philosophers will have any luck at all analyzing or explaining. Presumably, if humans make identity judgments about K's, it must be a relation we can determine to hold, or at least think we can.

The various theories of personal identity briefly mentioned in essay 3 can be put into this format:

> x is the same person as y iff x and y are persons and x has the same body as y
>
> x is the same person as y iff x and y are persons and x remembers y's thought and action
>
> x is the same person as y iff x and y are persons and x has the same soul as y

Given this picture, we can understand the "two faces" of identity. There is the relation of identity whose logical features completely circumscribe it. There are various conditions of identity which differ from kind of object to kind of object. It is these for which we search when looking for an explanation of K-identity.

6. The Circle of Reference and Individuation

But there are difficulties with this way of looking at things.

One question immediately arises when we look at the conditions of K-identity in this way. How can the relation in question guarantee indiscernibility? Why should the two faces of identity conform with one another? This they must do, for the identity condition guarantees K-identity, K-identity is identity restricted to K's, and identity guarantees indiscernibility. But why should, say, rocks that are spatiotemporally continuous have all their properties in common? The problem is not so much that this question cannot be answered, but that the answer leads into another circle, the circle of reference and individuation.

At too casual a glance, we may think that something has gone terribly wrong, for the various conditions of identity might seem not to guarantee indiscernibility at all. The rock that was on my desk a moment ago and the rock beside the paint pail are spatiotemporally continuous; that is, a rock-filled continuous path stretches from one to the other. But they are hardly indiscernible: the one was gray, and the other is red; the one was on the desk, and the other is on the floor.

But this is just our old fallacy again. The red rock on the floor was on the desk and was gray, and that's just what we said about the rock that was on the desk. That the red rock was gray seems to depend importantly on its identity, on the present assumptions, on the fact that it is spatiotemporally continuous with the rock that was on the desk and was gray. To understand what it is for a rock to have been gray seems to involve understanding what it is for a rock to be identical to a rock that was gray. One who did not understand that spatiotemporal continuity was the condition of rock identity would not realize that the red rock had been gray, even if all the facts were readily available.

These reflections seem to provide an answer to our question. The identity condition of K's guarantees indiscernibility, because the identity condition is involved in what it is for a K to have a property. If rock A is gray at t and spatiotemporally continuous with the rock on the floor at t', then the rock on the floor at t' also has the property of being gray at t. Metaphysically, properties flow along the relation of identity. If A and B are K's and the condition of identity is met, then they will share all properties, because the properties of the one become by that fact the properties of the other.

Like much that is strictly speaking incoherent in philosophy, this all makes a point. The point is that the identity condition secures indiscernibility, because the scheme of K-individuation, the identity condition for K's, is a part of the scheme of K-predication, the condition under which K's have various properties and stand in various relations.

This is really the same point, made earlier, when we wondered why knowing that indiscernibility was a condition of identity did not solve our problems with regard to Julia, Mary Frances, and Mary-Julia. To check on indiscernibility, we have to understand under what conditions persons have properties, and this involves understanding personal identity. If we don't know whether Mary-Julia is Mary Frances, we don't know whether Mary Frances had the property of having already known French.

Given this intimate connection, can we really have evaded the circle of predication and individuation? It seems that although the understanding of some properties (such as having known French) and relations (such as having been taught French by Madame Foucault) presuppose an understanding of identity conditions, understanding other properties and relations does not. For example, we can determine that Mary-Julia speaks French without solving the problem of who she is, Julia or Mary Frances. Similarly, we may understand what it is for *person* x *to have the same body as person* y or for *person* x *to remember something that person* y *did* without understanding the conditions of personal identity. Though we cannot explain personal identity in terms of sharing *all* properties and relations, as long as we confine ourselves to the properties and relations that can be understood independently of individuation, we can explain it.

7. Explaining Identity Conditions

But another set of problems begins to emerge with the suggested format if we press our examples a little. Consider the claim that spatiotemporal continuity is the condition of identity for material objects. How would this be stated more precisely? We might say that where K is a kind of material object, say, rocks,

> A is the same rock as B iff A is a rock and B is a rock and there is a spatiotemporally continuous path from A to B with a rock at each point along it.

But, now, this is really a very curious thing to say. If A and B are identical, they are in exactly the same place. A path from one to the other would be too short to be worth mentioning.

Perhaps the problem is that we need descriptions that locate the rocks identified in different places and times: "The rock that broke my window Saturday is identical with the rock that broke your window Sunday if and only if there is a spatiotemporally continuous path from the one to the other with a rock at each point."

But this is no better. If the rock mentioned first is identical with the rock mentioned second, they are now in exactly the same place. And wherever the one has been, the other has been, too. No path has ever needed to stretch between them. A good thing, too—there has never been any room.

The problem seems to be this. When we say that rocks are identical if spatiotemporally continuous, or if a continuous rock-filled path stretches from one to the other, we must be thinking of two things.

But if the path constitutes rock identity, there aren't two things, but only one. But the relation we were trying to use, that of there being a continuous path between, seems to be a relation that can hold only between an object and another object. As soon as we accept this relation as our condition of identity, it becomes incoherent that it should be such. Or, if we say that everything has the "null path" between it and itself, trivial.

Consider the theory that Mary-Julia is Julia only if she can remember Julia's actions. To see if this relation obtains, it seems we have to go to the referent of "Julia" and the referent of "Mary-Julia" and see if the relation obtains between them. If we don't understand the terms "Julia" and "Mary-Julia," we don't understand the left side of the explanation of identity as couched in the current format. But to understand a term such as "Julia" is to be able to determine which person is Julia, to know to whom "Julia" refers. But if we could do that, we would already understand the identity conditions for persons. I called this the circle of individuation and reference. To explain the identity conditions for K's, we need to talk about them. To talk about them, we need singular terms that refer to them. To understand these terms is to be able to pick out which K's they refer to. But to do that we need to understand the identity conditions for K's.

Now, this seems like it must be some sort of confusion rather than a deep problem. What is intended by the explanations of identity in terms of spatiotemporal continuity or memory seems clear enough. We do seem to be able to explain identity conditions in the way suggested.

Clearly, to understand the left side, for example, "the rock that struck your window at 5:00 P.M. Saturday," what we need to do is to be able to determine which rock this refers to from among the rocks inspectable at that time. We could do this without being able to *trace* the rock, without knowing its identity condition. And similarly for Julia.

However, an important point emerges. The circle of individuation showed that until we understood the identity conditions for persons, we don't fully understand the ascription of properties and relations to persons. We partly understand it: we know under what conditions *this* person speaks French. But we don't fully understand it; we don't understand what it is for this person *to have been able to speak French yesterday*. The understanding of ascriptions of the first sort plus an understanding of individuation yield an understanding of ascriptions of the second sort.

This second problem, the circle of reference and individuation, was that we don't fully understand reference to K's until we understand the conditions of K-identity. Again, we have a partial understanding. I can pick out, from among the objects before us now, after the operation, the one we refer to with "Mary-Julia." The problem isn't epistemological; it's not that I think identical twins might be involved. Even given full information, I can't trace Mary-Julia back.

It's clear that identity conditions can be explained by the format

A is the same K as B iff A has R to B

But these considerations suggest that the format misleads us as to exactly what we do understand. My understanding of the singular terms A and B on the left side of "iff," prior to being told that R is the condition of identity, differs from my understanding of them after I have learned this. Just as my understanding of "knows French at t" was limited to being able to apply it at t, so my understanding of "Mary-Julia" is limited. Again, it seems that a partial understanding of reference plus an understanding of the conditions of identity yield a full understanding of reference. The fact that the right side is only partially understood, it seems, should be represented in the format.

8. Partial Understanding of Identity

We need a format that makes clear that to understand an explanation of K-identity, only a partial understanding of K-predication and a partial understanding of K reference can be presupposed, and only a partial understanding need be presupposed.

One way to represent this is to suppose that on the right-hand side of our present format, the singular terms have, as their reference, not K's but *K-stages* and that the relation used on the right is not a relation between K's, but between K-stages. For example, in the case of the rocks, what the "path" stretches between is not rocks (or a rock and itself) but rock-stages (which might just be taken to be those place-times occupied by rocks). To understand the right side, I need only to be able to tell rock-occupied place-times from place-times that are not rock occupied, to know the boundaries of rock-stages, and to be able to understand when two rock-stages are joined by a continuous path of rock-filled stages.

On this approach, what is misleading about the format is that the singular terms are used ambiguously on the left and right sides. On the right side, they refer to rock-stages, on the left to rocks.

Our account of rock identity looked like this:

The rock at p^t is the same rock as the rock at $p^{t'}$

iff

p^t is rock occupied and $p^{t'}$ is rock occupied and there is a continuous sequence of place-times between p^t and $p^{t'}$, each member of which is rock occupied.

Here we have given necessary and sufficient conditions for a statement about rock identity in terms of statements not about rocks, but about place-times. We introduce K-identity without presupposing K-individuation.

Before criticizing this idea, let's develop it somewhat.

We have a class of entities, place-times, that stand in a certain relation, *being occupied by,* to rocks. Every rock determines a class of place-times, those place-times p^t such that the rock was in p at t. And each place-time is either occupied by exactly one rock or none. Let us call place-times the class of "rock occurrences" and "occupying" the occurrence relation. And generally I will speak of the class of K-occurrences. Note that, somewhat unnaturally, K-occurrences are not K's. Place-times are not rocks.

Next we have a relation among rock occurrences. This relation is not identity. This is a complex relation for which it will be handy to have a simple name; let's call it "being rock-connected." This relation, like identity, is transitive and symmetrical. It is *weakly* reflexive; any place-time that is rock-connected with any place-time is rock-connected to itself. Thus rock-connectedness is an equivalence relation. It partitions the set of rock-occupied place-times into mutually exclusive sets. Each member of one of these equivalence sets is rock-connected to all the other members.

To understand the left side or our explanation, one needs to understand what it is for a place-time to be rock-occupied and what it is for place-times to be rock-connected. Now, in fact, a place-time is rock-occupied only if there is a rock in the place at the time. It seems one could understand the notion of a place-time being rock-occupied without having a fully developed concept of rocks as temporally enduring objects. And, further, place-times are rock-connected only if the rock that occupies one is identical with the rock that occupies the other. But, again, it seems one could identify the place-times that are rock-connected without yet having the full concept of a rock.

We have, then, two skills or competencies which are presupposed by the explanation of rock identity. I shall say that one who has these skills has a "preindividuative" understanding of rocks. The concept of a rock plays, in this conceptual scheme, only a predicative, and not a referential, role. The explanation of rock identity introduces, on the basis of the preindividuative concept of a rock, an individuative concept.

To generalize, an explanation of K-identity requires the following:

a class of K-occurrences

an occurrence function

a unity relation—now conceived as an equivalence relation among K-occurrences

The explanation introduces the notion of "the K that has the occurrence relation to the occurrence"—that is, an apparatus for reference to K's—and gives the condition of K-identity for K's thus identified.

Note that this way of looking at the matter corresponds to the format of the analyses of personal identity provided by Grice and Quinton, discussed in essays 3 and 5. Grice provides us with a relation between "total temporary states"—slices of consciousness, so to speak. They are states of a person (occurrence relation) and are states of the same person if the latter contains or could contain memories of experiences in the former (unity relation). This isn't quite an equivalence relation, but one can be built from it: the one state contains or could contain memories of an experience in the other or contains an experience of which the other does or could contain a memory. We seem to have found a format for identity explanations that fits the work of a revered philosopher.

9. A Regress of Individuation?

This way of looking at the matter is not completely satisfactory either, however. For, to introduce a concept of K-identity, for any kind of object K's, we seem to presuppose a mastery of reference, predication, and individuation of another kind of entity, K-occurrences. But where did this understanding come from? It seems that the identity conditions of K-occurrences would also have to have been learned. But this would presuppose an understanding of reference, predication, and individuation of some further sort of entity, the occurrences of the occurrences. We have escaped the circles of individuation, it seems, at the cost of a regress of individuation. And the regress is vicious, since understanding reference, predication, and individuation at each level presupposes an understanding of these items at the next level down.

Though vicious, the regress is perhaps not infinite. Maybe there are minimal entities, with no spatial or temporal spread whatsoever, that could terminate the regress. Hume, perhaps partly because of some perception of these problems, seems to suppose that in the end what we perceive and think about are such minimal sensibilia. And Wittgenstein's (1921/1961) simples, as well as Russell's (1929) transitory sense data, seem also suited to terminate such a regress.

But the emerging picture of individuation seems, if not logically incoherent, simply false. The idea that we begin with a secure understanding of reference, predication, and individuation of some minimal sensibilia, whether conceived of as transitory mental phenomena, total temporary states, or the smallest portions of space-time capable of arresting our attention, is just bizarre.

The problem, I believe, is this. We were right in saying that only a preindividuative understanding of K-reference and predication can be, and need be, presupposed to understand K-identity. But the current scheme represents a partial understanding of K-reference and predication as a *full* understanding of some *other* scheme of reference and predication, of an alternate scheme of individuation. What we need to do is represent it as just what it is: partial understanding. I try to do this in the next part of this essay.

10. Entity without Identity?

Quine famously said, "no entity without identity" (1981, p. 102). We can certainly have a partial understanding of a system of reference, predication, and identity for a kind of object K, however. A helpful idea here is Strawson's (1959) concept of *feature placing*. Suppose I am an American midwesterner in the 1950s traveling in Europe. I am confronted with a large playground full of soccer fields. I know that there is a game, soccer, called "football." I know it involves kicking and scoring goals and is played on a larger field than American football. But suppose, for the sake of an illustration, that I have no idea whether the entire playground constitutes one soccer field, two, or several. I have the ability to point out various features. I can point and say, "This field has a muddy spot here" and "This field has a big metal structure with a net there." I manage thereby to say something truth-evaluable, even if I do not know whether "this field (pointing one place) is that field (pointing another)." Hence, I do not know whether "the field with a muddy spot here has a metal structure there." The limits of my ability are not due to the fact being hidden from me; the relevant facts are open to view, but I don't know the rules. I have a partial understanding of the conditions of reference, predication, and identity for soccer fields, the system of individuation and predication.

This partial understanding suffices for me to ask the questions and learn the answers that will take me to a full understanding. I can ask, "Is this field the same as that one" or "Does this goal go with the field it opens to or the field behind it?" The process of learning the scheme of individuation and predication will be just a part (usually a very early part) of understanding how the game works. When I learn that the metal structure is a goal and that the requirement is to get the ball into the inner part of the net from the direction it faces (like hockey) and not from behind (analogous to basketball, where to get the ball through the opening it has to change direction), I'll naturally grasp that each field will incorporate a pair of facing goals and probably get the hang of it pretty quickly after that.

Consider a checkerboard, with sixty-four squares, thirty-two black and thirty-two red; eight rows of eight alternating red and black squares; eight columns of alternating red and black squares; eight left-leaning diagonals, four all red and four all black, varying in length from one square to eight; and eight otherwise similar right-leaning diagonals. I put my finger on a square and say, "That is red there." This could mean "This square is red," or it could mean "This column (or row) is red at this square" or that "this right-leaning (or left-leaning) diagonal is red." But it really doesn't mean any of these things; it means something that is neutral between them. We can imagine the feature placing sentences, that I have mastered, to be a neutral bottom level that can be used with superstructures that determine which of the entities we are talking about.

Clouds are an interesting example. Take a typical Nebraska summer afternoon, building up to a glorious thunderstorm, with a sky full of different kinds of clouds stretching this way and that.[1] We seem to have a sky full of entity, but there is not very much identity. Is this huge expanse of darkness over in the west a part of the same cloud as this other part over here, a bit to the east? The two parts do not constitute one clear, homogeneously colored bulgy mass—a sort of paradigm case of cloud identity. But there is a continuous stretch of cloud stuff between them, with the color gradually changing. "Cloud" seems to be clearly a count noun, not a mass term. There are many clouds, not a lot of cloud, in the sky. But the identity conditions for clouds seem to be greatly underdetermined.

This is true not only for cloud identity at a time, but cloud identity over time. Anyone who spends a good part of an afternoon watching clouds can testify that although there can be clear cases of a single cloud moving across the sky, there are many cases where the way clouds combine and split and change shape leaves our concept of cloud identity without much of a hold. The problem is not that you or I only have a partial understanding of an existing system of cloud individuation and predication, but that there is no such system. We get by with a partial system. There is no abiding need for a set of rules that would cover a wide variety of cases. If there is, say for the purposes of an art class (you must paint at least two clouds), additional conventions can be manufactured on the spot.

How do we model the partial understanding in these cases? In each case, there is a confident identity in a small region—in the cloud case, also over a small period of time. This is tied to the system of features that we are placing. We could say that each placement of a feature is an existential quantified statement, to the effect that there is a thing of the kind in question that exhibits such and such a property; for example, "There is a soccer field here where I'm pointing, and it is muddy." Another way is to simply suppose that the speaker is talking about small spatial or spatiotemporal parts of roughly the size

---

[1] It is an odd convention that counts permanent dramatic features, such as mountains, in favor of a state's natural beauty, but not reliable but transient features, such as clouds. Thus the Colorado Rockies, which cover only a portion of the sky, cause Colorado to be considered a beautiful state, while the regular shows that Nebraska's clouds provide, stretching from horizon to horizon with fireworks several times a week all summer long, are discounted.

of the region of confidence: small soccer field parts, squares, and cloud-stages.

The way out of the circle of predication and individuation is then to realize that talk of occurrences is a way of modeling partial understanding, or partial implementation, of a system of predication and individuation.

We said earlier that an explanation of *K*-identity requires the following:

a class of *K*-occurrences

an occurrence function

a unity relation—now conceived as an equivalence relation among *K*-occurrences

This explanation of *K*-identity does not mean that talk about *K*'s is thus revealed as or shown to be talk about *K*-occurrences. It is, rather, an explanation in the sense of giving us another way of looking at the phenomena that the institution of *K*'s and *K*-identity is a way of dealing with. This alternative system need not itself be complete, particularly efficient, or good for anything at all except the needs of the theorist. It will allow us to see the actual system of *K*-individuation and predication against a background of alternative possible systems for dealing with the same phenomena.

However, much the same effect can be achieved by continuing to talk about *K*'s but simply limiting the predications that we make to those that are not based on feature flow along the lines of identity. We can talk about the people, Mary, Julia, and Mary-Julia. We can say that all of them speak English, but we can't say that two of them speak French. The first doesn't require anything but checking on features. The second would require a negative decision as to identity, namely, that Julia and Mary-Julia are different. Likewise, we can't say that only one of them speaks French. We can say that Julia speaks French, Mary-Julia speaks French, and Mary does not speak French. Most philosophers who talk about identity conditions will talk this way, with a sense of which explanations are fair and which are not, revealing a sense of what attributions count as placing features and which require identity judgments. We have then done what philosophy should do: free the natural way we talk about and explain identity from a host of problems that bother philosophers who obsess about the topic but that do not often get in the way of profitable discussion.

11. Return to Dividing Selves

In essay 3 I discussed the case of dividing selves. B and C emerge from surgical shenanigans with equal claims on being A, the presurgical source of their memories. But there is no inclination to suppose that B and C are identical, for there is no unity of consciousness nor of body. They are separate people, with mental lives flowing in different directions, sitting in different rooms; eventually, no doubt, they will sue one another, a strange thing for someone to do to himself.

I posed the issue as one about which of three languages we speak. The stage language said that B and C are not identical, and neither are A and B or A and C. This is the way David Lewis looked at the case. The branch language says that there were two persons all along, A is B, or A is C, but not both. Perhaps there is a metaphysical link that may be impossible to establish (Chisholm 1969). Or one may be the overall "closest competitor" (Nozick 1981). Finally, there is the lifetime language—the alternative I defended. According to the lifetime language, before the operation all of the things that happen to B and C after the operation were in A's future, and after the operation all the things that happened to A before the operation were in B's past and in C's past. But nothing that happened to B after the operation was ever to be in C's past and vice versa. Each view has its pluses and minuses. I argued in the article that my view—that we implicitly speak the lifetime language—did the best job providing a home for our various "intuitions" about the case. However that may be, it seems to be a very difficult position for people to swallow. There is a certain tendency to suppose that there are really three people involved, the Y-shaped one we called A before the operation and the two branches that we call B and C, and that only tricks I built into the mechanism of reference make it the case that before the operation "There is just one person here" is true in the lifetime language.

Perhaps I marched by the most plausible solution, without noticing it, under the banner "no entity without identity." I want to say that A should anticipate everything that happens to B and to C after the operation; he *will* do those things. And both B and C should take credit for everything that A did before the operations; they *did* those things. And I should say that this way of spreading properties around is consistent, because it could be done consistently, as both the lifetime and the person-stage languages show. And perhaps there I should have stopped. The article provided the machinery for seeing that ordinary language may simply be undetermined on the crucial question; its language may be only partially defined on all of the possibilities we can think of, even though it takes care of virtually all of the cases that have ever arisen. Whether we should spread properties around without identity or insist on identity, and go against some intuitions about how many people there are, may be quite undetermined, even if the question of who would have done what is not, as I tend to think.

Perhaps, but I am not yet convinced. The intuitions we have about identity are not all equal. The strangeness of being able to say, from a sort of atemporal perspective, that there are three people before the operation is real enough. But that is because we expect more out of identity than logic puts into it. The surplus comes from the well-behaved nature of most unity relations under most circumstances that we need to worry about. If the unity relation is not well behaved, we will get surprising results. I still think my solution keeps the surprises to a minimum and the logic to a maximum.

II. PERSONAL IDENTITY

5

Personal Identity, Memory, and the Problem of Circularity

> When it is asked wherein personal identity consists, the answer should be ... that all attempts to define would but perplex it. (Butler 1736/ 1975)

When he said this, Joseph Butler was thinking of Locke's (1694/1975) attempt to define personal identity in terms of memory; if his opinion about a future state, which motivated his interest in personal identity, proved correct, he has doubtless since had similar thoughts about more recent "memory theorists," such as H. P. Grice (1941) and Anthony Quinton (1962/1975). For, in spite of such perceptive critics as Butler and Reid (1785/1975), the thought that personal identity is analyzable, and analyzable in terms of memory, has been periodically revived.

In this essay, I try to discover the strengths and weaknesses of the memory theory by defending the best version of it against arguments that could be raised by those who feel, as Butler did, that the concept of personal identity is primitive. The memory theory emerges from this defense with its letter intact but its spirit scathed.

1. Grice's Theory

Locke suggested that A is the same person as B if and only if A can remember having an experience of B's.[1] The sufficient condition implied is plausible: if I really can remember going to the store

---

"Personal Identity, Memory, and the Problem of Circularity" was originally published in *Personal Identity*, edited by John Perry (Berkeley: University of California Press, 1975), pp. 135–55. Reprinted by permission.

[1] Locke's actual words are, "as far as this consciousness can be extended backwards to any past action or thought, reaches the identity of that person." (1694, sec. 9).

yesterday, then I must have gone to the store. That is, I must be the same person as someone who went to the store. But the implied necessary condition is much too strong, as Reid and other critics have pointed out. That I cannot remember going to the store yesterday does not mean that I did not go. Forgetting, even beyond the possibility of recall, is possible.

Later memory theorists have concentrated on weakening the necessary condition to the point of plausibility. Grice, whose account is, in my opinion, the most subtle and successful, in essence takes Locke's relation, disjoins it with its converse, and takes the ancestral of the result. Grice adopts the notion of a total temporary state, or "t.t.s.," which is a set of simultaneous experiences of a single person, and conceives of his task as finding the relation that must obtain between t.t.s.'s that belong to one person. In Grice's terms, with A and B now being t.t.s.'s and not persons, the relation Locke uses in his analysis is this:

R_L: A contains, or would contain given certain conditions, a memory of an experience contained in B.

The relation that results from Grice's weakening maneuvers we can express this way:

R_G: There is a sequence of t.t.s.'s (not necessarily in the order they occur in time and not excluding repetitions), the first of which is A and the last of which is B, such that each t.t.s. in the sequence either (i) contains, or would contain given certain conditions, a memory of an experience contained in the next or (ii) contains an experience of which the next contains a memory, or would contain a memory given certain conditions.[2]

---

[2] Grice actually describes the series, comembership in which is required of A and B, as follows: "Every member of the series either would, given certain conditions, contain as an element a member of some experience which is an element in some previous member, or contains as an element some experience a memory of which would, given certain conditions, occur as an element in some subsequent member; there being no subset of members which is independent of all the rest" (1941, sec. C). The condition imposed on A and B by R_G is equivalent to this. A series of the sort Grice describes would result from the R_G sequence by putting the members in chronological order and eliminating repetitions; and R_G sequence can be obtained from a series of the sort Grice describes by starting with any t.t.s. and building an

A set of t.t.s.'s which can be formed into a sequence of this sort, and to which no more t.t.s.'s can be added (which I shall call a "Grice-set"), is a person or self.

Grice's account avoids the Brave Officer Paradox (Reid 1785/ 1975) and other stock counterexamples to memory theories of personal identity to which his predecessors and successors have fallen prey. But it is not at all obvious that he avoids objections of another sort, in the spirit of Butler's criticism of Locke: "Memory presupposes, and so cannot constitute, personal identity" (1736/1975). In this essay I will examine three charges of circularity, each maintaining for a different reason that Grice implicitly uses the concept of personal identity in his analysis of it.

I shall not examine every interesting objection of this sort that could be made against Grice; in particular, I shall not examine the objection that experiences themselves, the ultimate building blocks in Grice's constructions of persons, must be individuated in terms of persons. I do not believe this objection is fatal, but discussion of it would lead us away from the topics I wish to discuss, into the difficult problem of the individuation of events.

2. Circles and Logical Constructions

Before settling down to specifics, we must satisfy ourselves that Grice's enterprise is of a sort for which circularity is a vice. He explicitly defends the view that persons are logical constructions from experiences. Whether he held this view as a part of a generally phenomenalistic philosophy is not disclosed in the article on personal identity, and Grice may well have had special views about the nature of the logical constructor's enterprise and special motivation for holding persons to be so constructable. But it will be helpful and only fair, given a lack of contrary evidence, to suppose Grice involved in a logical construction of a "standard" sort.

The logical constructor attempts to analyze sentences about objects of some category into sentences about objects of some other category. Examples of such analyzed and analyzing categories are

---

appropriately linked sequence, repeating a multiply linked t.t.s. when necessary in order to continue until all the t.t.s.'s are used. For a comparison of Grice, Quinton, and Locke, see the introduction to Perry (1975).

numbers and classes, material objects and sense data, and persons and t.t.s.'s. The analyzing sentences may themselves be thought analyzable—for example, sentences about classes into sentences about propositional functions or sentences about t.t.s.'s into sentences about experiences. At the bottom of the structure are sentences with a favored epistemological status, as, for example, that they can be directly known, because the objects they are about can be directly inspected. Through analysis this favored status, or at least some status more favorable than was originally apparent, is transmitted up the structure to the analyzed sentences. Talk about persons might have seemed to involve us in talk about pure egos, or substances of some other obscure sort, but when we see that talk of persons is, really, just talk of t.t.s.'s and, ultimately, of experiences, our knowledge is revealed as more secure than it seemed.

Sentences about experiences seem to be directly knowable, by the people who have the experiences, at the time they occur. Now, a present-tense sentence about persons, or material objects, cannot be plausibly regarded as merely a remark about present experiences. But it has been thought that it could be plausibly regarded as asserting no more than would be asserted by a string of sentences about past, present, and future experiences. While not all of these sentences could be directly known at one time, each of them could be directly known at some time. The complex of assertions, into which a sentence about persons or material objects can be analyzed, will not have as favored an epistemological status as a sentence about a present experience. But it will have a more favored status than a sentence that asserted things never directly knowable by anyone at any time.

In both the construction of material objects and of persons, it soon becomes clear that past, present, and future experiences do not provide sufficient materials: possible experiences, the experiences someone would have had, had things been different than they were, are also needed. And it is not clear that sentences about possible experiences have much favored epistemological status to transmit upward.

On Grice's conception of logical constructions, if all goes well, the analyzed sentence (say, "Someone heard a noise") and the analyzing sentence (say, "A past hearing of a noise is contained in a t.t.s. which is a member of a Grice-set") will have just the same truth conditions. If this were the only condition of a successful analysis, the analyzed sentence could serve as the analysis of the analyzing sentence, for "has the same truth conditions" expresses a symmetrical relation. It is the favored status of the analyzing sentence which gives the logical construction its noncircular structure.

A charge of circularity against Grice, then, will consist of two claims. First, the analyzing sentence does not seem to have the favored status and so must itself be analyzed. Second, its analysis will have to employ sentences about objects of the category constructed, that is, sentences about persons. This would show that even if Grice has produced an analysis free from counterexample, it is a failure: the mystery of personal identity is transmitted downward to memory, rather than the clarity of memory being transmitted upward to personal identity.

3. Three Charges of Circularity

The core of Grice's analysis is R_L. R_L is in itself a disjunction; the first charge of circularity will concern the first, simpler, disjunct:

> A contains a memory of an experience contained in B.

The second and third charges of circularity concern the second disjunct:

> A would contain, given certain conditions, a memory of an experience contained in B.

For simplicity, I explain these charges in an assertive tone, but the reader should keep in mind that ultimately I shall reject them.

(i) Smith examines a green cube and later vividly describes his examination of it. Jones has never examined a green cube; he is hypnotized and told that when he awakes he will remember examining one. Jones later vividly describes examining a green cube. To observers who do not know the whole story, Smith and Jones both seem to be remembering, in vivid detail, a past examination of a green cube.

Smith is really remembering; Jones is not. Their present experiences, the occurrence of which they know directly through introspection, are indiscernible. Jones cannot discover he is mistaken through careful attention to his own mind. Their outward behavior, the sentences they use, their facial expression, etc., is also indiscernible. And yet Smith's experience is a memory of a past experience, and Jones's is not. Saying of an experience that it is a memory is thus a complex attribution and not just a report of what is directly observed through introspection. That a person is really remembering at a given time, and not just seeming to, cannot always be determined solely on the basis of observations of the person made at that time, whether by that person or others.

That we are seeming to remember a past experience can be known directly; that we are really remembering involves more. And this "more" is not just the occurrence of a past experience of the appropriate sort directly knowable when it occurred. For there was a past experience of the sort Jones seems to remember—Smith's experience of examining the cube. What further must be added? The example suggests that one further necessary condition is that the same person who is seeming to remember have had, in the past, the experience in question. But then, spelled out, with the full analysis of memory incorporated into the condition, the first disjunct of R_L would look like this:

A contains an apparent memory of an experience contained in *B*, and *A is a t.t.s. of the same person of whom B is a t.t.s., and . . .*

The ". . ." represents whatever further conditions may be found necessary for an analysis of memory. But we need go no further. The italicized condition is sufficient to doom Grice's analysis to circularity.

(ii) Even if the last objection is somehow overcome, Grice's analysis would still be circular. The problem is the subjunctive conditional contained in the second disjunct of R_L: "would contain, given certain conditions."

Let us look at the kind of example that makes this disjunct necessary. Wilson is asleep. His present t.t.s. contains only a vague blissful feeling, which he will never remember after awakening. Thus there are no actual memory links between Wilson's present t.t.s. and his past (because his present t.t.s. contains no memories), and there never will be any actual memory links between Wilson's future t.t.s.'s and his present one. So the analysis cannot rely solely on the first disjunct of R_L.

Had we shaken Wilson a moment ago and asked, "What thrilling things did you do today?" he would now be telling us about seeing Wynn hit a home run at Dodger Stadium earlier in the day. Although his sleeping t.t.s. contains no memory of this past experience, given certain conditions (our having shaken him and asked him the question), it would now contain such memories. It contains, we might say, only possible memories of the past t.t.s. The second disjunct asserts that there will always be at least a chance of possible memory links where there is personal identity.

Now, the problem with this conditional is not simply that its truth cannot be known through any sort of direct observation, but that, taken literally, the sentence "T.t.s. A would, under certain circumstances, contain a memory of seeing Wynn hit a home run" makes no sense. To make sense of it, we will have to use the concept of personal identity.

It makes no sense, taken literally, because the identity of a t.t.s. must be determined by the experiences it contains. T.t.s. A is a set of experiences, and a set's whole identity is wrapped up in its membership.[3] The t.t.s. or set of experiences Smith would have had, if he had been awakened and questioned, and the t.t.s. he actually has, while asleep, are different t.t.s.'s. When we say, "The t.t.s. would have contained a memory," we can only mean something like "The person would have had a different t.t.s. than he did have, and that different t.t.s. would have contained a memory." And in making sense of the conditional, we have had to talk about persons.

An analogy may help to make this point clear. When we say, "If the meeting had been advertised, the number of people in the hall would have been greater," we don't mean to imply that there is a certain number, say 50, which would have been greater if the meeting had been advertised. The number 50 will always be a little greater than 49 and a little less than 51, no matter how well advertised meetings are. Rather, we mean that a different number, say 101, would have fit the description "number of people in the room" had the advertising been more thorough. So with the t.t.s. Wilson had and the t.t.s. Wilson would have had. They are not the same t.t.s. but different t.t.s.'s, one which deserves, and one which would have deserved, the description, "Wilson's t.t.s."

In order to state a conditional such as the one about the meeting or the one about Wilson fully and explicitly, we need some "anchor"—some entity that retains its identity under the imagined change in circumstances and in terms of which the number or t.t.s. is identified. In the case of the meeting, the meeting itself is the anchor:

---

[3] Grice does not say explicitly that a t.t.s. is a set. But it seems clear that if a t.t.s. is not a set, it is nevertheless some other sort of entity the identity of which is determined by the experiences contained in it.

the same meeting would have drawn a different number of people. And in the case of Wilson, Wilson himself seems the natural anchor: the same person would have had a t.t.s. that contained a memory . . . had he been awakened and questioned. But then, fully spelled out, the second disjunct of R_L is, "Given certain conditions, the same person of whom A is the t.t.s. would have had a t.t.s. that contained a memory of an experience of B's." But this uses the concept of personal identity, and so the analysis is circular.

(iii) Even if charges (i) and (ii) are somehow circumvented, the phrase "given certain conditions" leads to a third problem. Should Grice tell us which conditions it is, under which t.t.s. A would contain a memory of an experience contained in t.t.s. B? If he simply means "There is at least one condition such that, if it obtained, t.t.s. A would contain memories of an experience contained in t.t.s. B," then he owes us no such list; the analysis is complete as it stands. But if not just any condition will do, he should tell us which ones will. But it seems quite clear that Grice cannot mean simply "There is at least one condition such that . . ." by the phrase "under certain conditions." For, if he does mean this, "Under certain conditions, t.t.s. A could contain a memory of an experience of t.t.s. B's" would not mean anything like what it is supposed to mean, namely. "The person, of whom A is a t.t.s., can remember an experience of B's." Consider this example. Johnson saw a flash of lightning in the sky last Thursday; immediately afterward he received a serious head injury. As a result he cannot remember seeing the flash—the injury, we may suppose, interfered with the consolidation of short-term memory which makes memory of such events for more than a few seconds possible. In this case, we would not say, "Johnson can remember seeing the flash of lightning." No amount of reminding or prompting will bring it about that Johnson remembers. But we can state a condition such that, if it had obtained, Johnson would now be remembering the flash of lightning: that he didn't receive an injury and was just asked if he had ever seen lightning. (We may suppose Johnson had never seen lightning before and would surely have remembered it if not for the injury.) But the fact that the conditional "If Johnson had not been injured, and had just been asked about it, he would now be remembering seeing the flash of lightning" is true does not show that Johnson can remember seeing the lightning, even though the truth of some other conditional, such as "If Johnson were not asleep and had just been asked about it, he would remember . . ." would show that he can remember seeing it. So some conditionals of the form "If C, then Johnson would remember . . ." are relevant to the claim that he can remember, and some are not. So the words "t.t.s. A would, given certain conditions . . ." must mean "there are certain conditions, C_1, C_2, . . . C_n, and under one of these conditions t.t.s. A would . . ." Grice owes us a list, or some other specification, of these conditions.

I wish to make, but not press here, the point that it is unlikely this could be done. The point essential to this charge is that, even if the conditions were exhaustively listed, it seems inevitable that the concept of personal identity would be required. The only example we have discussed so far of such a condition is that the person with t.t.s. A was awakened a few moments ago and questioned; if under those conditions the person would remember, then under actual conditions he can remember. Now, it is hard to see how this condition, or any of the conditions involving prompting, reminding, or threatening, all of which typically occur somewhat before the occurrence of the t.t.s. in question, could be expressed without requiring that it be the same person who is prompted, etc., who is later to remember. If the phrase "given certain conditions" were cashed in, as it must be, for a list of conditions, the second disjunct of R_L would look like this:

> T.t.s. A would contain, *if the same person who has A* had been awakened and asked or if the same person who has A had not just taken a powerful drug or . . ., a memory of an experience contained in B.

And so, again, we see that Grice's analysis makes implicit use of the concept of personal identity and is circular.

4. Memory

Memory can be analyzed without use of the concept of personal identity and Grice thus cleared of these charges of circularity. I sketch such an analysis here, focusing first on the ordinary way of expressing event memory, as in "MacKenzie remembers Wilbur's marriage" or "Sandy remembers seeing her high marks," and later considering Grice's rather specialized locution.

The analysis of memory requires three sorts of conditions having to do, in turn, with what must happen at the time of the remembering, what must have happened at the time of the remembered event, and what the link between the remembered event and the event of remembering must be.

The first condition I call the Representation Condition. Representation is a notion I borrow from Martin and Deutscher's (1966) excellent discussion of memory. It has been thought, for example, by Locke (1694, book 2, chap. 10: "Of Retention"), Hume (1741/1968, book 1, part 1, sec. 3: "Of the Ideas of Memory and Imagination"), and Russell (1921, chap. 9: "Memory") that mental imagery is required for memory of an event. This is a mistake. Someone giving a vivid verbal description of a past event, or painting a picture of it, could be said to be remembering that event, whether or not he was having, or could produce, mental imagery of the event. But something separates the rememberer and the apparent rememberer from the common run of humankind. Martin and Deutscher introduced the term "represent" to cover the many ways a person can indicate the past occurrence of an event of a certain type, and I follow them not only in adopting this notion, but in apologizing for not giving a fuller account of it.

The first step in our analysis of "A remembers e," then, is

(1) A represents the past occurrence of an event of some type E.

What sort of thing is A? A is to be a live human body, or a human being. The difference between this concept and that of a person has been emphasized by many writers on personal identity and is a point of agreement between memory theorists and Butler and other critics who think personal identity an unanalyzable concept. So I shall feel free to use the concept of a live human body, and of bodily identity, in the analysis of memory, without fear of circularity.

Condition (1) is satisfied by both the real and apparent rememberer, as well as others who comment on the past: factual rememberers, liars, historians, and the like.

The second condition required for memory is the Witnessing Condition, that the rememberer witnessed the remembered event. We need to state it in a way that avoids circularity, however. So, the second condition is a detoxified version of the Witnessing Condition:

(2) B witnessed event e.

I shall call this the Weak Witnessing Condition. It makes no claim of identity between A and B.

Now, suppose we had added, as held necessary in the first charge of circularity, the (strong) Witnessing Condition. This would have disqualified Jones as a rememberer, but the analysis would still be deficient. Hennig examined the green cube, then received an electrical shock that wiped out his memory. The Electrical Company, in compensation, had him hypnotized and given the same posthypnotic suggestion as Jones. Hennig satisfies (1) and the Witnessing Condition but is not a rememberer. So, even if we had the (strong) Witnessing Condition in the analysis, we would still need a third condition, a Linking Condition, to rule out Hennig. It seems clear that what would be further required is some condition to the effect that the past witnessing brings about the present representing. My strategy, in what follows, is to beef up the Linking Condition in such a way that the Witnessing Condition is not needed.

With or without the Witnessing Condition, it is not easy to see what exactly the Linking Condition should be. I believe that the view Martin and Deutscher defend, that the link is a causal one, is correct.[4] But, as they point out, merely requiring that if the witnessing had not occurred, the representing would not be occurring, will not do. If Hennig had not examined a green cube, the Electrical Company would not have underwritten his hypnosis, and he would not be representing. (And Smith, the rememberer, would be representing, even if he had not examined the cube, for in that case I would have had him hypnotized and treated like Jones.) The witnessing must not just cause the representing, it must cause it in a certain way.

Scientists are trying to discover the causal mechanisms involved in memory. Suppose they discover that a certain process is involved in memory. Could our Linking Condition simply be that that process led from B's witnessing to A's representing? No, for in analyzing the concept of memory, we seek beliefs common to all who use with understanding the formula "x remembers E," and knowledge of, or even specific beliefs about, the processes involved in memory are not at all common.

But we may believe that memory involves some characteristic process without having a belief about which process, or what kind of process, that might be. In fact, I think we do believe this. Some who have the concept of memory may be sure the process is not, or not merely, a material one; this was apparently Bergson's (1912) view.

---

[4] But I do not accept their final version of this condition.

Others may believe it certainly is a material process, an electrochemical process of the central nervous system. Perhaps most have no opinions on the matter. But in accepting, as we all do, that "He remembers it" is an explanation of representing; in predicting, as we all do, that in certain circumstances people are likely to remember the past and in other circumstances unlikely to; and in seeking, as we all do, alternative explanations for representing of the past when circumstances make memory unlikely ("He can't have remembered, he was too young—his mother must have told him"), we indicate that we do believe there are certain processes involved in memory which can be expected to occur in some circumstances and not in others. This is a hypothesis, a speculation if you will, for no such process can be observed by the ordinary human, introspectively or otherwise. But it is an irresistible hypothesis.

Let us say that a witnessing and a representing are *M*-related when they are the beginning and end of such a process. Then our analysis is simply

> *A* remembers *e* if and only if
> (1) *A* represents the past occurrence of an event of type *E*;
> (2) *B* witnessed *e*; and
> (3) *B*'s witnessing of *e* is *M*-related to *A*'s representation of the past occurrence of an event of type *E*.

But is it fair to use, in the analysis, a relation the nature of which we haven't disclosed? It is fair only if we can identify the relation independently of the concept analyzed. This I have not done, for all I have said about the *M*-relation is that it is the relation involved in memory. But I shall now try to provide such an independent identification of the *M*-relation.

"Recollection" I shall use purely as a technical term for which I stipulate this definition:

> *A* recollects *e* if and only if
> (1) *A* represents the past occurrence of an event of type *E*;
> (2) *B* witnessed *e*, and *e* is of type *E*; and
> (3) *B* and *A* are the same live human body.

Recollection, so defined, occurs often. One of the things we all know about live human bodies is that they are quite likely to recollect, and we know the conditions that make recollection more and less likely. But recollection is a significantly different notion from memory. Returning to the case of the green cube, both Smith and Hennig recollect examining the cube, though only Smith remembers. With regard to cases that actually occur, memory is a more restrictive concept than recollection. Oddly enough, with regard to cases produced in the imagination of humans, memory seems less restrictive. Philosophers thinking about personal identity, seeing no contradiction in transbodily memory, have produced many characters who remember what they do not recollect: Locke's prince, (1694/1975, sec. 15), Shoemaker's Brownson (1963, p. 23), and Quinton's no longer fat but still self-indulgent Pole (1962/1975, sec. 3). And the occupants of the Hereafter are regularly conceived as remembering earthly events, although the "resurrected" bodies of these occupants must not be the very same bodies as were buried and rotted away on earth. So the concept of memory is not simply more restrictive and not simply less restrictive than recollection, but sits askew of it.

An *unaided* case of recollection is one in which the representing of A is not explained by provision of information about e other than B's witnessing of it. Now, any ordinary human is drawn to the belief that there is an explanation for the frequent occurrence of unaided cases of recollection, that there is some process, material or immaterial, gross or sublime, complex or simple, which frequently occurs when a human being witnesses an event and leads to that same human's later representation of it. When the witnessing of an event leads by this process to a later representation of it, the witnessing and the representation are M-related.

I now have identified the M-relation not just as the relation that links the witnessing and representing in memory, but, noncircularly, as the relation that explains the great bulk of cases of recollection. And, of course, it is not an accident that the M-relation plays both roles.

My view is that the key to understanding memory is seeing it as an explanatory concept, not merely in that individual cases of past-representing are explained by memory, but that a generalization about human behavior, the frequency of recollection, is explained by a hypothesized process and that this process is incorporated into the very concept of memory. This conception of memory explains its skewed relation to recollection. Memory is a more restrictive concept in that more is required; the witness and the representer must not just be the same human being, but a certain process must have occurred. But by distinguishing between the M-relation and the relation of being or belonging to the same human body and by virtue of our lack of knowledge of the nature of the M-relation, it becomes possible to think of the two as separate; we are able to imagine the possibility that certain witnessings and representings might be M-related, though not experiences of the same human body. It does not follow, after all, from the fact that the M-relation is regularly associated with sameness of human body that it must always be so associated. And, indeed, we can, through use of the M-relation, extend the class of rememberers. We can let A and B in our analysis stand for not just human bodies, but human bodies and any other sorts of things, ghosts or even gorse-bushes that might, for all we know, become M-related to them.

There is another dissimilarity between memory and recollection. In a case of recollection, the representation must be accurate; the event recollected must be of the type represented, but no such condition has been placed on memory. We do not require a person's memory of an event to be accurate. Smith may be rattling on about the time he met the Prince of Wales in London; Jones may quite correctly observe that Smith never met the Prince of Wales, and has never been to London, but is really remembering the time when, as a part of a hoax that defies summary, he met Stanky in Philadelphia. The point is not that Smith speaks truly when he says, "I remember meeting the Prince of Wales in London." His claim, remember, is twofold, that he remembered a certain event and that it has a certain type, that it was a meeting of a Prince of Wales in London. The point is, rather, that Jones speaks truly when he says Smith is remembering meeting Stanky in Philadelphia, even though Smith is not representing the past occurrence of an event of *that* type. The event remembered need not be of the type represented. This too is explained by the suggested relation between recollection and memory. We build the concept of memory on a relation, the M-relation, in which we are interested largely because it so often leads to accurate past-representing. But we allow that the processes involved, when conditions are less than ideal, may not inevitably lead to accuracy.

If we add to the three conditions of memory these two,

(4) *e* is of type *E*

(5) *A* believes (1)–(4)

we shall have what I call a paradigm case of memory. Paradigm cases explain our interest in memory as a source of knowledge about the past; only when a person is remembering accurately and knows he is remembering, and not, say, imagining, can he derive knowledge of the past from his own tendency to represent it.

What is the relation between "A remembers e," the concept just analyzed, and "t.t.s. A contains a memory of an experience of t.t.s. B," the expression Grice uses? I take it that experiences are a species of events. But it will not do simply to say, as an explication of Grice's notion, "A remembers e, and e is an experience." For, suppose Wilson remembers Wynn watching the ball go over the fence. Then Wilson is remembering an experience, but Wilson's present t.t.s. does not contain a memory of an experience contained in Wynn's earlier t.t.s., in Grice's intended sense, or else Grice's analysis is in more serious trouble than contemplated so far. The experience we are after is not the event remembered, even if it is an experience, but the witnessing of it. Now, given our peculiar use of "witnessing," the witnessing may be the event remembered. Wynn remembers watching the ball go over the fence, and it is this very watching of the ball which, in virtue of our extended use of "witnessing" as including participation in the past event, is, in his case, the witnessing of the remembered event. But when the witnessing and the event remembered are distinct, it is the witnessing, and not the event witnessed, that belongs in the rememberer's biography. So I shall take "t.t.s. A contains a memory of an experience contained in t.t.s. B" to mean "A is representing the past occurrence of an event of some type E, and this representing is M-related to B's witnessing of some event e."

Now we must turn to the charges of circularity to see if Grice has been cleared.

(i) This charge rested on the claim that the Witnessing Condition must be incorporated into the analysis of memory. But I have argued that with a properly formulated Linking Condition, the Weak Witnessing Condition is sufficient. The Witnessing Condition is not rejected. It remains true, a consequence of the analysis of memory plus Grice's analysis of personal identity.

(ii) This charge was that in order to make sense of the conditional used in the expression of possible memory, we had to take the person as the "anchor," the entity that stayed the same under the imagined change of conditions. We could, I think, answer this by simply taking the human being involved to be the anchor. But in replying to the third charge, we shall eliminate the use of subjunctive conditional in the expression of possible memory, making the present charge irrelevant.

(iii) We certainly have a concept of possible memory, of persons who could remember a certain event, although they are not in fact doing so. And there are certainly conditions such that if their obtaining would lead a person to remember, then it is true of him that he can remember. But it would be a mistake to approach the concept of possible memory by trying to list these conditions.

A better approach to the problem begins with the notion of an inclination to believe that an event of type E occurred. Someone who is inclined to believe that an event of type E occurred will be disposed to represent that such an event occurred at that time. We do not need to have an exhaustive list of the conditions under which this disposition will be triggered in order to understand what it is to be so disposed, any more than we need to have an exhaustive list of the conditions under which a belief will be expressed in order to know what it is to believe. Now, just as we believe that humans often represent the occurrence of past events of a certain type as a result of a certain process set in motion by a past witnessing, we also, I think, believe that a person may have such a disposition to represent as a result of such a process. Indeed, we believe that having such a disposition is a part of the process that eventually leads, in some cases, to representation. Thus we can introduce the M'-relation, which obtains when the processes that lead from witnessings to dispositions to represent occur, and analyze A's possible memory of e as follows:

(1) A is disposed to represent the past occurrence of an event of type E;

(2) B witnessed e; and

(3) B's witnessing of e is M'-related to A's being disposed to represent the past occurrence of an event of type E.

For this analysis to be legitimate, we should provide an independent identification of the M'-relation; this could be done along the lines used before, by first constructing a notion of possible recollection and introducing the M'-relation in terms of the processes that explain the frequency of unaided possible recollection.

5. Logical Constructions and Inferred Entities

Although I have defended Grice against the charges of circularity, the concept of memory I have used does not fit well with his conception of a person as a logical construction from experiences. If a person is a logical construction from experiences, the existence of a person should follow, as a matter of logic, from the occurrence of the experiences of which the person is composed. The existence of a person entails nothing more than the existence of those experiences, related in a certain way, a way that itself could be immediately read off from experience. Thus Russell (1929, pp. 155ff.) contrasts logical constructions with "inferred entities," where the word "inference" carries the implication of a nondemonstrative inference, incorporating some element of probability, or some explanatory hypothesis, that goes beyond the directly known facts. But when I say that my toothache this morning and my headache of last night belong to the same person, because my toothache belongs to the same t.t.s. as a memory of the headache, we are saying, according to the concept of memory just defended, that a certain process, the nature of which we do not know, led from the headache to this morning's toothache-accompanied memory impression. The occurrence of this process does not follow from the occurrence of the headache, the toothache, and the memory impression. The occurrence of the process, and so of the person who both had the headache and has the toothache, is in fact an inference, not something directly known at all. We believe that there is such a process at all since that seems the most likely explanation of the frequency of recollection. We believe such a process was involved in this case because of a lack of alternative explanations and because it seems very likely that such a process should have occurred, given the other things we believe, including things believed on the basis of memory; for example, that given last night's other activities, a headache was to be expected; that given last night's sleep, with no evidence of interruption by electrical shock, mad scientist, brain transplanter, or hypnotist, a memory of it was to be expected.

Also, in the explanation of possible memory, that which might be directly knowable was sacrificed for what can only be inferred. A memory impression, an "occurrent" belief, and a representing may perhaps be objects of direct observation for the person who has them. But beliefs in the ordinary sense, in which I have many beliefs with which my mind is not now occupied, are not. Dispositions to represent and possible memories are states we ascribe to persons, including ourselves, as a way of systematizing and explaining the conditions under which more directly observable phenomena occur. Indeed, in using subjunctive conditionals in his formulation, Grice had already left the realm of what, in any reasonable sense, can be directly known.

So neither the primitiveness of memory nor the primitiveness of personal identity is suggested by our investigation, but only the derivative nature of both concepts. And they are derivative, not from the conception of a world of atomistic experiences, but from our scheme of a material world of which human beings are a part. And the nature of the derivation is not logical construction, but generalization and theory building in the service of explanation and prediction. And if such theories as the belief in a process that explains recollection lead us to speculations and even convictions that carry us well beyond the material world that forms their evidential base, that is a danger of the natural human bent for such theory building against which must be weighed its utility in the mundane tasks from which these speculations provide an occasional relief.

I end with two disclaimers. I do not think Grice's theory, even freed from its origins in the project of logical construction and incorporating the concept of memory defended here, is fully satisfactory. As Quinton saw, ways in which a person's past are expected to influence his future, other than just event memory, should be incorporated into our account of personal identity. The pattern used in doing this, however, could be one suggested by our investigation of Grice: first elaborating generalizations about human behavior after the pattern of our concept of recollection and then introducing the relation which is believed to underlie them and forms the basis of our concept of a person. But this is a large project.

Second, the approach that has emerged from our investigation of Grice is not inimical to Locke's original scheme, for Locke was not a logical constructor and had a place, in his version of the memory theory, for unknown processes and inferred states. This fact has often been sighted as a sign of his faintheartedness, in not banishing from his philosophy the last traces of the notion of substance, but I think it is rather a sign of his level-headedness. And Locke would also, I think, be sympathetic with the first point, for it is only by generalizing from the memory theory and incorporating somehow into our account of personal identity the sort of character development, stability of ideals and values, influence of past intentions, and the like, which we normally expect to find in humans, that the forensic and moral importance of personal identity, which Locke so rightly emphasized, can be explained.

6

Williams on the Self and the Future

Is personal identity simply bodily identity? Or is it based on a different principle, continuity of consciousness or links of memory? Locke (1694/1975) thought the latter, and so, with various important qualifications, do Sydney Shoemaker (1963; 1970a, b) and a number of other contemporary philosophers who have written on the problem of personal identity. Both Locke and Shoemaker bolster the case for the memory theory by appealing to cases of putative body transfer. In a body transfer case, a person has one body at one time and a different body at a later time. In other words, there is personal identity without bodily identity. The advocate of the view that personal identity consists in, or at least implies, bodily identity must resist taking these cases to be real cases of body transfer. This Bernard Williams has done in a number of essays, culminating in the imaginative and elegant "The Self and the Future" (1970/1973). In this essay, I raise some doubts about the arguments Williams has given for resistance.

1. Putative Examples of Body Transfer

The most famous examples of putative body transfer are Locke's cobbler and prince and Shoemaker's case of Brownson. Locke doesn't explain why the cobbler he imagines comes to have memories of a prince, but says that the cobbler would be the same person as the prince, but not the same man. Shoemaker gives us more details. Brown's brain is transplanted into Robinson's cranium. The survivor of this operation Shoemaker calls "Brownson." We can represent this

---

"Williams on the Self and the Future" is a reworked version of a review of Bernard Williams's *Problems of the Self,* which appeared in *The Journal of Philosophy* 73, no. 13 (1976): 416–28.

sort of case with a diagram in which the horizontal rows represents sameness of body:

Earlier Time	Later Time
Brown	Brown's body, no brain
Robinson	Brownson [Person with Robinson's body and Brown's brain]

Shoemaker's Case

The diagram is neutral as to the question of personal identity. We can ask whether Brownson is Brown, Robinson, or neither. Shoemaker says that assuming Brownson has the memories of Brown, we should cautiously conclude that Brownson is Brown. If we conclude this, then this is a case of body transfer, though Brown still has part of his original body, his brain.

Since Shoemaker put forward the Brownson case, writers, including Shoemaker, have considered more abstract examples in which the brain itself isn't transferred. The properties of the brain that are relevant to memory (and any other mental traits deemed important) are somehow duplicated in another brain, whose owner is imagined to have a mental life exactly similar in relevant respects to that which actual brain transfer would have produced. Williams discusses variations of this more abstract case I'll call "the basic case":

Earlier Time	Later Time
A	Left open
B	B-body person [B's body, A's memories]

The Basic Case

Is the B-body person A? or B? Or neither? In Shoemaker's case, it was the memories and not the brain that were important in arguing that Brownson was Brown. The brain's importance derived only from the fact that it was the physical basis of the memories. It seems, then, that the same arguments would apply in the basic case. Williams himself states these arguments very effectively in "The Self and the Future" (pp. 47–50)—but only as a preparation to rejecting them.

Williams thinks that persons are material objects, that personal identity is bodily identity, and that the putative cases of body transfer should not be accepted as real. His strategy is to lead us to consider variations on the basic case. When we explore our intuitions about these variations, we find the force of the arguments for the memory theory based on simpler cases fading away. In an early paper, "Personal Identity and Individuation" (1957), he puts forward his reduplication argument.[1] Later, in "The Self and the Future," he puts forward what I shall call the nonduplication argument. I shall consider each of these.

2. The Reduplication Argument

In the reduplication argument, Williams asks us to consider a variation on the basic case. Instead of having one person at the later time with *A*'s memories and someone else's body, we imagine having two. Given that the basic case does not involve an actual transfer of the brain, we can suppose that the very same process that in the basic case led to the *B*-body person having *A*'s memories is applied twice. Thus both the *B*-body person and the *C*-body person have *A*'s memories.

---

[1] I am ignoring certain historical niceties here. In "Personal Identity and Individuation" (1957), Williams doesn't discuss why the competing survivors both (seem to) remember being Guy Fawkes, so it wasn't quite presented as a variation on what I call the basic case.

As Wiggins points out in *Identity and Spatio-Temporal Continuity* (1971), we can imagine this sort of duplication even in the original case if we suppose that the halves of the brain are roughly equivalent in function and imagine them being transplanted to different recipients.

The first version of the reduplication argument appears to be due to Samuel Clarke, in his controversy with Antony Collins about the merits of Locke's approach to personal identity within the context of the issue of whether matter can think (Clarke and Collins, 1736).

For treatments of reduplication cases, see Wiggins (1967), Parfit (1971), essay 3 of this book, David Lewis (1976), and Terrence Leichti (1975).

Earlier Time	Later Time
A	No person has A's body
B	B-body person [B's body, A's memories]
C	C-body person [C's body, A's memories]

The Reduplication Case

This sort of case presents the memory theorist with a dilemma. Both the B-body person and the C-body person have that relation to A that was deemed sufficient for personal identity in the basic case. But then both of them should be A. But they clearly are not identical with each other. They have different bodies, will have different perceptions when they awake from the operation, and so will soon have different memories. They can't find out what each other is thinking or doing by introspection. But since identity is a "one-to-one" relation, we can't consistently maintain all of the following:

(1) the B-body person = A

(2) the C-body person = A

(3) the B-body person ≠ the C-body person

Which of these will the memory theorist give up? It would be absurd to give up (3). Giving up either (1) or (2) undermines the idea that personal identity consists of links of memory. (There can be no sufficient reason for giving up (1) and (2) without the other, since the claims have exactly the same basis.) Thus the reduplication argument forces us to rethink the power of the basic case.

The logic of this argument seems to be this: A description of some basic case is given, neutral on questions of personal identity. From this description, we can see that some relation obtains between the memory donor and the survivor (A and the B-body person). Is this relation sufficient for identity? If it is, changing the example in ways that do not affect it should not affect the question of identity. But certain changes give us a variation in which the relation is clearly not sufficient for identity, namely, adding another survivor (the C-body person) who also has the relation in question to the memory donor.

Of course, one can make these changes only if the relation in question is "duplicable"—is the sort of relation that can obtain between A and both the B-body person and the C-body person.

In Williams's "Personal Identity and Individuation," Charles claims to be Guy Fawkes and supports this claim with detailed memory-like reports of Fawkes's life. "Appears to remember events from Fawkes's life in great detail" is a duplicable relation which two people might have to Fawkes. But this relation would surely not be supposed, even by those most sanguine about transfer of bodies, to be sufficient for personal identity. Any inclination to suppose that Charles is Fawkes must be based on the assumption that this relation is good evidence for some other relation, itself sufficient for identity. The real question is the duplicability of this other relation.

Consider the Shoemaker case. Suppose Charles is to Fawkes as Brownson is to Brown: Charles actually has Fawkes's brain, which has somehow survived with all of its memories intact. The possibility of a competitor with similarly accurate sensory impressions is not a problem for the advocate of body transfer. This competitor would simply seem to remember being Fawkes. But Charles, because his current memory impressions have the right sort of causal link to Fawkes's life, could be said to really remember. The advocate of body transfer could say that the important relation, the one that permits there to be one person where there are two bodies, has not been duplicated.

Williams notes that it is an advantage of the Shoemaker example that it does not seem to admit of the reduplication problem. But he points out that a natural extension of the example does: "Consider, not the physical transfer of brains, but the transfer of information between brains" (1970/1973, p.79). The relevance of this to the Shoemaker case, and to the project of rebutting the argument that personal identity is not bodily identity, is not perfectly clear, because it seems that only one successful example of bodily transfer needs to be provided to disprove the claim that bodily identity is sufficient for personal identity. The following line of argument is open to Williams. Whatever considerations there are in favor of counting brain transfer as body transfer are also reasons to regard information transfer as body transfer. But the reduplication argument shows we cannot regard information transfer as body transfer, so these reasons must not be good enough. Further, as Williams points out, the reduplication argument is certainly an embarrassment to any memory theorist who doesn't want possession of a particular brain to be a condition of personal identity, and the motivations behind memory theories are such that most would not.

But what sort of embarrassment is it? Williams says the principle of the argument is that "identity is a one-one relation, and that no principle can be a criterion of identity for things of type *T* if it relies only what is logically a one-many relation between things of type *T*" (1960/1973, p.21). What the reduplication case shows (with the details suitably filled in to be relevant to a particular account of personal identity in terms of memory) is that the memory relation proposed as the criterion of identity is not logically one-one.

Does it follow from the fact that identity is logically one-one that any criterion for identity must be logically one-one? It is not even clear that it follows that it must be, as a matter of fact, one-one. For example, having *the same fingerprints* is perhaps, as a matter of fact, but surely not as a matter of logical necessity, a one-one relation, yet this is certainly, in the ordinary sense, a criterion of personal identity. It would still be so, even if in every couple of million cases two or three people did share the same fingerprints. A relation that is not one-one can be quite good evidence for one that is one-one, so long as there are not too many exceptions. Presumably, then, some special philosophical notion of "criterion" is at work here. Even if we require some "conceptual" or "logical" connection between the criterion and what it is a criterion for, the inference in question may not hold. Using, for example, Shoemaker's explanation of the term in *Self-Knowledge and Self-Identity* (1963), a criterion for personal identity would be a relation that could not possibly not be good evidence for personal identity. All that seems to be required of such a relation is that, in each possible world, it is good evidence for personal identity. All this seems to require is that in each possible world the relation in question be one-one with but a few exceptions.

Perhaps a "criterion of identity" is to be some relation between persons which the memory theorist produces as giving an analysis of the very meaning of "is the same person as." Williams's remark, that his point could be made more rigorously in terms of "sense and reference of uniquely referring expressions," suggests this (1960/1973, p. 21). Such analyses are often developed in terms of equivalence relations and equivalence classes.

An equivalence relation is one with the following properties: It is transitive, which means that if x has the relation to y and y has it to z, then x has it to z. It is symmetrical, which means that if x has it to y, then y has it to x. And it is weakly reflexive, which means that if x has it to anything, x has it to x. Equivalence relations break populations up into equivalence classes. These classes contain only things that have the relation in question to everything inside the class, including themselves, and nothing outside of it. For example, *having the same mother* is an equivalence relation among children. If we pick any child and consider the class of things that have the same mother as her, they will all have the same mother as each other, and none will have the same mother as anything outside of the class. On the other hand, suppose we say that x is y's brother if x is a male and x and y have the same mother or the same father. Then *having the same brother* would not be an equivalence relation, because it is not transitive. It will not break a population of children up into equivalence classes. If we start with one child and consider the class of children that share a brother with that child, we may have people in the class that have this relation to people outside of it.

Memory theorists often explain the notion of personal identity by starting with a relation that obtains among stages or phases of persons or their minds. Persons are then taken as being or corresponding to equivalence classes of these entities, generated by the relation given as the "criterion of identity," or, as I prefer to call it, the "unity relation." For example, with an analysis Grice suggests, the relation is roughly "A and B are end points of a series of person-stages each member of which has an experience of which the next could have a memory" (Grice 1941).[2]

In this framework, Williams's requirement for a logically one-one relation amounts to the following: the unity relation must be an equivalence relation not merely as a matter of fact, but as a matter of logical or metaphysical necessity. But I don't think the memory theorist needs to accept this requirement.

In the actual world, if we take a person-stage and consider the class of other states that have Grice's relation to it, the population of person-stages breaks up into equivalence classes. Now, suppose that in some other possible world w, this is not so because there is frequent "fissioning" in the following sense: A person-stage A has an experience, which two successor person-stages B and C can remember. B and C have experiences, which successors of theirs, B' and C', can remember. But no successor of B remembers any of C's experiences and vice versa.

---

[2] An exposition of Grice's views can be found in essay 5 and in the introduction to Perry (1975).

Now, if we start with C and generate the set of stages that have Grice's relation to it, A will be included. And if we start with B, A will be included. But C will not be included in B's set and vice versa.

In world w, the notion of a person will not be as useful as it is in ours. We might say that the presuppositions of using it the way we do, to pick out individual nonbranching streams of thought and experience, are not met. But the fact that this notion would not be very useful in w does not mean it doesn't work fine in the world the way it actually is. It does not mean that this is not the notion of a person that we actually have in our world, where R is an equivalence relation.

The memory theorist can be even more flexible about the logical properties of the unity relation. Suppose that such "fissionings" of streams of experience happen in our world, but only very occasionally. The notion of a person could still be very useful, even though not applicable in a clear-cut way to those particular cases. Consider the notion of a *nation*. This is a pretty useful notion, although occasionally, as in the cases of Germany and Korea, a sort of fissioning takes place. When we are talking about the history of Germany or Korea, we have to be careful about the way we use the concept of the *same nation* to describe things. If streams of experience were occasionally to split, as is imagined in the reduplication case, we would have to be careful in applying the concept of *same person* to those cases. This does not show that an analysis, such as Grice's, that allows the logical possibility of fission is mistaken.

So, I think it is open to memory theorists to reply to Williams's reduplication argument by saying that it imposes a requirement on analyses of personal identity that they do not need to accept. The possibility of body transfer only requires that our notion of personal identity may be correctly analyzed in terms of a relation that is, as a matter of fact, an equivalence relation and could obtain between person-stages that involve different bodies.

The memory theorist can go further, I think, and note that the analysis implied by those who reject the possibility of bodily transfer is also subject to the reduplication argument. Williams himself notes that one could claim that "even a criterion of identity in terms of spatio-temporal continuity is itself not immune to this possibility. It is possible to imagine a man splitting, ameba-like, into two simulacra of himself" (1960/1973, p. 23). He states that there is "a vital difference between this sort of reduplication . . . and the other sorts of cases." The difference is that the procedure of tracing the continuous path between two occurrences of what is taken to be a single person will inevitably reveal the duplication if "ideally carried out." Thus, "in this case, but not in the others, the logical possibility of reduplication fails to impugn the status of the criterion of identity" (p. 24). This is unconvincing for several reasons. Even if we grant that the spatiotemporal continuity requirement has the advantage described, having that advantage does not make it "logically one-one." How can such a difference between the spatiotemporal continuity criterion and others exempt it from what are alleged to be logical requirements of a criterion of identity? Perhaps the force of the "logical requirement" simply reduces to this advantage. But why should we think, after all, that this advantage is not shared by the memory criterion? Among other things, we should have to know what it is to "ideally carry out" the application of that criterion. Williams asserts that memory is a causal notion (p. 47). As Shoemaker has observed, this seems to suggest that application of the memory criterion, ideally carried out, would disclose the existence of competitors, since the causal chain involved would presumably involve a spatiotemporally continuous chain of events.

I conclude that the reduplication argument does not show that memory theorists are incorrect in allowing for the possibility of body transfer. Let us now turn to what I shall call the "nonduplication argument."

3. The Nonduplication Argument

Williams begins his discussion in "The Self and the Future" by introducing an example whose structure is that of two basic cases superimposed:

Earlier Time	Later Time
A	A-body person [A's body, B's memories]
B	B-body person [B's body, A's memories]

Master Case
(Superimposed Basic Cases)

Williams then poses a problem for the A and B. Each is asked, at the earlier time, to choose one of the bodies to be tortured at the later time, the other to receive $100,000. This choice is to be made on selfish grounds. Williams assays the results of various possible combinations of choices and seems to find in them a strong argument for describing the case as one of body transfer. For example, if A chose that the B-body person be rewarded and this is done, then the B-body person will be happy about a choice he will seem to remember making. It is natural to report this as "Someone got what he wanted," and this someone must be someone who had body A and then had body B. Williams's discussion from page 47 to page 50 puts the case for the possibility of body transfer about as effectively as it has been put.

But then he pulls the rug out from under us. "Let us now consider something apparently different. Someone . . . tells me that I am going to be tortured tomorrow . . . when the moment of torture comes, I shall not remember any of the things I am now in a position to remember . . . but will have a different set of impressions of my past" (p. 50). To be tortured is a frightful prospect, and the additional bits of information about loss of memory and acquisition of false belief just make things worse. But this is just a variation on the master case. Instead of adding a character, as in the reduplication argument, characters are subtracted—or at least knowledge of them. We represent this variation by simply striking out half of the last diagram:

Earlier Time	Later Time
A	A-body person [A's body, but not A's memories]
B	~~B-body person~~ ~~[B's body, A's memories]~~

**Nonduplication Case
(Top Half of Master Case)**

(With the information in the bottom half left out, the force of "B's memories" in the previous case is simply "memories that are not A's"; for all A is to be told, the memories of the A-body person might not belong to anyone.) As Williams says, "For what we have just been through is of course merely one side, differently represented, of the transaction which was considered before; and it represents it as a perfectly hateful prospect, while the previous considerations represented it as something one should rationally, perhaps even cheerfully, choose out of the options there presented" (pp. 52–53).

Going back to the choice about torture and money in the master case, Williams tells us that these and other considerations leave him "not in the least clear which option it would be wise to take if one were presented with them before the experiment" (p. 61). But his cautious advice is that "if we were the person *A* then, if we were to decide selfishly, we should pass the pain to the *B*-body person" (p. 63).

Williams suggests that his opponent might claim that in terrifying *A* with his one-sided description of what is to happen, it is the omission of mention of the *B*-body person that clouds the issue. The objector would maintain that this "is to leave out exactly the feature which, as the first presentation of the case showed, makes all the difference: for it is to leave out the person who, as the first presentation showed, will be you" (pp. 55–56). Williams challenges this objector to draw a line somewhere in the following series. At which point should *A*'s fear of torture give way to anticipation of $100,000?

(i) *A* is subjected to an operation that produces total amnesia;

(ii) amnesia is produced in *A*, and other interference leads to certain changes in his character;

(iii) changes in his character are produced, and at the same time certain illusory "memory," beliefs are induced in him; these are of a quite fictitious kind. . . .

(iv) the same as (iii) except that both the character traits and the "memory" impressions are designed to be appropriate to another actual person *B*;

(v) the same as (iv) except that the result is produced by putting the information into *A* from the brain of *B*, by a method that leaves *B* the same as he was before;

(vi) the same happens to *A* as in (v), but *B* is not left the same, since a similar operation is conducted in the reverse direction. (pp. 55–56)

It is case (vi) that the memory theorist seems to suppose should leave *A* looking forward to receiving $100,000. This is, it must be admitted, an odd reaction to (vi) if we take everything up to (v) as describing an increasingly troubling description of surviving as an amnesiac. But should we react to cases (i) to (v) in this way? This depends, I suggest, on what we mean by "total amnesia."

Let's return for a moment to the diagram of the master case and the nonduplication case to note a crucial point about the logic of Williams's argument. For the nonduplication argument to work, there must be a certain relation that obtains between A and the A-body person both in the master case and in the nonduplication case, which is supposed to be part of the master case differently presented. The relation will have to be clearly sufficient, in the nonduplication case, for the identity of A and the A-body person. Then the argument will be that the addition of B and the B-body person to make the master case should make no difference—just as eliminating the strike-throughs in the bottom of the diagram would not alter the top. The A-body person would still be A and not have suddenly become B instead.

I believe the plausibility of the nonduplication argument turns on leaving the details of the master case hazy. I shall argue that filling them in one way leaves the argument with no force, while filling them in the other way reduces the argument to a fancy version of the reduplication argument, which I found unconvincing in the prior section.

The haziness derives from the ambiguity of the term "amnesia" and the phrase "extracting information." "Amnesia" is a slippery word. It means one thing to a physician, another to a television writer, and perhaps something still different to Williams. In ordinary fiction, amnesia is consistent with, and indeed implies, survival of memory traces. The picture is of a person whose memories are inaccessible but, in some sense, still there. The disposition to remember is present, but not triggered by the ordinary conditions. Photographs, diaries, and the sight of loved ones will not do the trick; perhaps a fortuitous blow on the head or electric shock therapy will. In introducing the procedure whose consequences he wishes to discuss, Williams says, "[S]uppose it were possible to extract information" (p. 47). This is ambiguous. Compare photocopying a book to ripping its pages out. In either case, one has extracted information from the book. A possible interpretation is this: The information is extracted in a way that leaves the brain with all its memory dispositions in some way intact, although no longer capable of being triggered in the usual ways. On this interpretation, the case he envisages seems to involve a sort of programming of new memory dispositions over the old, in such a way as to leave the old dispositions no longer capable of being triggered. I'll call this the "information overlay."

A second interpretation I'll call a "brain zap." The information in the brain is extracted in the "ripping out the pages" sense. The information and the dispositions to speak, imagine, infer, and the like are destroyed. The brain is "wiped clean" to be a suitable receptacle for a completely different set of memory dispositions. Efforts to trigger the disposition would be to no avail because the disposition is not there to be triggered.

If we think of Williams's case as an information overlay, it simply leads to a complex version of the reduplication argument. A plausible analysis of personal identity in terms of memory will have to be flexible enough to allow for amnesia, even amnesia together with delusions of an alternative past. The identity theorist who allows for these possibilities will be confronted with two reduplication cases. Stage A will have the unity relation to the A-body person-stage and to the B-body person-stage. Stage B will also have the unity relation to both of these stages. We have two intertwined cases where the presuppositions of the concept of person have broken down. The memory theorist should certainly not say, in this case interpreted this way, that A should have unalloyed feelings of joy about getting $100,000. He will have a ready explanation, in terms of the breakdown of the presuppositions of the concept of a person, of our feeling of not knowing where to draw the line in the series (i) to (vi). This feeling of bafflement is just what the memory theorist could predict. Personal identity is analyzable in terms of a certain relation, and if Williams's case involves a double-intertwined breakdown of an empirical presupposition of that concept, namely that the relation is an equivalence relation, then we have a case in which we should not expect to be able to readily apply our ordinary concepts.

I think there is good reason to suppose that Williams was giving "amnesia" a reading closer to what I am calling a brain zap, however. If Williams intended an information overlay, the whole point of his discussion becomes rather obscure. Let us review the logic of the situation. The interest in putative cases of body transfer is as counterexamples to the necessity of bodily identity as a condition of personal identity. If a case is presented as a counterexample, it's no good to pick another case something like it, but different in essential respects, and point out that this new case is not such a clear-cut counterexample. I think we have a right to assume that Williams's example is intended to be more or less the same sort of example that advocates of body transfer have offered. Moreover, the fact that he develops his example as a sort of moderate alternative to Shoemaker's original case, where a brain was transferred and there was no question of superimposition of one set of memory dispositions over another, and the fact that he speaks of replacing the information extracted from each brain with information extracted from the other suggest that a brain zap is what is involved.

This suggests it might be a relevant and helpful exercise to think through the nonduplication argument as applied to Shoemaker's original case. The removal of a brain and its replacement with a different one, with no transfer of information between them, seems like just an extreme way of achieving the same effects, so far as information goes, as a brain zap. Let's suppose for a moment that in the master case the A-body person has the actual brain B had at the earlier time. Then the relation between A at the earlier time and the A-body person at the later time is "having the same body but not the same brain." This will also be the relation in the nonduplication case, the variation where B is left out. Consider what we should tell A were we to fully represent to him one side of the transaction: "Tomorrow your brain will be removed from your body. Another man's brain will be put in its place. Then your body will be tortured." This certainly represents a frightening prospect. But it is not torture that is to be feared, but death and defilement. We could, of course, give a superficial description that would both be true and inspire fear of pain: "Your body is going to be whipped, and it won't be a corpse when it happens." But the fear of torture inspired by this description might be a consequence of the omission of such details as the removal of the brain. The principle, to which Williams appeals in considering his case, is that "one's fears can extend to future pain whatever psychological changes precede it" (p. 63). It's a little hard to get a grip on how this principle is supposed to work, since it seems that fear can extend to any future pain whatsoever, no matter whose it is, so long as the fearful person believes it will be his pain. The principle is surely only dubiously applicable to the Shoemaker case, for loss of one's brain is not, in the ordinary sense, a "psychological change." Williams's argument, that addition of another body to the scenario in the nonduplication case cannot affect the identity of A and the A-body person, has no force unless the identity is clear to start with. If we were dealing with a brain transplant case, it would not be clear at all.

Perhaps this is all irrelevant, since Williams explicitly chooses not to deal with a case involving a physical transplant. He says, "if utterances coming from a given body are to be taken as expressive of memories . . . there should be some suitable causal link between the appropriate state of that body and the original happening" (p. 47). But one need not imagine, in order to secure this link, that a brain has actually been transplanted. "[S]uppose it were possible to extract information from a man's brain and store it in a device while his brain was repaired or even renewed, the information then being replaced: it would seem exaggerated to insist that the resultant man could not possibly have the memories he had before the operation. . . . Hence we can imagine the case we are concerned with in terms of information extracted into such devices from A's and B's brains and replaced in the other brain" (p. 47).

Thus the relation between A and the A-body person is not as it would be in a transplant case: having the same body but different brains. The relation is that they have the same body and the same brain, but information about A's life has been extracted from this brain and other information has replaced it.

But should this make any difference, either to A or to the memory theorist? I cannot see that the situation is importantly changed when we deal with a brain zap rather than a brain transplant. When it's not clear that A's brain will be zapped, he fears torture. When that is clear but he is left to assume the worst about the survival of the information in his brain, he fears death or perhaps doesn't know what to fear. When he is told that this information will be appropriately put into another brain, itself previously zapped, that might change the focus of his fear considerably.

Consider now the nonduplication case in which B has been left out. What is the relation between A and the A-body person? Is it psychological change, through which A's fears could, by Williams's principle, appropriately extend? Or is it simply the death of A? Or something else? For the nonduplication argument to work, it must be psychological change. A would react to the description of what is to happen with fear, because he regards what is to happen to his body as something like his forgetting and assimilates how he will be to a "completely amnesiac state" (p. 52).

If the relation between A and the A-body person is that the latter has the very brain the former had but it has been zapped, then the case seems unimportantly different from a case in which they share no brain at all. A superficial description of the case might evoke fear of pain, but when the details are known, fear of death seems more appropriate. If one were tempted to draw a line between the case in which A and the A-body person do not share a brain and one in which they share a brain but it gets zapped between the earlier and later time, we could appeal to a point Williams makes. He argues that if the sort of information-parking operation he envisages were possible, "a person could be counted the same if this were done to him, and in the process he were given a new brain (the repairs, let us say, actually required a new part)" (1970/1973, p. 80). Apparently, so long as no transfer of bodies is at issue, it is the retention of information, and not of the brain, that is crucial for survival. Why shouldn't the same be true for nonsurvival?

In considering the series (i) to (vi), the memory theorist can simply point out that if a brain zap is involved, "amnesia" in (i) to (v) is simply a euphemism for "death." After all, it is the cessation of the sort of activity of the brain whose role is to preserve that which has here been destroyed that is known as "brain death." The use of the pronoun "him" simply begs the question at issue. In case (vi) the trauma of gaining a new body should probably be feared, offset perhaps to some extent by gaining $100,000 if one made the right choice.

If we understand that a brain zap is involved, Williams's nonduplication argument fails. The nonduplication case was supposed to remind us that A really was the A-body person. Then the argument is that A doesn't cease to be the A-body person simply because the B-body person is hanging around. Since, given that it involves a brain zap, the nonduplication case doesn't show that A is the A-body person, it's possible that, when the facts about B and the B-body person are added, A will be seen at the later time to be the B-body person, an unusual but unambiguous case of personal identity with transfer of bodies.

7

Personal Identity and the Concept of a Person

Philosophers approach the concept of a person from two directions. In ethics and political philosophy, it often is taken as primitive, or at least familiar and not requiring elucidation, but persistent inquiry and difficult problems make a deeper look inevitable. In discussing abortion, for example, one can hardly invoke principles about rights and welfare of persons concerned without facing the question about which concerned parties are, in fact, persons and what that means. One moves remorselessly from issues of rights and responsibilities to questions of consciousness, self-awareness, and identity—from the moral to the metaphysical.

From the other direction, no comprehensive epistemology or metaphysic can avoid the question of what persons—our primary examples of knowers and agents—are and how they fit into the universe, whether as illusion, phenomena, or things in themselves. Answers to this question will have consequences in the ethical sphere.

These approaches meet in the problems of freedom and in the problem the recent history of which I discuss: personal identity. It is the identity of the knower over time that seems to be both the ground and the result of empirical knowledge and identity of the moral agent that seems presupposed by notions of responsibility, guilt, decision, and freedom.

I shall discuss a number of contributions by philosophers to our understanding of personal identity. I shall follow a specific path through the literature, which means I shall have to ignore a number of contributions that lie to one side or the other. The discussion is

"Personal Identity and the Concept of a Person" originally appeared in *Contemporary Philosophy: A New Survey*, vol. 4, *Philosophy of Mind*, edited by Gottorm Floistad (The Hague: Martinus Nijhoff, 1983), pp. 11–43. Reprinted, with revisions, by permission.

mainly metaphysical and epistemological, but questions of ethical significance are posed.

1. Personal Identity from Locke to Shoemaker

Our path will begin with Sydney Shoemaker's seminal book, *Self-Knowledge and Self-Identity*, published in 1963. But before starting on the path proper, it will be helpful to glance at the historic sources of the problems Shoemaker discusses. Although questions of personal identity are central to Idealism, from Kant to Royce, Shoemaker's book skips over this tradition (except, perhaps, as it enjoys a twilight existence in Wittgenstein's thought) and, like so much of twentieth-century analytical philosophy, picks up the problem as it was left by empiricist and commonsense philosophers of the seventeenth and eighteenth centuries. The most important of these was John Locke, who added a chapter on personal identity to his *Essay Concerning Human Understanding* in 1694 (1694/1975). Identity of persons consists in continuity of consciousness, and this seems to be provided by links of memory: "As far as this consciousness can be extended backwards to any past action or thought, so far reaches the identity of that person . . ." (sec. 9). Thus Locke appears to analyze self-identity in terms of self-knowledge and provides the theme of Shoemaker's book and the dominant topic in the discussions to follow.

Locke distinguished identity of person from identity of spiritual substance on the one hand and identity of human body ("identity of man") on the other. The second distinction he argues for with a striking thought experiment:

> For should the soul of a prince, carrying with it the consciousness of the prince's past life, enter and inform the body of a cobbler, as soon deserted by his own soul, everyone sees he would be the same person with the prince, accountable only for the prince's actions." (sec. 15)

The use of thought experiments which are putative cases of "body-transfer" was to become a focus of discussion 270 years later, but at the time Locke wrote, his distinction between identity of person and identity of soul or spiritual substance was more controversial.

> Let anyone reflect upon himself, and conclude that he has in himself an immaterial spirit, which is that which thinks in him, and, in the

constant change of his body keeps him the same; and is that which he calls himself: let him also suppose it to be the same soul that was in Nestor or Thersites, at the siege of Troy . . . but he now having no consciousness of any of the actions either of Nestor or Thersites, does he conceive himself the same person with either of them? Can he be concerned in either of their actions? attribute them to himself, or think them his own, more than the actions of any other man that ever existed? (sec. 14)

Locke also held that it is possible, for all we know, that consciousness can be transferred from one substance to another, so "two thinking substances may make but one person" (sec. 13). This outraged Joseph Butler:

[I]n a strict and philosophical manner of speech, no man, no being, no mode of being, nor any thing, can be the same with that, with which it hath indeed nothing the same. Now sameness is used in this latter sense when applied to persons. The identity of these, therefore, cannot consist with diversity of substance. (Butler 1736/1975; see also Reid 1785/1975)

The idea that personal identity could be analyzed in terms of memory was used by twentieth-century empiricists who attempted to analyze the self as a logical construction from momentary experiences. This project, more Humean than Lockean, requires a relation between those experiences which will group them into sets of "co-personal" experiences. Though Hume (1741/1968) rejected Locke's memory theory and Locke himself did not hold a bundle theory, the two doctrines seem to fit together naturally: we use memory to hold the bundle together through time. The clearest expression of this view comes from H. P. Grice in his fine essay "Personal Identity" (1941). Grice labors to discredit the pure ego theory of the self, a descendant of the view that personal identity consists in sameness of spiritual substance, and to put in its place a "modification of Locke's theory of personal identity." We can understand Grice's subtle and sophisticated theory as the result of successive accommodations to counterexamples, starting with Locke's view. Reconstructing Locke's view within Grice's framework, we begin with experiences. Those that can be known by introspection to be simultaneous belong to the same total temporary state, or "t.t.s." (p. 88). Thus, we may imagine the realm of experience broken into discrete bundles, each t.t.s. being the experiences belonging to a single person at a given time. Locke's theory then is seen as giving us a principle for stringing these bundles together through time, giving us persons as enduring entities. His view is simply that t.t.s. *A* and t.t.s. *B* belong to the same person if and only if the latter contains an experience that is a memory of some element of the earlier. But this permits Thomas Reid's (1785/1975) famous brave officer paradox: the boy is the officer (for the officer remembers stealing apples), and the general is the officer (for the general remembers leading the charge), but, since the general doesn't remember anything the boy thought or did, the general is not the boy.

Grice's final theory goes roughly as follows. Consider the relation t.t.s. *A* has to t.t.s. *B* if either one could contain a memory of an experience contained in the other. Any set of experiences which is closed under this relation, and contains no subsets closed under it, we may call a Grice set. (A set x is closed under a relation R if anything that has R to any member of x is in x.) Two t.t.s.'s are members of the same Grice set if and only if they are stages of a single person. The theory gets around the brave officer paradox, and other problems of Grice's own devising, by allowing indirect memory links, such as that between the general and the boy, to confer identity.

Between the publication of Grice's article and the publication of Shoemaker's book, Ludwig Wittgenstein exerted tremendous influence on philosophy, and Shoemaker's perspective and theoretical approach were very Wittgensteinian in some respects. In particular, Shoemaker makes heavy use of the concept of a criterion and of the asymmetries between first- and third-person reports. Shoemaker is also sympathetic to Butler and Reid, trying to bring out epistemological insights that motivate their criticisms of Locke without adopting their metaphysics of immaterial substances. Shoemaker did not conceive of himself as building on Grice's work and was in fact severely critical of aspects of Grice's view and of much that Locke had said. Yet, perhaps ironically, a chief effect of Shoemaker's books was to precipitate an increasingly productive reexamination of their ideas.

2. Self-Knowledge and Self-Identity

A main theme in Shoemaker's book is that problems about self-knowledge have led philosophers to misconceptions about self-identity and about the nature of selves in general. Self-knowledge is that which would be characteristically expressed in sentences containing the word "I." The problems have to do with the asymmetry between such statements and the third-person statements which are, in some sense, equivalent to them. One who says "I see a tree," for example, will normally find a tree in his visual field, but will not find himself looking at one in his visual field. And yet someone else who reports the same episode of vision in the third person by saying, for example, "Jones sees a tree" will have to see a person and identify that person as Jones, as well as seeing a tree. Now, one who thinks that in the first instance, one must have seen, or somehow been aware of, or at least inferred the presence of, the tree seer as well as the tree seen and must have identified the person so perceived or inferred as a person appropriately referred to with "I" is likely to be led to the conception of the self as a nonphysical thing, simply because no physical thing seems available to fill this role. Shoemaker finds such conceptions in McTaggart, Russell, and others. But these theories, he thinks, all wrongly assume that in order to be entitled to say "I perceive an X," I must perceive more than an x. In fact, says Shoemaker, it is a distinguishing characteristic of first-person experience statements that their being true entitles one to assert them. The problem of identifying the perceiver as "me" does not arise, and so the mysterious thing so identifiable need not be found nor postulated. That there should be this entitlement Shoemaker accounts for in two ways. First, that such first-person statements are generally true when made is not contingent, but necessary. Second, it is simply a fact, indeed, a very general fact of the sort it is easy, as Wittgenstein had emphasized, to overlook, that we can teach individuals to use such sentences as "I see a tree" just when they see a tree, and in doing so we need not be and would not be providing them with criteria which they can use to identify themselves.

Similarly, in the case of a statement such as "I remember going to the store" or "I broke the window," there are no first-person criteria which one must apply to determine who is remembering, went to the store, or broke the window. Now, philosophers such as Locke and Grice, who are drawn to the view that personal identity consists of links of memory may have been led to this view by supposing that we must have criteria of personal identity that we apply in our own cases and finding nothing but memory that could play this role. Philosophers, such as Reid and Butler, who emphasize the special and undefinable nature of personal identity may have seen that no criterion is applied in our own case but misinterpreted this to mean that identity is directly observed and consists in the identity of immaterial substance.

In both cases, philosophers have been led away from the view that persons are physical beings by the fact that one need not use a bodily criterion of personal identity in a first-person report of what one did, or remembers doing, in the past.

But if we see that rather than a nonbodily criterion being applied, or a nonbodily fact being observed, it is simply the fact that one is doing the remembering that entitles one to say that it is oneself who went to the store, we shall be free to agree with Shoemaker that identity of body is the fundamental criterion of personal identity.

Although Shoemaker criticizes the memory theorists severely as being motivated by a mistaken epistemology, and defends bodily identity as the fundamental criterion of personal identity, he does allow that memory is a criterion of personal identity and one that can conflict with the fundamental criterion. Early in the book he introduces the case of Brownson, a twentieth-century version of Locke's cobbler and prince—a case that was to perplex and intrigue philosophers for years to come:

> It is now possible to transplant certain organs . . . it is at least conceivable . . . that a human body could continue to function normally if its brain were replaced by one taken from another human body. . . . Two men, a Mr. Brown and a Mr. Robinson, had been operated on for brain tumors, and brain extractions had been performed on both of them. At the end of the operations, however, the assistant inadvertently put Brown's brain in Robinson's head, and Robinson's brain in Brown's head. One of these men immediately dies, but the other, the one with Robinson's head and Brown's brain, eventually regains consciousness. Let us call the latter "Brownson." . . . When asked his name he automatically replies "Brown." He recognizes Brown's wife and family . . ., and is able to describe in detail events in Brown's life . . . of Robinson's past life he evidences no knowledge at all. (1963, pp. 23–24)

Shoemaker does not say that Brownson is Brown. But he does say that if people did say this, they would not be making a mistake, nor even necessarily deviating from our present criteria or denying the primacy of the bodily criterion. They might simply be allowing it to be overridden by other criteria in some circumstances (p. 247).

At this point, some feel a certain frustration with Shoemaker's conclusions. If Brownson is Brown, or even if that is something we might decide was true without inconsistency, then personal identity is not bodily identity and, it seems, persons are not simply live humans.

What then is personal identity? Here the notion of a criterion of identity and other notions and modes of argument reflecting a Wittgensteinian merger of epistemological and metaphysical questions seem to obscure rather than illuminate issues. That memory is a criterion of personal identity means that it could not be discovered not to be good evidence for personal identity (p. 4). But that does not mean that memory is logically necessary or logically sufficient for personal identity. The same goes for bodily identity. So the identity of Brown is not settled: we have a conflict of criteria that usually don't conflict, and it appears we must leave it at that.

But it is not clear why Locke's theory, or Grice's modification of it, could not take hold here. Grice might agree with Shoemaker's main conclusions but argue that his theory is consistent with them and partly explains them. Memory is a criterion simply because personal identity consists in links of memory. Shoemaker argues that we cannot apply the memory criterion, or even have a concept of memory, without presuming a stable relation between bodily identity and links of memory. That is why the bodily identity criterion is fundamental. But Grice, it seems, could accept that bodily identity was the fundamental criterion of personal identity, and that the assumption of a close correlation between bodily identity and links of memory is a premise of the whole enterprise of talking about persons, without giving up the claim that personal identity consists in links of memory. Just this strategy was adopted by Antony Quinton in "The Soul" (1962), in which a version of the memory theory is defended.

A key consideration against the memory theory in Shoemaker's book is that since we employ no criterion of identity in first-person reports of past thought and action, we do not employ the memory criterion. But while being misled about this might have played a role in motivating the memory theory, it does not seem to provide a decisive objection, as Shoemaker was to point out later himself. Grice's view is that if I remember an experience, it is mine. This is not to say that I use the fact that I remember it as a criterion for deciding that it is mine.

In spite of Shoemaker's criticisms of the memory theorists and his reluctance to unequivocally allow Brownson to be Brown, the overall effect of his book on most philosophers was not to produce the conviction that personal identity is simply bodily identity. In the first place, the example of Brownson takes on a life of its own in the mind of the reader; to many, Shoemaker's reluctance to straightforwardly identify Brownson with Brown underestimates the force of his own example. Second, Shoemaker's probing studies of various examples, claims, and positions, while not always proving the conclusions he draws, always impress one with the depth of the problems involved. Third, Shoemaker's point that we typically apply no criterion in first-person judgments about the past has seemed a point in favor of the memory theory, in spite of his own use of it as a contrary argument. Finally, Shoemaker does allow that memory is a criterion. Locke had part of the truth. Even though memory may not be enough to make Brownson unequivocally Brown, even Shoemaker admits it is enough to prevent him from clearly being Robinson.

3. Dividing Selves and Multiplying Minds

Before publication of Shoemaker's book, Bernard Williams had put forward a clever argument against the memory theory. In "Personal Identity and Individuation" (1957/1973) Williams constructs the case of Charles, a twentieth-century man who shows every sign of remembering the actions and experiences of Guy Fawkes:

> Not only do all Charles' memory-claims that can be checked fit the pattern of Fawkes' life as known to historians, but others that cannot be checked are plausible, provide explanations, and so on. (p. 7)

The case is designed to give us all the evidence we might want to say we have a case like that of Locke's cobbler. But, Williams points out, we are not forced to say that Charles remembers what Fawkes did, rather than merely that he claims to do so. And he comes up with an impressive argument to clinch the point:

> If it is logically possible that Charles should undergo the changes described, then it is logically possible that some other man should simultaneously undergo the same changes, e.g., that both Charles and his brother Robert should be found in this condition. What should we say in this case? They cannot both be Guy Fawkes; if they were, Guy Fawkes would be in two places at once, which is absurd. Moreover, if they were both identical with Guy Fawkes, they would be identical with each other, which is also absurd. . . . We might instead say that one of them was identical with Guy Fawkes . . . but this would be an utterly vacuous maneuver, since there would be ex hypothesi no principles determining which description to apply to which. So it would

be best, if anything, to say that both had mysteriously become like Guy Fawkes. . . . If this would be the best description of each of the two, why would it not be the best description of Charles if Charles alone were changed? (p. 8)

In a reply to an article of Robert Coburn's (1960), Williams makes the principle behind this argument explicit.

The principle of my argument is . . . that identity is a one-one relation, and that no principle can be a criterion of identity for things of type T if it relies only on what is logically a one-many or many-many relation. . . . "being disposed to make sincere memory claims which exactly fit the life of . . ." is not a one-one, but a many-one relation. (1960/1973, p. 21)

Williams's "Reduplication Argument" provided an interesting challenge to those who wished to defend some version of the memory theory. But it also stirred interest in more general problems of identity and individuation, problems on which attention was also focused as a result of Peter Geach's provocative writings on identity (1962; 1969). David Wiggins, in his pioneering study *Identity and Spatio-Temporal Continuity* (1967), adopts a condition very much like Williams's requirement that a criterion of identity be one-one:

If f is a substance concept for a then coincidence under f must be a determinate notion, clear and decisive enough to exclude this situation: a is traced under f and counts as coinciding with b under f, and a is traced under f and counts as coinciding with c under f while nevertheless b does not coincide under f with c. (p. 38)

Wiggins distinguishes the concept of a person from that of a human body and a person from his or her body. And he incorporates into his notion of a person the memory criterion of personal identity. But, he claims, in opposition to Shoemaker's analysis of the Brownson case,

that no correct spatio-temporal criterion of personal identity can conflict with any correct memory criterion or character-continuity of personal identity. (p. 43)

Wiggins, then, accepts both the importance of memory and Williams's condition on criteria of identity. How can he escape the reduplication argument?

In Williams's notion of the memory "criterion," there is again a merging of epistemological and metaphysical considerations. Surely, it is not *claiming* to remember that Locke or Grice thought constituted identity, but some relation of memory for which such claims are evidence. Wiggins is quite clearheaded about this. He generally keeps questions of what constitutes identity and questions of how it is known clearly distinguished. In the present case this is manifested by his adoption of a causal theory of memory, adopted from Martin and Deutscher (1966). Note, it is much easier to imagine two persons sincerely claiming to have done what one person did in the past than it is to imagine two persons whose claims are both caused by the previous action in the way appropriate to be memories. The memory criterion, interpreted as a causal criterion, is much more plausibly one-one.

Even if this were enough to avoid the reduplication argument, it would not vindicate Wiggins's claim that the memory criterion, properly conceived, cannot conflict with the spatiotemporal continuity requirement. For, in the Brownson case the causal requirement appears to have been satisfied.

Wiggins says that they cannot conflict because when the memory criterion is properly founded in the notion of causation, the two criteria inform and regulate one another reciprocally:

> [I]ndeed they are really aspects of a single criterion. For the requirement of spatiotemporal continuity is quite empty until we say continuity under what concept . . . and we cannot specify the right concept without mention of the behavior, characteristic functioning, and capacities of a person, including the capacity to remember some sufficient amount of his past. (p. 46)

In the final analysis, Wiggins says, we should

> analyze person in such a way that coincidence under the concept person logically requires the continuance in one organized parcel of all that was causally sufficient and causally necessary to the continuance and characteristic functioning, no autonomously sufficient part achieving autonomous and functionally separate existence. (p. 55)

Thus, as I understand it, Wiggins allows that Brownson is Brown, the brain being the "organized parcel."

Wiggins points out, however, that building causality into the memory criterion does not totally preclude the reduplication problem:

Suppose we split Brown's brain and house the two halves in different bodies . . . there is memory and character and life in both brain transplants. . . . In this case we cannot simply disregard their (claimed) memories. For we understand far too well why they have these memories. On the other hand, if we say each is the same person as Brown, we shall have to say Brown I is the same person as Brown II. (p. 53)

Wiggins reasons that we cannot take both Brown I and Brown II to be the same person as Brown, for they are not the same as each other. And he reasons that even if half of the brain is destroyed and the other half transplanted, we do not have identity.

[O]ne of the constraints which should act on us here is the likeness of what happens to the surviving half in this case to what happens in the unallowable double transplant case. (p. 56)

Wiggins here agrees with the key move in Williams's original argument. If there were two survivors, we could not say they both were the original. But both would have just the relation to the original that a sole survivor would have. So the relation the sole survivor would have cannot be identity, or enough to guarantee identity. Now, one might criticize this by pointing out that the relation differs, in the latter case, in that there is no competitor. And Shoemaker, in an article to be discussed later, does take just this attitude towards the reduplication case: causally based memory without competition is sufficient for identity. It is natural to reply, on Wiggins's behalf, that this added element of lack of competition does not seem the right sort of difference. Why should who I am be determined by what is going on elsewhere in the world—the presence or absence of a competitor to the identity of the person whose thoughts and actions I remember? This line of thinking will lead us naturally to the insistence not only that the criterion or principle of identity for persons (and perhaps for anything) be logically one-one, but that it be, in some sense, intrinsically so rather than as a result of an ad hoc stipulation that competitors defeat identity. Here, however, there is a problem. It is not clear that there are any such intrinsically one-one empirical relations. As Richard Gale (1969) points out, it is not even clear that Williams's favored criterion of bodily continuity is logically and intrinsically one-one. Can we not imagine a situation in which there are two bodies, either of which by itself would be clearly reckoned as a later stage of a given body?

Another alternative is to allow both of the survivors to be the original. This is assumed to be incoherent, due to the logical properties of identity, by Williams, Wiggins, and Shoemaker. In "Can the Self Divide?" (Perry 1972; essay 3 in this book), however, I argued that if we were careful we could allow this without incoherence—or that at least we could say everything we wanted to say, giving each of the survivors full credit for the past of the original.

Like Wiggins's, my views were set within a general approach to individuation developed as a response to Geach's thesis of relative identity, the thesis that there is no such thing as identity, but only different kinds of "relative identity," and that objects can be identical in one of these ways and not in another (Geach 1962; 1969). My point of view was derived from Frege (1884/1960) and Quine (1973) and emphasized the distinction between identity, a relation that is a part of logic and which every object or entity of any kind or type has to itself, and various relations, unity relations, which were closely related to identity but which were different for various kinds and types of objects.

The undeniable phenomenon motivating doctrines of relative identity is the relativity of individuation (see Essay 3). Imagine a checkerboard. We can think of it as eight rows, as eight columns, as sixty-four squares, or in a variety of other ways. That is, we can individuate it, break it up into individuals for the purpose of description, in different ways. To these different ways of thinking of the same hunk of reality, there seem to be different relations that correspond to identity. Imagine pointing to a checkerboard, saying, "This is the same as that." If one is thinking of rows, the sentence will only be true if the pointings are side by side, the same distance from the bottom of the board (roughly). If we are thinking in terms of columns, one pointing must be above the other. This suggests that identity is a different relation, depending on whether we are talking about rows or columns. It appears that we need to distinguish between row identity and column identity. This crude example captures one motivation people have had for accepting Geach's doctrine; indeed, the conclusion seems almost forced upon us. If I point at the very same places, side by side, saying first, "This is the same row as that" and next, "This is the same column as that," what I say first will be true and what I say second will be false. So the relations asserted to obtain between the identified individuals must, it seems, be different. (Geach has more sophisticated arguments, of course.)

If we think of rows and columns as sums of squares grouped according to different relations—being above and being beside—and consistently follow through on this, all of these difficulties, and the motivation for relative identity, will disappear. Being beside and being above are not two kinds of identity, but relations between squares used to construct two different kinds of objects. The problem with "This is the same as that" is not that it hasn't been said what sort of identity is at stake, but that the objects referred to have not been fully identified. And "This is the same row as that " and "This is the same column as that" do not assert different relations of the same objects, but the same relation, identity, of different objects, a row in the first case and two columns in the second. Thus, like Wiggins, I was unconvinced by Geach's doctrine. In many ways Wiggins's view is that of well-behaved relative identity; however, he does not emphasize, and in some cases (where temporal parts are needed to make the distinction) seems not to allow, the distinction between the unity relations and identity. (See Shoemaker 1970b.)

This distinction, however, allows us to see a fundamental flaw in Williams's reduplication argument. Williams claims that any criterion of identity must be logically one-one. Now, it seems perfectly clear that the evidential relations we have for identity need not be one-one. If x looks exactly like you, that is good evidence that x is you, not because of logic, but because of the rarity of what are called "identical twins." What Williams has in mind are clearly the relations that are constitutive of identity, the relations that parts have if they are parts of the same person (as I would put it). That is, his principle is that unity relations must be one-one because identity is.

But, in fact, unity relations need not, and often do not, share the logical properties of identity. It is more convenient to think about this in terms of the traditional conception of identity as an equivalence relation (reflexive, symmetrical, and transitive), for the notion of one-one becomes awkward when comparing relations between parts (the unity relations) to relations between wholes (identity). Many unity relations are not, even as a matter of fact, much less as a matter of logic, equivalence relations. In general, where K's are a certain kind of entity with spatiotemporal parts, the formula "x and y are parts of a single K" gives us the unanalyzed unity relation for K's. Now consider, for example, highways. The roadbed of the Golden Gate Bridge and the portion of U.S. 101 that goes by Candlestick Park are parts of a single highway, as are the roadbed of the Golden Gate Bridge and that part of California Highway 1 that goes by the Pillar Point Fishing Pier. But the part of 101 that goes by Candlestick and the part of 1 that goes by Pillar Point are not parts of a single highway. (The situation is the familiar one of different highways merging to cross an expensive bridge.) It might seem that if the unity relation for highways is not an equivalence relation, then highway identity also must not be. A counterexample to the one should provide a counterexample to the other. But one finds that an attempt to produce a counterexample is blocked by a failure of reference. "The highway that crosses the Golden Gate Bridge," or "This highway" as said on the bridge, fails to refer, for there are two highways that cross the bridge. Thus, mechanisms of reference act as fuses, which by failing keep the logical shortcomings of unity relations from being passed on to identity.

In "Can the Self Divide?" this idea was worked out in some detail in a way that allowed us to say, without contradiction and without abandoning any of the traditional properties of identity, that each of the survivors of a reduplication case did all of the things the original had done and that he was to do all of the things each of them did. The abstract point that unity relations need not share the logical properties of identity has been more convincing than the particular solution proposed, however. Criticisms by David Lewis (1976) and Terence Leichti (1975) have weakened my faith that my intuitions about what to say in a reduplication case were as inevitably the product of careful reflection, and that my scheme embodied them in so completely an unobjectionable way, as I had thought. I would now prefer to speak of "individuative crises" occasioned when unity relations that have been reliably equivalence relations (though not logically) cease to have that character, to which we can respond in a number of ways, the present concept underdetermining the matter (see essay 4). I still think my solution is the best response to the crisis, however.

"Can the Self Divide?" was one of three papers (essays 3, 5, and 8) in which I defended Grice's memory theory. It seemed to me that Grice had been clearer about the structure of identity than his successors and that since a careful distinction between identity and unity was built into his account, the reduplication argument did not touch it. This still seems to me correct, even if we adopt the view that what to say in a case of reduplication is left indeterminate by our concept of personal identity rather than being as intuitively clear as I had supposed. In essays 5 and 8, I argued that Grice's point of view, when stripped of its goal of logical construction, leads to a plausible causal theory of personal identity and that an account can be given, within this framework, of the importance of personal identity. In my thinking on each of these matters, the distinction between the unity relations and identity loomed large; I thought it was a necessary first step to clarity on these issues. In reviewing the literature for this article, I find my earlier attitude rather unfounded and think it must have led me to be insufficiently appreciative of others, particularly Shoemaker and Wiggins, who manage to make pretty much the same points without explicitly appealing to the distinction. Perhaps emphasis on the distinction between unity and identity is not so necessary a first step as I had thought! It's a very helpful first step, however.

Another approach to the reduplication case is taken by Roderick Chisholm (1976). Chisholm wondered how we might face the prospect of splitting like an ameba. He concludes,

> There is no possibility whatever that you would be both the person on the right and the person on the left. Moreover, there is a possibility that you would be one or the other of these two persons. And finally you could be one of those persons and yet have no memory at all of your present existence. (p. 179)

Chisholm draws on Shoemaker for support. He says he agrees with Shoemaker's contention that first-person psychological statements are not known to be true on the basis of criteria. He thinks a consequence of this is

> [I]t makes sense to suppose . . . that you are in fact the half that goes off to the left and not the one that goes off to the right even though there is no criterion at all by means of which anyone could decide the matter. (p. 182)

These reflections on reduplication come at the end of an article whose main object is to defend a version of Bishop Butler's claim that there is a "loose and popular," as well as a "strict and philosophical," sense of identity. Personal identity, unlike the identity of ships and carriages and trains and rivers and trees and in general "compositia" or evolving systems thereof, is identity in the strict and philosophical sense. Identity in the loose and popular sense is typically vague, open ended, defeasible, and, ultimately, a matter of convention, of how we choose to talk. In puzzling cases, decision by courts or other agencies is appropriate. But none of this is applicable to personal identity, according to Chisholm. He considers Peirce's (1935, p. 355) example of someone who is to be operated upon, without anesthetic, with a drug administered beforehand which wipes out memories during the operation and one administered after that restores these but leaves no memories of the operation. Chisholm has no doubt that it is the person in question who will feel pain during the operation, but he considers someone—perhaps someone tempted by Grice's theory—who is not so sure. He says it ought to be obvious to such a person that the adoption of a convention, a way of talking or a practice by a judge or a whole community, cannot in the least affect the question he is worrying about.

In his reply to Chisholm's paper at the Oberlin Colloquium, Shoemaker (1969) begins to develop a line of thinking which goes significantly beyond his book and introduces ideas and problems that dominated the study of personal identity for the next decade. "What we need to clarify," he says, "is the nature of that interest we have in personal identity, and in particular that special concern that each of us has for his own future welfare" (p. 117). Shoemaker entertains the idea that it might be appropriate for one who knows he is to undergo fission to anticipate the experience of both offshoots while not supposing that he would be identical with either. These themes are developed in an important paper Shoemaker was to publish three years later.

4. Persons and Their Pasts

In "Persons and Their Pasts," published in 1970 (1970a), Shoemaker gives a much more sensitive and sympathetic treatment of the memory theory than he had in *Self-Knowledge and Self-Identity*. He says that he is defending Locke's view that persons have, in memory, a special access to facts about their own past histories and their own identities and he is also defending the nontrivial nature of Grice's claim (suitably interpreted) that "one can only remember one's own experiences." This would be trivial if there were some general mode of access to past experiences, our own and others', and "remembered" were simply a title for the subset of experiences so known that happened to have been ours. It is nontrivial if memory (of some sort) is an independently specifiable mode of knowing of past experiences and what we mean, or part of what we mean, by calling an experience "ours" is that it is remembered. In that case, the limited access we have in memory would be constitutive of the notion of a single person. Shoemaker considers two criticisms of the memory theory. One is that it is circular, a charge originally made by Butler; Shoemaker had earlier made a version of this criticism himself. The other is the reduplication argument, not in the form in which Williams originally advanced it, but as put forward by Wiggins and Chisholm, with appropriate causal links between the survivors and the original.

Those who charge the memory theory with circularity acknowledge a strong conceptual link between personal identity and memory but see this as simply the upshot of the fact that personal identity is a logically necessary condition for memory. If it is a part of our concept of memory that one can only remember events one witnessed or participated in, then it is hardly surprising that memory is a sufficient condition for identity with a past witness or participant. But the analysis of personal identity in terms of memory would be circular.

Shoemaker suggests an analysis of memory for the purposes of considering this charge, which goes more or less as follows:

X remembers event e if and only if

(1) X is in a cognitive state S;

(2) Y was aware of e when it happened, in virtue of being in cognitive state S';

(3) cognitive state S' corresponds to S;

(4) Y's being in S' and X's being in S are elements in an M-type causal chain; and

(5) $X = Y$.

The cognitive state mentioned in (1) is intended to be the sort of state one could be in whether remembering or only seeming to; to distinguish apparent from real memory, we need the rest of the analysis. Clause (2) captures part of what is called the "previous awareness condition": if one remembers an event, one must have been aware of it at the time it occurred. By using "Y" instead of "X" in its statement, the part of the analysis that seems to lead to circularity, the condition that the previously aware person be the remembered, is split off for separate consideration. Clause (3) makes the plausible point that what is remembered must correspond to what one perceives or experiences, though exactly what this involves is not explained at any length. Clause (4) requires that the present memory activity be caused by the earlier perceptual activity in the right way, that is, in the way that it is usually caused in memory. Clause (5), finally, is the identity condition split off from the previous awareness condition, the element in the analysis that makes the use of memory to analyze identity seem circular.

Shoemaker then introduces two new notions. X q-remembers e if conditions (1)–(3) are satisfied. X quasi-remembers e if conditions (1)–(4) are satisfied. Thus the statements that one can only q-remember one's own past experiences or that one can only quasi-remember one's own experiences would certainly not be trivial. If we find that either of these notions assigns the same past event and experiences to a person as does the "unstripped" notion of memory, then we can say that the additional clauses are really just redundant. If, for example, we find that one quasi-remembers just those past events that one would be said to remember, then one can say that clause (5) is really not necessary for the analysis of memory: memory is just quasi-memory. Clause (5) would be true, but now we could look on its truth as a consequence of the nature of memory as given by (1)–(4) and the noncircular analysis of personal identity in terms of that notion of memory.

Shoemaker isolates the strong conceptual links between memory and personal identity in two principles. The first is the (unstripped) previous awareness condition. The second is what Shoemaker calls preservation of immunity to first-person misidentification. This notion is a descendant of the idea in *Self-Knowledge and Self-Identity* that one needs no criterion for first-person identification. Used in the book as a basis for criticism of the memory theory, this immunity is now seen as something the memory theory goes some way towards explaining. Shoemaker brings in the helpful notion of memory "from the inside." When I remember a past thought or action from the inside, then I can identify myself as the past thinker or doer without identifying the thinker or doer as someone who fits a certain description or satisfies certain criteria. Now, insofar as we can understand q-memory at all, neither the previous awareness condition nor the principle of preservation of immunity to misidentification seem to hold for it.

For quasi-memory, however, the picture is quite different. When we add the causal requirement, we get a notion almost indistinguishable from ordinary memory. Virtually any situation I can imagine in which the conditions for quasi-memory are met is a situation in which the conditions for memory are met. This strongly suggests that personal identity can be analyzed in terms of quasi-memory, that clause (5) can be seen as a consequence of this analysis, and that the memory theory need not be circular.

The need for qualification comes from the second criticism of the memory theory that Shoemaker considers. The way the world is, M-type causal chains neither branch nor merge. Given this orderly behavior, quasi-memory seems indistinguishable from memory. But it is imaginable that M-type causal chains should not behave in such an orderly way; this is just what we imagine when, with Wiggins, we imagine halves of a brain transplanted to different bodies or, with Chisholm, we imagine splitting like an ameba. In these cases Shoemaker supposes that we

> cannot identify both of the physiological offshoots of a person with the original person, unless we are willing to take the drastic step of giving up Leibniz's Law and the transitivity of identity. (1970, p. 28)

Given such ill-behaved causal chains, I could quasi-remember from the inside an experience or action that wasn't mine. For this reason, the analysis of personal identity in terms of quasi-memory is not totally straightforward. But we can get a logically sufficient condition for personal identity: quasi-memory with no branching. Basically, Grice and Locke are vindicated.

Towards the end of the article, Shoemaker picks up the question he raised in the reply to Chisholm. In a case in which there has been branching, Shoemaker thinks that neither of the branch persons is identical with the original. But each would quasi-remember the experiences and actions of the original person. Now, which of these facts is important? That they do quasi-remember or that they are not identical? As Shoemaker puts it,

> If I [quasi-remember] from the inside a cruel or deceitful action, am I to be relieved of all tendency to feel remorse if I discover that because of fission someone else [quasi-remembers] it too? (p. 284)

Shoemaker thinks not. It is the quasi-memory that is important, not the lack of identity. As against this, we might appeal to such facts as that identity is a necessary condition of responsibility for past actions. But then Shoemaker could simply repeat the identity-stripping investigation for the concept of responsibility and argue that the operative concept is really quasi-responsibility. No concept has identity more "built into it" than that of survival. Shoemaker thinks that if one is to fission, one will not be identical with either of the survivors. And yet,

> The prospect of immanent fission might not be appealing, but it seems highly implausible to suppose that the only rational attitude toward it would be that appropriate to the prospect of immanent death. (p. 284)

The idea emerging here is that personal identity is important to us because it involves certain relationships to past and future persons, rather than these relationships being important because they constitute identity. This idea was to undergo explicit statement and dramatic development in an important article by Derek Parfit (1971/1975) published shortly after Shoemaker's. Before looking at that, however, we must look at an article by Bernard Williams (1970/1973) published the same year as "Persons and Their Pasts" (1970a), in which, once again, the argument against according memory too much importance in personal identity is made subtly but forcefully.

5. The Self and the Future

In "Persons and Their Pasts," Shoemaker says that Brownson is Brown and that his former reluctance to conclude this was a result of overlooking the causal component in the notion of memory—an element which, as we have seen, was emphasized by Wiggins, who himself seems to have accepted that Brownson is Brown. Though remaining more certain of the puzzling nature of the questions raised than of his own conclusions, Bernard Williams remained unconvinced, and in "The Self and the Future" (1970/1973) he argued against the possibility of body transfer and the considerations about memory and personal identity that seem to allow it. Since I have discussed this paper at length in essay 6, I have omitted the discussion of it originally included in this survey.

While I argue in essay 6 that Williams's argument against Shoemaker and the possibility of body shifting is not convincing, his subtle and stubborn argumentation forces to one's attention what might be called the phenomenological difficulties of accepting one's identity as the sort of thing which could be a matter for decision. Chisholm (1969), it will be recalled, found it simply bizarre to imagine that one's identity could be a matter for decision, a matter that would be decided by convention or litigation or even by social practice. Though not drawn, as Chisholm was, by something like a pure ego or immaterial substance theory, and more in a mood to remind us of difficulties than to establish conclusions, Williams shares Chisholm's attitude towards the suggestion that personal identity could be a matter of convention.

> There seems to be an obstinate bafflement to mirroring in my expectations a situation in which it is conceptually undecidable whether I occur. . . . The bafflement seems, moreover, to turn to plain absurdity of we move from conceptual undecidability to its close friend and neighbor, conventionalist decision . . . as a line to deal with a person's fears or expectations about his own future, it seems to have no sense at all. (1970/1973, p. 61)

While Chisholm was drawn to a metaphysical solution to these problems, Williams seems to think that there is refuge in bodily identity. It seems to me, though, that he has put his finger on something that is not just a baffling consequence of one theory of personal identity, that which emphasizes memory, and is avoided by others, but rather on something that is simply baffling. Let any empirical relation R be the candidate for the unity relation for persons. Then some philosopher is clever enough to construct a case in the area of R-vagueness, that is, a case where our concepts leave it indeterminate whether R obtains or not, even given all the facts (see Swineburne, 1974). Then we will have an indeterminate case for the theory that maintains that R is the unity relation for persons. It may be easier to construct cases for links of memory than for links of body. But it seems that all of our concepts are formed, as Wittgenstein (1953, Ilxii) said, within the context of certain very general assumed facts; by imagining those facts to be otherwise, we can create cases the concept was not designed to handle.

We have seen, in the course of discussions, a shift of attention from persons and their pasts to persons and their futures, a shift called for by Shoemaker in his reply to Chisholm (1969), and initiated in the thoughts at the end of "Persons and Their Pasts" (1970a). A key concept in such an enquiry is that which Williams calls "the imaginative projection of myself as participant in [a future situation]" (1970/1973, p. 59). We can perhaps think of this as the future-oriented analogue of Shoemaker's "memory from the inside." Shoemaker's question, whether one should look forward to fission as death, given his belief that one will be identical with neither of the products of fission, is then a proposal to consider imaginative projection of ourselves as participants when we realize that no participant in the situation will be identical with us. Made sensitive by Williams of the baffling aspects of such questions and proposals, let us return to them.

6. Survival without Identity

If one is asked why one feels bad about an event of the previous evening and responds, "Because I am the one that committed the outrage," the identity asserted between the present speaker and the participant in the earlier event seems to be bearing an important explanatory role. But in "Persons and Their Pasts" (1970a), Shoemaker is on the verge of displacing identity from this explanatory role, putting in its place the "identity-stripped" concepts of quasi-memory, quasi-fear, quasi-responsibility, and the like. The importance of identity derives from the importance of these relations, which in our well-behaved world, with no M-fission or M-fusion, can be taken as constitutive of identity. The suggestion that identity is after all not so crucial is also considered by Terence Penelhum, in *Survival and Disembodied Existence* (1970), with special reference to what we really want when we hope for survival after death. But the step of pushing identity to the background was made most boldly and unequivocally by Derek Parfit in his profound, imaginative, and influential article "Personal Identity":

> Judgments of personal identity have great importance. What gives them their importance is the fact that they imply psychological continuity. . . . If psychological continuity took a branching form, no coherent set of judgments of identity could correspond to, and thus be used to imply, the branching form of this relation. But what we ought to do . . . is take the importance which would attach to a judgment of identity and attach this importance directly to each limb of the branching relation. . . .judgments of personal identity derive their importance from the fact that they imply psychological continuity. (1971/1975)

Parfit thinks that there are cases in which there is no correct answer to a question about personal identity. He refers to the examples of Locke (1694, sec. 18), Prior (1966), Bennett (1967), and Chisholm

(1976), but in particular to that of Wiggins (1967). "My brain is divided, and each half housed in a new body. Both resulting people have my character and apparent memories of my life. What happens to me?" (Parfit 1971/1975, p. 5). To say he does not survive seems odd, Parfit argues: "How could a double success be a failure?" For him to be only one or other seems arbitrary. But to say he survives as both is to violate the laws of identity, Parfit assumes. His solution is that we do not need to have identity to have survival, or at least not to have what is important in survival: "We can solve this problem only by taking these important questions and prizing them apart from the question about identity" (p. 9). When we do this, the results are dramatic. While identity is an all or nothing affair, the various identity-stripped relations that constitute it when well behaved, and are what really matters in any case, are often quite plausibly regarded as matters of degree. This is a matter of importance, not only in analytical metaphysics, but in the way we think of ourselves in real life:

> Identity is all-or-nothing. Most of the relations which matter in survival are, in fact, relations of degree. If we ignore this, we shall be led into quite ill-grounded attitudes and beliefs. (Parfit 1971/1975, p. 11)

Among these are the principles of self-interest and regrets about one's eventual death. He argues:

> Suppose that a man does not care what happens to him, say, in the more distant future. . . . We must say, "Even if you don't care, you ought to take what happens to you then equally into account." But for this, as a special claim, there seem to me no good arguments. . . . The argument for this can only be that all parts of the future are equally parts of his future. But it is a truth too superficial to bear the weight of the argument. (p. 26)

Parfit notes that in certain extreme puzzle cases—a network of "persons" who periodically fission and fuse, for example—we are naturally led to think not in terms of continuous persons, but in terms of more- or less-connected selves, reserving the word "I" for the greatest degree of psychological connectedness. This way of thinking could be applied even in normal cases and would embody a recognition that it is psychological connectedness that is what matters, and this would help in avoiding the ill-grounded attitudes and beliefs Parfit mentioned. In "Later Selves and Moral Principles"

(1973), Parfit argues that thinking in this way, or recognizing the possibility of doing so, undercuts certain arguments against utilitarianism.

In Parfit, we might say, Shoemaker's analytical tool of identity stripping has become an approach to life.

The question of the importance of identity seems to me greatly illuminated by general questions about identity and individuation and in particular by the perspective sketched in essay 4. Indeed, as soon as one adopts the perspective that identity is a logical relation, one is implicitly committed to the derivative importance of identity, although not necessarily to Parfit's claim that what matters are relations of degree.

After all, there are many conceivable ways of individuating the world—of choosing unity relations with which to unify our objects. That is, many are conceivable from the point of view of constraints imposed by logic, although most fanciful alternatives would not be possible ways for beings like ourselves (however individuated) to experience or deal with the world. Each way of individuating gives rise to a class of objects, members of which are identical to themselves in as literal and unsullied a sense as I am to myself. Thus, for example, we could think in terms of a kind of object which consisted, during any baseball game or inning thereof in which the San Francisco Giants participate, of the Giants' shortstop for that period. This would be a discontinuous object composed of stages of ordinary men, stages of Le Master and Metzger this season (1982). We could give rules for referring to and assigning predicates to these objects, adjusting things to preserve the indiscernibility of the identical. Let us call such entities "longstops." Then the longstop in the game gets an error or strikes out just in case the shortstop does. But the present longstop may have struck out in the last inning, even if the present shortstop didn't—if Metzger replaced a slumping Le Master, for example.

Last inning's longstop is identical with this inning's longstop in as pure a sense of identity as anything is identical with itself. But the identity is unimportant. That the longstop was injured last inning, and that the very same longstop is now playing, gives us no reason to expect limping. That the longstop who is playing now made a good play last inning gives us no reason to cheer when he comes to bat.

Clearly, the importance of the identity of objects of a given kind depends on the unity relation. The choice of a unity relation to be a part of our scheme, and so the presence of objects of the corresponding kind in the scheme, reflects its importance. The importance of identity is in this sense derivative; how could it be otherwise?

But we can also ask why a given unity relation is important—worth fashioning identity out of. In particular, if memory, or some more general kind of psychological continuity or connectedness, is important and the source of the importance of personal identity, why is this so? What is so important about it? I think this question is the one which is often on the minds of philosophers who resist the idea that personal identity is analyzable at all. For we can make the point about the derivative importance of identity from an even more general principle. If, as Locke supposed, personal identity may be analyzed, must not the analysands explain the importance of the analysandum? The idea that any such explanation of the special importance identity has for us must be absurd leads to the claim that identity is unanalyzable and primitive. Butler, for example, thinks that if personal identity is analyzable, then it is not strict identity after all but something else and that if this were so, it would be

> a fallacy upon ourselves to charge our present selves with anything we did, or to imagine our present selves interested in anything which befell us yesterday, or that our present self will be interested in what will befall us tomorrow. (1736/1975)

While I think that there is no distinction to be drawn between strict and loose identity of the sort that Butler imagines, if we hold that personal identity is analyzable, it seems his challenge must be met. Of Parfit's (1971/1975) analysis we might ask: "Why is it important, and why do we care in a special way about, what will happen to someone tomorrow who is psychologically directly connected with me?" Now, it is no longer open to us to say the most natural thing, that it is because psychological connectedness is sufficient for identity, and so he will be me if he is so connected with me. We have concluded that such an appeal to identity is not ultimate, but gives way to the explanation in terms of connectedness.

I tried to deal with this problem in "The Importance of Being Identical" (essay 8), which appeared in Amélie Rorty's anthology *The Identities of Persons* (1976). The attempt led to conclusions which I found peculiar at the time, and still find peculiar, but of which I reconvince myself each time I reflect upon the matter. It seemed clear that a theory of personal identity should be causal; I adopted a descendant of the memory theory that fully relied on the fact that memory is a causal notion. Now, in general, attempts to explicate concepts in causal terms make reference to the normal mode of causation. It is not enough for me to remember a past event that the event has caused my present memory impression; it must have done so in the right way. If I spill soup on my grandmother as a child and am told of it so often as an adolescent that as an adult I have a clear memory-like impression, then my spilling has caused the impression. But I do not remember, for it was not caused in the right way.

The account of why identity should be important was built around the fact that we know what to expect from ourselves in the normal case and can expect continued commitment to the values we have. But it is hard to see why an atypical causal chain that provides the same guarantees should not be just as good, even though, as seemed and seems clear to me, if it is atypical enough it doesn't provide identity. I came to the conclusion that it shouldn't matter:

> Suppose the following. A team of scientists develops a procedure whereby, given about a month's worth of interviews and tests, the use of a huge computer, a few selected particles of tissue, and a little time, they can produce a human as like any given human as desired. . . . I have an incurable disease. It is proposed . . . that a duplicate be created . . . and simply take over my life. . . . He would not be me. The relation between my terminal and his initial states is too unlike the [normal causal relations which preserve psychological continuity between earlier and later stages of humans] to be counted, even given the vagueness of the concept of a person, as an instance of it. But . . . I would have the very same legitimate reasons to act now so as to secure for him future benefits as I would have if he were me. (Perry 1976; essay 8, p. 224)

I meant to include by this the full appropriateness of "imaginatively projecting myself" into the benign imposter's future experiences. Such a position still seems to me a natural and inevitable outcome of Locke's original idea.

8

The Importance of Being Identical

1. Introduction

Most of us have a special and intense interest in what will happen to us. You learn that someone will be run over by a truck tomorrow; you are saddened, feel pity, and think reflectively about the frailty of life; one bit of information is added, that the someone is you, and a whole new set of emotions rise in your breast.

An analysis of this additional bit of information, that the person to be run over is you, is offered by theories of personal identity, for to say it is you that will be hit is just to say that you and the person who will be hit are one and the same. And so it seems that those theories should shed some light on the difference this bit of information makes to you. If it gives you more reason to take steps to assure that the person is not run over, our theory should help explain why that is so. And if this bit of information gives you reasons of a different kind than you could have, if it were not you who was to be run over, our theory should help explain this too.

The most famous theory of personal identity, Locke's (1694/1975) analysis in terms of memory, was criticized on just these grounds. Butler's most serious charge against Locke was that his account "rendered the inquiry concerning a future life of no consequence" (1736/1975, p. 99). And Butler did not just have in mind an inability to explain our interest in an afterlife, but an inability even to explain why we care about what happens to us in this life tomorrow. From a natural extension of Locke's "hasty observations," Butler draws the conclusion "that it is a fallacy upon ourselves to charge our

"The Importance of Being Identical" was originally published in *The Identity of Persons,* edited by Amelie Rorty (Berkeley: University of California Press, 1976), pp. 67–90. Reprinted by permission.

present selves with anything we did, or to imagine our present selves interested in anything which befell us yesterday, or that our present self will be interested in what will befall us tomorrow " (1736/1975, p. 102).

Butler's arguments for this conclusion are confused,[1] but the point remains that there is nothing in Locke's account of personal identity to explain why I care what happens to me tomorrow. That I will be run over by a truck means, says Locke, that the person who is run over by a truck will remember thinking and doing what I am thinking and doing now. But why would I care especially about that? Why should a person who is having such memories be of any more concern to me than anyone else? One is inclined to respond, "because to have such memories is just to be you," but now the explanation goes the wrong way round; isn't it fair to demand that the analysands shed light on why the analysandum has the implications for us that it does?

Some of the difficulties here can be brought out by noting that Locke's account (and any account which analyzes personal identity in terms of an empirical relation between person-stages or phases) will allow indeterminate cases. Our concepts of empirical relations, such as having a memory of an experience, are inevitably vague. This means I could conceivably be presented with facts which could only be interpreted as neither a clear-cut case of my own death nor a clear-cut case of my survival. But how should I feel about such a case? "There seems to be an obstinate bafflement to mirroring in my expectation a situation in which it is conceptually undecidable whether I occur." The quote is from Bernard Williams (1970/1973), who mounts a subtle and ingenious attack on memory theories of personal identity whose theme is reminiscent of Butler's.

Take, for example, what I have elsewhere called a "brain rejuvenation" case (essay 3). Smith's brain is diseased; a healthy duplicate of it is made and put into Smith's head. On the assumptions about the role of the brain usually made in these discussions, the survivor of this

---

[1] Butler thought that because Locke did not require identity of substance for personal identity and took the inquiry into the identity of vegetables to be relevant to the discussion of personal identity, it was clear that Locke was not using "same" in a "strict and philosophical manner of speech" (p. 259). Thus, on Locke's theory, we are not, in this strict sense, identical with ourselves tomorrow, not to mention ourselves in the hereafter.

process will be just like a healthy Smith. But will he be Smith? It seems that people of good faith can differ over the answer to this question (and, if this case is not one that is truly indeterminate, it points the direction in which such a case could be constructed). How is Smith to think about this indeterminacy? Lying in bed before the surgery, should he look forward to the painful convalescence of the survivor with terror or merely sympathy?

Is the need here for further conventions which will clear up the area left vague by our concept of personal identity? We can imagine the French Academy or the American Philosophical Association or the Supreme Court passing resolutions or handing down decisions which have this effect. (Perhaps the Court decides the survivor can cash checks on Smith's account.) And from one point of view, this seems perfectly reasonable. But from Smith's point of view, it seems insane. Whether he should think of the survivor's pain as something he himself is to endure, and so can without impropriety fear, or should think of it in some other way is not something to be decided by adopting a convention.

Perhaps any treatment of personal identity which admits of this sort of case must contain a fundamental mistake. But I do not think Locke's analysis is fundamentally mistaken. I wish, in this paper, to put forward a theory of personal identity which is a descendant of the memory theories of Locke, Grice, and Quinton and to show what kind of account can be built upon it of the intense and special interest we have in our own futures. And then, in the light of this account, I shall remark on the case just described, as well as others.

2. A Theory of Personal Identity

The theory of personal identity I advocate is a descendant of the memory theories of Locke, Quinton (1962/1975), Grice (1941), and others. A sophisticated version of such a theory might maintain that a sufficient and necessary condition of my having participated in a past event is that I am able to remember it; or that there be some event I am able to remember such that, at the time it occurred, the person to whom it happened could remember the event in question; or there be two events, such that at the time the first occurred, the person to whom it happened could remember the second and the person to whom the second occurred could remember the event in question; or there be three events . . .[2] I have argued elsewhere (essay 5) that by adopting a causal theory of memory, the advocate of such an account of personal identity can reply to the famous charge of circularity which Butler leveled against memory theories but that he does so at the cost of making "the self" an inferred entity, a result contrary to the intentions of some of the memory theorists. That my present apparent memory of a past event stands at the end of a causal chain of a certain kind leading from that event is not something I can directly perceive, but something believed because it fits into the simplest theory of the world as a whole which is available to me. Moreover, once one has moved this far, it becomes attractive to simply adopt a causal theory. In such a theory, all of the ways in which a person's past normally affects his future are built into the account and not simply the peculiarly discursive form of memory which preoccupied memory theorists. Such a theory I now proceed to sketch.

By "human being" I shall mean merely "live human body." It is a purely biological notion. Thus, in a "brain transplant" operation, the same human being acquires a new set of memories and personality, whatever we say about the persons involved. We are all in possession of a great deal of information about how human beings may be expected to behave—to move, to think, to feel—in various circumstances. We know that if we ask a human being if he would like his toe stepped on, he will probably say "no"; that when deprived of food for a long time, he will seek it; that shortly after observing something with care, he will be able to recall what he observed; and so forth. Some of the things we know about human beings we also know about rocks: if either is dropped from a cliff, they will fall. But there are a large number of principles, which I shall call the "human-theory," which have no application to rocks, or any of the lower forms of life, and a great many of which seem to have application only to humans. The principles of the human-theory are not ironclad rules; they are sprinkled with "probablys," and the theory as a whole is applied confidently only in relatively normal circumstances; there are many cases in which we have no idea what to expect from humans. It is, I shall say, "approximately valid."

Particular cases of human thought and action are explained by reference to the human-theory, but it is only human nature to suspect

---

[2] This approximates one of Grice's preliminary versions and is less flexible than his final proposal.

that what we may call the "approximate validity" of the human-theory itself has an explanation, that something about human beings, some relationship that a human's past states have to his present states, explains why the principles of human behavior to which we sub-scribe are as reliable as they are. In this inclination to have an explana-tion for the human-theory lies, I believe, the origin of our concept of a person.

Let us say that stages of a single human being are *H*-related. We can think of the human-theory as a theory about the effects earlier mem-bers of an *H*-related sequence have on the later members. But their being *H*-related does not explain the approximate validity of our principles concerning the effects earlier *H*-related stages have on the later. The human-theory tells us how humans may be expected to think and act; it does not tell us why humans do think and act that way. Our speculation is that there is an explanation, that *H*-related stages are, at least for the most part, related by some other relation (or at least by a relation which, for all we know, may not be the *H*-relation) and their being related by that other relation explains the effect of the earlier stages on the later. This new relation, under the description "the relation which explains (or, if known, would explain) the approximate validity of the principles about humans that we sub-scribe to," is my candidate for the analysis of personal identity. That is, it is the unity relation for persons, that relation which obtains between two stages if and only if there is a person of which both are stages.

I shall call this relation the *P*-relation. The entities that stand in the *P*-relation are stages of human bodies, the very same entities that stand in the *H*-relation (although it might turn out that the *P*-relation, unlike the *H*-relation, can relate a human body stage to something other than another human body stage). But there is nothing about the way we introduce the *P*-relation which makes it necessary that human-stages which stand in the *P*-relation invariably stand in the *H*-relation or vice versa.

How would we identify the *P*-relation? It should satisfy the follow-ing conditions: (i) in normal circumstances, human-stages are *P*-related if and only if they are *H*-related; (ii) in abnormal circumstances, when we have *H*-related stages that are not *P*-related, the human-theory breaks down; and (iii) in unusual cases, when we have *P*-related stages that are not *H*-related, the *P*-related stages exemplify relationships that the human-theory leads us to expect in the normal circumstances of *H*-related stages. We might summarize these points by saying that the person-theory—the set of principles we obtain by substituting "the *P*-relation" for "the *H*-relation" in the human-theory—should be more accurate than the human-theory. Finally, (iv), the nature of the entities or processes involved in the relation should explain the kinds of events involved in the human theory.

A philosophical theory about the mind (that, for example, it is an immaterial substance, operating not by efficient causality but by some other species) will generate views about what the *P*-relation turns out to be; but all, or at least many, such views would be compatible with the analysis of personal identity I have given. But if the assumptions about the role of the brain made by recent philosophers who discuss personal identity are correct, the relation of having the same brain is at least a promising candidate for the *P*-relation. For, in normal circumstances, human-stages are *H*-related (are stages of the same body) just when they have the same brain. In abnormal cases, when we have *H*-related stages that do not have the same brain (e.g., Shoemaker's Robinson and Brownson), the human-theory breaks down (Brownson doesn't remember what Robinson carefully observed). And in abnormal cases when we have stages with the same brain that are not *H*-related (Shoemaker's Brown and Brownson), relations are exhibited which are usually found in *H*-related stages (Brownson remembers what Brown carefully observed). And the nature of the human brain may account for the special kinds of events that humans participate in.

The advantages of this view are as follows:

(1) As just pointed out it allows for the possibility that two human body stages which are not stages of the same human body may be, nevertheless, stages of the same person. This is the puzzling feature of the puzzle cases (Locke's cobbler and prince; Shoemaker's Brownson) which have played such an important role in philosophizing about personal identity. All that our account requires is that there be a general correspondence between the *H*-relation and the *P*-relation; there is no reason that it might not turn out that stages could be related by *P* which are not related by *H*. What we count as a case of this will depend on what we take the relation *P* to be; if, for example, we think that the nature of the human brain explains that which is characteristically human about human behavior, we will be likely to suppose that in the case of a brain transplant, the relation *P* will obtain between the non-*H*-related stages that share a brain.

(2) The account explains the importance of bodily identity. Bodily identity is neither a necessary nor a sufficient condition for a personal

identity; but bodily identity is nevertheless importantly involved in our concept of personal identity. We know the P-relation only as the relation which explains the validity of the theory we have about how earlier and later stages of a single human body are related. The stable relation between persons and bodies is, in this sense, not an accident, although purely contingent; if the P-relation was not generally accompanied by, and causally related to, the H-relation, we would not have the concept of a person we do have.

(3) This account explains the plausibility, and the limits, of attempts to analyze personal identity in terms of memory. The problems with memory theories are, briefly, these: any theory which requires a continuous path of overlapping memories is too stringent, for personal identity is preserved in amnesia and, for that matter, in sleep. This can be avoided by reference to possible memories—the memories the amnesiac person would have if he hadn't been conked on the head or the sleeper would have were he awake, etc. (as the theory mentioned on page 147 did, in virtue of the phrase "is able to remember"). But to do so is to covertly bring in a causal requirement, for it is only in terms of causal counterfactuals that possible memories can be understood. But once we have introduced a causal relation as the principle of personal identity, there is no reason not to widen the kind of causal relationship required. The memory theory is plausible, because memory is one of the most important effects that the past of a human body has on its future.

(4) Finally, this account puts the vagueness in our concept of a person in the right place. I believe there are conceivable cases in which we do not know what to say, or in which people of good will differ over what to say, even though they pretty much agree about the way human beings work. Many philosophers who are perfectly willing to accept that the brain donor and the survivor in a "brain transplant" operation (of the Shoemaker sort) are the same person are not willing to say in the brain-rejuvenation case, described in section 1 of this essay, that personal identity is preserved. This, I think, reflects the vagueness of "the relation which explains. . . ." There are a number of relations at different levels of abstraction which fit the description of the P-relation: having the same brain, having brains with certain relationships (i.e., the relationships stages of the same brain usually have with one another), and so forth. The more abstract we take the relation to be, the more bizarre will be the circumstances in which we are able to say it holds. There may be several equally acceptable candi-

dates, given the concept we actually have. If indeterminate cases become common, linguistic decisions will have to be made.

3. Can We Explain Self-Concern?

It may seem that whatever virtues this account may have in sorting out various real and imagined cases the way we more or less feel they should be, it shares with Locke's the defect noted by Butler. For why do I care so particularly and intensely about that future self which has the P-relation to my present self? And how could the appropriateness of the feelings in indeterminate cases be decided by linguistic decisions?

But I believe there is an explanation for its peculiar importance to us. I shall reconstruct the question of the interest we have in our own futures in this way: what reasons would we have for present action which would ensure future benefits for ourselves? Thus I shall phrase the question in terms of my having a reason to act so as to promote or prevent my having a certain property in the future. To keep as many things constant as possible, I shall take the future time to be tomorrow; the property, being in great pain; and the present act which will prevent it, pushing a button. If I am told that by pushing a button I will prevent someone from being in great pain tomorrow, I will have a reason to push it. But, intuitively, if the person is me, I will have more reason, or perhaps special reasons, for pushing it. What basis can the theory of personal identity sketched provide for this feeling?

A person has a reason for an act if he wants some event to occur and believes his performance of that act will promote the occurrence of that event. I shall call any events a person at a given moment wants to occur in the future his "projects" (at that moment). (I mean to use the words "events" quite broadly to include processes, states, etc. And so my use of the word "project" is much wider than its ordinary use.) Assume I will be in pain unless I push the button. If I am not in pain tomorrow, I will contribute to the success of many of my projects: I will work on this article, help feed my children, etc. If I am in great pain, I will not do some of these things. Thus, I have what I shall call "project related" reasons for pushing the button.

It is a principle of the human-theory that personality, values, character, and so forth change only gradually along sequences of H-related human-stages in normal conditions. And since the P-relation is that which explains the approximate validity of the human-theory, we expect the same of sequences of P-related human-stages, that is, persons. Our concept of a person does not require that no one, in any circumstances, undergo dramatic changes in personality and character. But the theory, in terms of which the concept of a person is introduced, maintains that this will be exceptional. That persons usually do not undergo such dramatic changes is a straightforwardly contingent fact. But this fact is importantly connected with our concept of a person, for it is a condition of our having the concept of a person we do have.

In this sense, then, it is part of our concept of ourselves, as persons, that we are reliable. I expect to have tomorrow much the same desires, goals, loves, and hates—in a word, projects—as I have today. There is, in the normal case, no one as likely as me to work on my article, love my children, vote for my candidates, pay my bills, and honor my promises.

Thus, it is a consequence of the theory of personal identity that I have offered that we probably have more reasons to push the button when it is us who will be in pain then when it is any other arbitrarily chosen person. (I say "arbitrarily chosen" because there may, of course, be some persons who are more essential to certain of our important projects than we ourselves.)

This goes, I think, some way to responding to Butler's demand.

4. Identification

But, one feels, the sorts of reasons just adumbrated certainly do not exhaust the sorts of reasons I might have; indeed, they are not the crucial ones at all. I can imagine being told that someone a lot like me, perhaps even with delusions of being me, will want to do just what I want to do tomorrow, will make as much or more of a contribution to my projects as I will, and will be hit by a truck. I would feel sympathy, but not terror; I would not think of the event as happening to me. And, surely, this is what is crucial.

Discussion of this requires introduction of the concept of identification. I shall say a person identifies with the participant in a past, future, or imaginary event when he imagines perceiving the event from the perspective of the participant; that is, when he imagines seeing, hearing, smelling, tasting, feeling, thinking, remembering, etc., what the person to whom the happened event did (or will or might) see, hear, smell, taste, feel, think, remember, etc., as the event occurs. Identification is a matter of degree. I imagine seeing what Napoleon saw and hearing what he heard while losing the battle of Waterloo, but I'm not up to imagining the smells, tastes, feelings, and memories. Perhaps I imagine having my own feelings and memories, or perhaps my imagining doesn't concern itself with feelings and memories.

When we remember events in our past, we do not always identify with the participant in those events; when we expect things to happen to us, we do not always identify with the participant in those future events. When we do so identify, the memory or expectation has more "impact" on us. As long as I think of tomorrow's pain as something that's going to happen to me but refrain from imagining being in pain, I keep my equilibrium; but when I begin to imagine being in pain, I become fearful or terrified. Similarly, certain attitudes towards our own past, such as guilt, seem to arise with identification with the doer of the past misdeed.

If I am identifying with myself, feeling pain tomorrow, I am more likely to push the button than if I am not. It is not, I suggest, that so identifying gives me additional reasons for pushing the button. Rather, it is a condition which makes it more likely that I will be motivated by the reasons I have. (Just as, although I am more likely to be motivated by my reasons for pushing the button if I am awake than if I am asleep, my being awake does not provide me with additional reasons for pushing the button.)

What is the relation between identification and personal identity?

Identity is not a necessary condition of identification. I can identify with the participant in events I did not do, will not do, and would not do, even if they were to be done. I can imagine losing the battle of Waterloo; I can imagine giving the 1973 inaugural address; and I can imagine being hung in 1850 for stealing a horse. Nor is it necessary even to believe, or imagine, myself identical with the participant with whom I identify. Imagining myself to have won the battle of Waterloo does not involve the difficult feat of imagining the course of world history to be such that Napoleon and I are one. I cannot easily imagine a possible world in which one person is both Napoleon and John Perry. But it is quite easy to imagine winning the battle of Waterloo, that is, imagining having certain perceptions, thoughts, and so forth (Williams, 1966/1973, especially pp. 118ff.).

Neither identity nor the belief in identity, nor even the imagining of identity, are necessary for identification. What limits are there on our ability to identify with participants in past and future events? Virtually none at all, insofar as the logic of the situation dictates.

Thus, the relation between identity and identification is not so intimate as one might have thought. But there are important relationships, which my theory of personal identity goes at least some way towards explaining.

I wish to consider two important questions. First, why are we so much more likely to identify with ourselves than with others? We are more likely, of course; that is why it is natural to borrow the cognate "identify" for the phenomenon in question. We might have expected this to be explained by logical constraints on identification, but I have denied that there are any. What, then, is the explanation? Second, why is our identification with our own "future selves" so likely to motivate us to act to prevent or promote the real occurrence of the imagined events, while our identification with others is not?

Let us suppose that there were beings more or less like us, except that the previous facts were not true of them. An individual of this species is no more likely to identify with, or be motivated to present action by identification with, his own future discomforts and pleasures than those of others. In the first place, note these beings would be significantly different from us; that is, it is a part of the human-theory, and so the person-theory, that most of us are not like that. Thus, in this sense, these truths are connected with our concept of a person. Second, note that in a world anything like ours, such beings would have difficulties surviving. We are, by and large, in a better position to watch out for ourselves than others. If I am not motivated to feed this body by thoughts of future hunger, I may starve. In that sense, then, it is not an accident that we are as we are—that the human-theory contains the principles about identification that it does. And this, again, is connected with out concept of a person. For, that I will in the future probably have this body is a part of the person-theory.

These explanations may seem to be inappropriate to what is explained. One wants, perhaps, a necessary truth, a transcendental argument, a reflection of the innermost structure of reality to get to the bottom of our intimate relation to our future self; I have offered only an empirical truth (which is, nevertheless, woven into our very concept of a person) and an evolutionary derivation of the facts explained. Butler would not have felt his demand met, I am sure. But I believe he would be wrong. My explanations explain, and my theory of personal identity allows the explanation of why we are more-or-less assured to have a preponderance of reasons for acting in our own behalf and strong motivation for acting on them. There is nothing left to explain.

5. Special Reasons

But, still, one may feel what is essential in the matter has somehow been missed, been passed over. The discomfort may take the following form: that I will make a contribution to some project of mine if I am not in pain tomorrow is perhaps a reason I might have for pushing the button. But it's the same sort of reason I might have for pushing the button to spare someone else pain. And, on the explanation given of identification, I might, without incoherence or conceptual impropriety, be motivated to spare another pain by identifying with him in pain. So neither my reasons for my act nor my motivation are special and unique in the case where my act is selfish, where it is me who will feel the pain if I do not act. But, surely, my reasons for acting in such a case are special. They are not the sort of reasons I can have for sparing someone else pain.

I believe that the claim that there are such special reasons can be expressed within the framework of projects, as consisting of either one or both of the following claims: (i) that there are some projects I might have to which I will (or may) make a contribution that no one else could make; if so, my project-related reason for pushing the button to spare myself pain will be one I could not have for pushing it to spare someone else pain; (ii) further, that some of these projects are such that I will be in a position to make my special contribution no matter what I am like tomorrow; my reason for pushing the button to spare myself pain will be one I will have whatever I think I will be like tomorrow.

Now, to satisfy the first condition, the description of the project would simply have to include my being in a certain state, for there is a contribution to any such project only I can make, namely, existing and being in that state. Such projects I shall call "private projects." And, to satisfy the second condition, the project merely needs to require my existence. We might call this "the ego project"—I may want tomorrow's world to find me alive, whatever I may be like, whatever I may remember, and whatever desires I may then have. It seems clear that many of us have the ego project and most of us dozens of other projects that satisfy condition (i). For example, I want not merely that this article be completed, but that it be completed by me.

What sorts of challenge do these "special reasons" pose for the account I am trying to construct? On the one hand, we might want an explanation of why we have such special reasons. On the other, we might want a justification. We feel that the desires which are a part of these special reasons are rational for us to have and irrational for us not to have.

With regard to projects meeting the first condition, the responses to each of these demands are, for a ways at least, coordinate. In the normal case, it will be reasonable to want not merely that my article be completed but that I complete it. For if I do not do so, but someone else does, that could only be because of a variety of catastrophes, which will leave other projects uncompleted and this one, perhaps, ill-completed. We may say, in this case, that I am derivatively justified in having the private project (that I finish the article), because I have the relevant nonprivate project (that the article be completed) and beliefs that if the nonprivate project is not contributed to by me, others of my nonprivate projects will fail. And that such desires are reasonable is an explanation of why they occur. But as we move from the ordinary case to the metaphysical, what we can explain, and what we can justify, begins to diverge. Suppose I believe that not just my article, but everything I will do tomorrow, and for the rest of my life, will be done, and done as well and done in just the same way, by someone else. Still, I want that I complete it, and not this benign imposter. The retention, in the metaphysical case, of the same sorts of desires, which are reasonable in the ordinary case, can be explained as habit; usually, surviving is the only way to achieve a good part of what we want done, and it is natural that the desire, fostered in the real world, is not extinguished when we enter the fairyland of contemporary discussions of personal identity. And to this habit we can add another; we identify usually with our own doings, and not those of others, however similar to us they may be. This habit too, ingrained in us as it is by the demands of evolution and its utility for achieving our purposes in ordinary circumstances, stays with us even when contemplating the metaphysical example.

This will, I realize, leave many unsatisfied. They will maintain that, in contemplating the case of the benign imposter, it is not only to be expected and natural and only human that I should not feel I have just the reasons for pushing the button for him as I would for myself, but also that these reactions are completely justified. As long as it is not I who will do all of these things, I not only will not but should not have the reasons and the motivation for sparing him pain I would have for myself. My desire that it be I who finish the article is justified in the metaphysical circumstances, just as it is normally.

I deny this.

The only justification for a private project that seems at all compelling to me is a derivative one: I have the relevant nonprivate project, and others as well, and believe that if it is not I who survives and contributes to the project in question, the others will not succeed.

Do I maintain that such unsupported private projects—those which remain, even as we move to the metaphysical case—are irrational? Not in the sense of being incoherent or self-contradictory. I am inclined to think they are irrational in that sense analyzed by Brandt: they "would not survive . . . in the vivid awareness of knowable propositions" (1969–70, p. 46). But I do not wish to argue that here. My claim is simply that our having such private projects can be explained by what I take to be the correct theory of personal identity, as the result of habit and the demands of evolution. But there is no justification for these projects in the way one might have felt there clearly must be. It is not, I think, at all irrational not to have them. The importance of identity is derivative. Apart from those other relationships it normally guarantees, it need be of no interest to us.

This strikes many as quite implausible. Its plausibility may be enhanced by noticing how extreme a metaphysical case has to be for the sort of derivative importance, which I claim is all that personal identity has, to be completely absent. Two lines of argument are particularly important here.

First, in order for there to be no justification for private projects, it has to be not merely that there will be a benign imposter ready, willing, and able to do what I will do if I survive, but also that I believe it and that my belief is justified. That x will finish my article tomorrow gives me a reason for pushing the button to spare him pain only if I believe that he will. And I will not have as strong of a reason to spare my benign duplicate pain, as I do myself, unless I believe it is as likely that he will do what I want done as it is that I would were I to survive. And my reason for pushing the button for him will only be as reasonable as my reason for pushing it for myself would be if my belief about what he will do is as justified as my beliefs about what I will do usually are. But if he is to be created by accident, or supernatural chicanery, it is difficult to see how these conditions could be met.

A second consideration requires some preliminary remarks. The properties that a person has at a given time can be divided into those he has just in virtue of events occurring at that time and those which he has in part in virtue of events occurring at other times. For example, I could not now have the property of sitting in a forty-year-old house unless some houses had been built forty years ago. If they had not been built, nothing I or anyone else could do now could make it true that I now have this property. And for some such properties, the past events must have happened to me. I could not now have the property of having been born a certain number of years ago unless that many years ago I had been born. And, finally, some of the properties that are now mine are so in virtue of my having a relation to past events no one else has. Since these events are in the past, no one else can ever be so related to them. Tomorrow, anyone could have the property of believing he worked on this article today. But only I can have the property of truly believing that I worked on this article today. There are certain properties which, given the history of the world until today, no one but me can have tomorrow. There are properties which if a person has them tomorrow, he has them partly in virtue of having the *P*-relation to one of my person-stages. But then he is me.

Suppose I am writing an autobiography. Tomorrow I plan to write the sentence "And Fido died." I desire not just that the sentence be written, but that I write it. And I desire that I write it in part because I want the event in question reported by someone who remembers it and, given that I am the only one who observed the event, no one else but me can do that. This is a property, then, which I wish the contributor to this particular project to have. Having this property does not, in and of itself, require being me; anyone could have watched Fido die. But given the contingent fact that only I did, no one but me can have this property.

This possibility might be used to argue that the theory of personal identity in question can, after all, justify private projects. For, surely, one's devotion to accuracy, to honesty, to truth telling, to freedom from illusion, and the like themselves constitute projects, and these might impose constraints on who is to say the things I want said, write the things I want written, and so forth, which only I could satisfy. My duplicate, however benign, will be deluded, claiming to be who he is not, saying he did things he did not do.

But this will not quite do. For the question of the importance of personal identity must simply emerge as a question about the importance of the properties that require it. Why is it important, for example, that people say they did only what they did? Perhaps because of the unfortunate nature of the ordinary consequences and causes of saying one did what one did not do. But in the case of the benign imposter, these ordinary implications may be absent: he may be honest, and what he says may never mislead anyone. Perhaps because the act of saying he did what he did not do has some other property. But then we need to be assured that this property attaches to just the act in question, and not any of the other sorts of acts which a person would normally be performing when he says he did what he did not do but which the benign imposter would not be performing (such as lying, being intentionally misleading, and so forth).

But, in terms of showing the conditions a case of the benign duplicate must meet, in order to cancel all of the special but derivative reasons I might have for preferring my own survival, this line of argument does get us somewhere.

These considerations, I think, suggest that such a case will have to be one in which the explanation of the benign duplicate's being like me is that he was produced "from me" by a process I know to be reliable. By saying "from me," I mean that my being in the states I am in is a part of the explanation of his being in the states he will be in. And by a reliable process, I mean one which, as reliably as the natural processes involved in aging another minute or another day, preserves accurate information. In short, the duplicate's initial stages will have to be related to mine by a reliable causal relation—and this means the relation will be not the same as, but will be of the same "species" as, the P-relation.

So my theory can justify the difference we feel between surviving and being replaced, where the replacement is incomplete or accidental or unsure. And it can explain the difference we feel, in any case.

But suppose the following. A team of scientists develops a procedure whereby, given about a month's worth of interviews and tests, the use of a huge computer, a few selected particles of tissue, and a little time, they can produce a human being as like any given human as desired. I am a member of the team, have complete (and justified) confidence in the process and the discretion of my colleagues, and have an incurable disease. It is proposed that I be interviewed, tested, and painlessly disposed of, that a duplicate be created, in secret, and simply take over my life. Everyone, except my colleagues, will think he is I (the duplicate himself will not know; he is made unlike I would be only in not remembering the planning of this project), and my colleagues, who have all studied and been convinced by this article, will treat him as me, feeling that the fact that he is not is, in this case, quite unimportant.

He would not be me. The relation between my terminal and his initial states is too unlike the P-relation to be counted, even given the vagueness of the concept of a person, as an instance of it. But, on my account, I would have the very same legitimate reasons to act now so as to secure for him future benefits as I would if he were me.

I believe that this is not a defect to be charged to my account, but an insight to be gained from it.

6. The Ego Project

What then, of the ego project? Suppose I believe that tomorrow I will be struck by amnesia incurable in fact, though not in principle; that my character and personality will suddenly change, so I will hate what I now love and work against what I now hope for. If the person I am to be were not me, I would have no reasons at all to push the button and spare him pain except those that derive merely from his being a sentient being. What additional reasons am I given by the fact that it is me?

The common feeling that we do have additional reasons seems to me clearly not accounted for by my analysis in any direct way. That is, the fact that I do especially care about this fellow is not made clear when I see that his being me consists in his stages having the P-relation to mine. It's quite the other way around; believing that his stages have the P-relation to mine produces concern only when and because I realize that if that's so, then he is me.

But, as before, it can be explained in terms of habit. We take identity always to be a good reason for care and concern, because usually it is.

At this point, one may be inclined to speak of the "ineffable me-ness" of the fellow which would survive any change and which is the real object of our concern. But this ineffable me-ness, when it is not the remnant of a bad theory of personal identity, is simply the shadow of the enormous contribution that we are in the habit of expecting ourselves to make to the projects we have.

7. Conclusions: Smith, Methuselah, Lewis, Parfit

My central claim is that the importance of identity is derivative. In ordinary cases, identity will guarantee innumerable special relationships. Particularly important, I will in all probability be assured that the person who is me will be a major contributor to my projects, and I will find it difficult to avoid identifying (in my technical sense) with him. Any of these relationships I could have to someone else. But it is incredibly unlikely that I should have all of those I will have to myself to anyone else. And all of this is, in a sense, no accident, for it is a part of the human-theory that H-related stages have these special relationships in ordinary circumstances and the P-relation is that relation which explains this. That these special relationships will probably obtain is part of our concept of a person.

It should now be clear what to say to Smith, whom we left unsure of his feelings in section 1 of this essay. Smith is about to undergo a brain rejuvenation, with his survival uncertain, not for medical but for conceptual reasons.

Smith should go ahead and be fearful of the painful convalescence, whether or not he is to survive. His survival is a question for linguistic decision or linguistic evolution to take care of. We may think of our concept of personal identity as designed to meet many conditions. In cases such as Smith's, a variety of these considerations pull us in different ways. By saying that Smith survives, we keep the intimate connection between identity and that complex of special relationships it guarantees in the normal case. But the more abstract relation we would thereby be choosing for our unity relation for persons does not have the empirical guarantee of transitivity that normal maturation does, and such consideration as this may pull in the other direction (see essay 3, section 7).

But, for Smith, such subtleties are irrelevant. He can expect to have as tight of a web of special relationships to the survivor of the operation as personal identity in its purest form could provide. And this, I think, is all that need matter to him.

I believe my account may also shed some light on an example discussed by two recent writers on personal identity: Methuselah.

David Lewis (1976) and Derek Parfit (1971/1975) have recently claimed that "what matters" in survival is not present in the case of Methuselah, since (as they assume) Methuselah at 930 will have no memories of Methuselah at 27, Methuselah at 27 should not consider his living to 930 to be survival. Parfit takes this to show that there can be *identity without survival;* Lewis wants to say that each 137-year stretch of Methuselah is a separate person (137 years, Lewis imagines, is the time it takes memory to completely fade). According to Lewis, when Methuselah celebrates his 300th birthday in his room alone, there are really "continuum-many" persons in the room.

Lewis's view, and perhaps Parfit's too, results from confusing two senses of "what matters in survival." The insight is that *what is of importance* in survival, need not occur in every case of survival or of identity. Thus, identity is not "what matters" in survival. But by "what matters in survival" we might also mean "what makes a case of survival a case of survival." I think the view that Methuselah is a case of identity without survival, or that (in order to insure the common-sense equivalence of identity and survival) we must reckon there to be "continuum-many" Methuselahs, result from confusing these two senses.

It seems to me that my analysis illuminates all of this. When I said that the human-theory tells us the stages of the same body are likely to have the "special relations" to one another, and likely to identify with one another, I oversimplified. For it will tell us (or would, if what Lewis imagines about memory were true) that under certain circumstances this is not to be expected at all, and one such circumstance is that of human-stages that, though stages of the same body, are separated by 900 years.[3] That is to say, our concept of the P-relation is not just of a relation that explains why various special relations, such as sharing of projects and identification, are likely to obtain among H-related stages, but also why, in certain circumstances, they cannot be expected to obtain.

We expect then that Methuselah at 27 will not find it easy to identify with Methuselah at 930. He won't expect Methuselah at 930 to have much in common with him. He won't have many special reasons to care about the old man he is to be nor as much motivation to act on them. Does he have any special reason, say, to refrain from smoking, knowing that if he does, it's quite likely that by 930 he will have lung cancer? Perhaps, for he alone, by refraining now, can help the old man's health. But this is more like the obligation I have to an office mate with whom I have little in common, not to blow smoke in his face than the special and intimate concern I have for myself. There are a lot of reasons we ordinarily have for concern for our

---

[3] Parfit actually discusses beings that never die.

future that Methuselah at 27 doesn't have in thinking about life at 930; enough, I think, to vindicate the opinion that it's quite possible that "what matters" in survival does not occur in the case of Methuselah's survival to 930.

I agree with some of Parfit's central claims in "Personal Identity." But I think one of the claims, or suggestions, which Parfit makes has little merit. Having recognized the importance of the various special relationships and the only derivative importance of identity, should we adopt, as Parfit proposes, a "new way of thinking," which (as I reconstruct it) involves taking the special relations themselves to replace the P-relation as our unity relation for persons?

This would guarantee that "what matters" in survival in the first sense mentioned is just what matters in the second. I mentioned one problem with this early in this section with regard to Smith's brain rejuvenation. Further objections are as follows.

Although Parfit describes this as giving up the language of identity, it really amounts to trading talk of one kind of object, persons (P-related sums of human-stages, perhaps), for another, let's call them "Parfit-persons," which are S-related sums of human-stages, where S is the complex of special relationships which "matter" in the second sense, in personal identity. There will be identity among the new objects as much as among the old. As long as one has predication, one will have identity; one merely needs to look and see under what conditions sentences ascribing past or future states to a presently existing Parfit-person are reckoned as true to find out what kind of objects these are.

Parfit does not tell us enough about the rules of predication involved in his "way of thinking" for us to determine exactly what Parfit-persons will be. They are not to be, I think, just Lewis-persons—the objects Lewis found continuum-many of at Methuselah's birthday party. But of both Lewis-persons and Parfit-persons, I think it is clear that it's much easier and simpler to talk about persons. The reasons for dropping talk about persons for talk about Lewis-persons or Parfit-persons will have to be enormously strong.

Notice, for example, that certain simplifying assumptions Lewis makes are pretty dubious. There are going to be no general truths about how long it takes memory to fade out or personality structure to undergo basic changes; this will vary from person to person and situation to situation. So, rather than counting 137-year stretches as Lewis-persons, we will have to make a separate determination in every case. Many of us undergo quite dramatic changes without taking 930 years to do it; others of us, I suspect, might actually make it through 930 years without many dramatic changes occurring.

Moreover, there is no reason to assume Lewis-persons or Parfit-persons will be composed of temporarily continuous stages. In the amnesia case, with later recovery, they would have to be reckoned as ceasing to exist for a time (for there is no one around during the period of amnesia with special relations to the preamnesiac) and then coming back into existence with his recovery.

Perhaps such numerous and ill-behaved entities would be worth talking about if our ordinary concept of a person locks us into various misconceptions. Parfit thinks it does. He maintains, I think insightfully, that the principle of self-interest is not especially compelling: "There is no special problem in the fact that what we ought to do can be against our interests. There is only the general problem that it may not be what we want to do." And he thinks that the compellingness of the principle of self-interest, and other misconceptions, is rooted in our concept of personal identity.

I think there is a point here. As I observed, identity comes by habit to be regarded as in and of itself a reason for special care and concern, even when it does not, or is not likely to, support the various special relationships which naturally give rise to this special concern. This habit has social importance and is reinforced: we teach prudence and saving for old age, even among those who don't particularly like old people. Philosophers do their part here. Thus we find the admirable Sidgwick saying,

> [M]y feelings a year hence should be just as important to me as my feelings next minute, if only I could make an equally sure forecast of them. Indeed this equal and impartial concern for all parts of one's conscious life is perhaps the most prominent element in the common notion of the rational—as opposed to the merely impulsive—pursuits of pleasure. (1907, p. 124)

But dropping the concept of a person would be neither necessary nor sufficient for removing these misconceptions. Not necessary, because we can explain the true importance of identity, and the true rationale of self-interest, without jettisoning the concept of a person. Not sufficient, for, the P-relation, as our only reasonable guarantee of the S-relation, is too important to be ignored; the concept of a person forces itself upon us.

Moreover, the habit of taking identity in itself, without consideration of whether the special relations will or won't obtain, has good effects as well as bad. There are characteristically human projects, such as settling on a long-range plan or dedicating one's life to a goal or making a promise, that depend on it. Let us say that a person's life is integrated to the extent that his various stages are S-related. The habit of taking identity itself as a reason for special concern promotes, as well as reflects, integration, for the sorts of long-range commitments and projects this habit makes possible are themselves the source of the continuity of character and personality and values that constitute integration.

And, finally, a remark that perhaps applies as much to what I have said so far as to Parfit. It would be wrong, however tempting, to take one's concern for his present self as a given, capable of shedding light on his concern for his earlier and later selves but not requiring and not capable of the same sorts of explanation itself. "My present self," that is, the currently existing person-stage belonging to me, far from being the immediate object of my concern, is an object that may answer only to a rather abstract conception we have when doing philosophy (but no less an object for that). It is an object, moreover, which if taken to exist "instantaneously," or even over a very short interval, cannot, for conceptual reasons suggested in the remarks in section 5, have many of the properties that make persons interesting. In a well-developed account of the concept of a person, of which the present essay is but a sketch of a part, concern for oneself generally would, I think, be explained in terms of the concepts of a project and of identification, and there would be room for a version of the claim that our concept of a person enjoys one sort of primacy, which excessive concentration on person-stages may, and no doubt in this essay does, obscure. [4]

---

[4] Versions of this paper were read at the University of California, Los Angeles; the North Carolina Colloquium; California State University at Northridge; and the University of Minnesota. In each case, the version emerged scathed and the paper improved. I am especially grateful to Marilyn Adams, Robert Merrihew Adams, Tyler Burge, Keith Donnellan, Sharon Hill, Tom Hill, Greg Kavka, and Peter McAllen for detailed comments on the penultimate draft and to John Bennett, Terence Leichti, Derek Parfit, and Michael Tooley for fruitful discussions on this topic over the past two years.

9

Information, Action, and Persons

1. Introduction

In essay 8 I put forward an account of personal identity that goes as follows. There is a theory, the "human-theory," we have about human beings and that we use to explain human thought and action, including language, memory, and intention. This theory allows us to explain and predict what people will do in the future based on the present and past. We think that there is some causal connection among the stages of human beings that accounts for this theory working as well as it does. The unity relations for persons, that is, the relation that obtains between human stages that are stages of the same person, is a matter of being causally connected in this way, whatever it is.

What I had in mind by "the human-theory" is basically "folk-psychology," the set of commonsense principles that we apply to explain and predict human behavior. This includes our doxastic concepts: belief, recognition, knowledge, know-how, habit, and so forth; our volitional concepts: decision, deliberation, choice, intention, and the like; the various pro-attitudes: want, desire, preference, lust, and the like; our catalog of emotions; and much else. It seems to me that this body of commonsense concepts and principles is an amazing intellectual accomplishment, and perhaps, even with all that science has brought us, it is still, together with commonsense physics, the most useful knowledge we have for navigating through an ordinary day.

Still, it is not a scientific theory, and it hasn't brought us scientific knowledge. As Lisa Hall puts it,

> Contrary to the Popperian ideal, it is a shallow and loosely-organized system with extremely vague conditions of application. . . . these features severely limit the value of common sense psychology as a tool in

"Information, Action, and Persons" was written for this volume.

scientific research. However, they do not give us reason to question the system's empirical adequacy. On the contrary, the very qualities that make common-sense psychology unsuitable for scientific purposes provide grounds for thinking that the theses to which it commits us are probably true. (1993, p. 41)

For our commonsense psychology to serve the purpose I have in mind within a theory of persons and personal identity, it does not need to be a scientific theory, or a theory of any sort, in the usual sense. The practices of explanation must, however, be capable of providing coherent and naturalistically plausible explanations and predictions to a sufficient degree to suggest an underlying causal principle of its success (see Hall, 1993 42ff.). I want to address one central puzzle about how this can be so, which I'll call the circumstantial nature of the attitudes. My approach may seem to stray from Hall's vision of the commonsense system as a sprawling, loosely connected set of principles encircled by special cases and hedges. Instead I simplify the underlying principle of explanation to a simple caricature:

belief + desire motivates action

My defense for dealing with this caricature, aside from intellectual limitations, is that by showing how this caricature could be coherent while at the same time make sense from a naturalistic viewpoint, I hope to provide a springboard for further work that will produce a picture more adequate to the sprawling, loosely connected system of principles and concepts.

2. How Can Circumstantial Attitudes Explain?

The view that our cognitive states are both causes of our action and provide reasons for it is central to a commonsense theory of persons. If a belief and a desire *motivate* an action, then the belief state and desire state *cause* the action, and their contents *rationalize* the action. A belief and a desire rationalize an action if the action will promote the satisfaction of the desire if the belief is true. The causal role and contents of our attitudes must *mesh*. Beliefs and desires must cause actions they rationalize.

Beliefs, desires, hopes, fears, and other attitudes seem to be located in the heads of the people that have them. Our attitudes are accessible to us through introspection. For example, Vice President Dick Cheney can tell that he believes President George W. Bush to be a Republican just by examining the "the contents of his own mind"; he doesn't need to investigate the world around him. We think of beliefs and desires as being caused at certain times by events that impinge on the subject's body, specifically by perceptual events, such as reading a newspaper or seeing a picture of an ice cream cone or having someone tell you, "I'm a Republican, just like my dad." These attitudes can in turn cause changes in other mental phenomena and eventually in the dispositions to behave and the observable behavior of the subject. Seeing the picture of an ice cream cone leads to my desire for one, which leads me to forget the meeting I am supposed to attend and walk to the ice cream shop instead. All of this seems to require that attitudes be states and activities that are localized in the subject where they do their causal work.

Propositional attitudes, however, seem essentially relational in nature. They are "directed at" propositions and at the objects those propositions are about. These objects are the subject matter of the belief or desires; facts about the objects determine whether the belief is true or the desire satisfied. They may be quite remote from the mind of the subject. An attitude seems to be individuated by the agent, the type of attitude (belief, desire, etc.), and the proposition at which it is directed. It seems essential to the attitude reported by (1),

(1) Cheney believes that Bush is a Republican.

for example, that it is directed towards the proposition that Bush is a Republican. And it seems essential to this proposition that it is about Bush. And it is facts about Bush that will determine whether Cheney's belief is true—the very same facts that determine whether (2)

(2) Bush is a Republican.

is true. But how can a local mental state or activity of a person essentially involve some other individual in this way?

The view I advocate is a two-tiered view. One must distinguish between cognitive states and attitude properties. Cognitive states are local, causally interact with one another, and explain how muscles and bodies move. Attitude properties are circumstantial, reported by attitude reports, explain actions by revealing their rationale, and are individuated by propositions—by the objects they are about and what their truth requires of those objects.

Cheney's belief that Bush is a Republican is a particular cognitive state he is in, a brain state. We can model it as a sentence of mentalese written in a box or, to use the vocabulary I prefer, an association in his mind between ideas. It makes sense to ask when he came to be in that state and about its causes and effects.

The way Cheney and those ideas are set into the world, the causes of the formation of the ideas, the ways they are related to perceptions and these perceptions are related to objects and properties, the way the ideas cause bodily movements, and the effects those movements have on situations in the world determine what the ideas are *of* and the content of the belief they comprise. That is, it is not only the internal state and its structure, but the wider circumstances of the belief which determine the proposition that Cheney believes. Believing the proposition that Bush is a Republican involves Cheney's brain states being related to a certain person, Bush, and a certain property, being a Republican. Believing that Bush is a Republican is a property of Cheney's, but not a "state" in the normal sense of the term, which connotes something internal and local. It is conceivable that Cheney could be in the very state he is in but have a different attitude property in virtue of being in that state. This is the lesson we learn from various "twin" cases.

Paralleling the distinction between cognitive states and attitude properties is one between two kinds of actions: *executing movements* and *bringing about results*. I'll call these "executions" and "accomplishments." The execution of a movement is a basic action, something that can be caused by internal brain states affecting the central nervous system, causing certain muscles to contract, etc. The philosophical paradigm is the movement of a finger. An accomplishment is something one does *by* executing a movement in certain circumstances, as one might bring it about that an elevator comes to the first floor by moving one's finger in the right circumstances, while it was just in front of the elevator button. One can also decide to think or calculate or daydream and do so without the train of causation going outside, so we'll include those as executions, although they don't feel very much like movements—movements of the mind perhaps, but that seems merely a metaphor.

On the two-tiered view, then, we have cognitive states causing executions and propositional attitudes rationalizing actions. But why should these two different levels, the local causal states and the circumstantial, rationalizing attitude properties, mesh? What coordinates them? There must be some sort of "preestablished harmony" between these levels for our cognitive life to make sense. To take an extreme case of noncoordination, suppose Cheney's belief that Bush is a Republican and his desire to have Bush reelected causes him to give a million dollars to the Democratic Party. If this happened, of course, our belief in coordination would lead us to try to close the gap between motivation and action. We would look for further beliefs. Perhaps Cheney believes the more money the Democratic campaign has, the worse it will do. Or we would look for further desires. Perhaps Cheney wants to have Bush win a very close race. We would not take the situation at face value, thinking, "Oh well, this is just one of those cases when the internal causal states weren't quite aware of their content." Commonsense psychology is deeply committed to harmony between cognitive states and attitude properties; they must somehow mesh.

3. Meshing

Here is a first shot at the meshing principle:

(3) If believing P and desiring Q cause A, then A promotes Q, given P.

This needs to be sorted out in light of the two-tiered strategy. Statement (1) has the attitude properties in the antecedent, causing action, and propositions in the consequent rationalizing it. We need states in the antecedent causing and circumstantially determined propositions in the consequent doing the rationalizing. Here is an improved version. B and D are internal cognitive states, M is a type of movement, and P, Q, and R are propositions:

(4) If belief states B and desire states D cause executions of movement M and, on a specific occasion, one believes P in virtue of being in B, desires Q in virtue of being in D, and brings about R in virtue of executing M, then, on that occasion, R promotes Q, given P.

Here I use "desire" and "belief" loosely and broadly. "Pro-attitude" and "doxastic pro-attitude" might be better. In our example, the total explanation of Cheney's making the movements necessary to make out the check to the Democratic Party and send it would include bits of know-how (he knows how to sign his name), recognition (he thinks *that* is his checkbook), attunement to background constraints (he doesn't act like he was in a spaceship, but rather as if he were in a normal earthly gravitational environment), and so forth. I don't think, however, that we need assume that the totality of Cheney's beliefs or cognitive states are involved in the causation and rationalization of each act. This is all discussed in more detail, although probably still not enough, in Israel, Perry, and Tutiya (1993).

Principle (4) helps to make the problem clearer. Since what a person believes in virtue of being in B, desires in virtue of being in D, and accomplishes in virtue of executing M will depend on the circumstances one is in, it would seem like a bit of a miracle, for all that is said in (4), if the antecedent guaranteed the consequent. To see that it need not be a miracle, we need to get inside the circumstances that determine the contents and results on a specific occasion to see how they might interact in a coordinated way.

Let Y_b be a function that assigns contents to belief states, considered in the widest sense, relative to agents, times, and circumstances. If

$$Y_b\ (a,\ t,\ F,\ B) = P$$

then if a at t is in belief state B and in circumstance F, then a believes proposition P at t. Similarly for Y_d and desires in the broadest sense.

Let P be a relation between agents, times, circumstances, movements, and results. If

$$P(a,\ t,\ F,\ M,\ R)$$

then if a executes M at t in circumstances F, a at t brings it about that R. Then I propose:

(5) If belief state B and desire state D cause movement M, then whenever there is an agent a, time t, circumstance F, and propositions P and Q such that

   (i) a at t is in states B and D and circumstances F,

   (ii) $Y_b(a,\ t,\ F,\ B) = P$, and

   (iii) $Y_d(a,\ t,\ F,\ D) = Q$,

there are also circumstances F' and a result R such that

(iv) $P(a, t, F', M, R)$ and

(v) a's bringing it about that R at t in F' promotes the satisfaction of Q.

Let's see how this works in a simple case. I see a glass c before me which I take to have water in it. Next to it is another glass, c' which I take to be empty. I want to quench my thirst. I reach out, pick up c, and drink from it. Here my perception causes me to go into an internal state B. The content of the state is P: that c is a certain distance and direction from me and has water in it. That state combines with the desire D, the content of which is Q: that my thirst be quenched. If my belief about the direction and distance of c from me are true, the result of these movements will be that the cup is brought to my lips and the liquid from it poured into my mouth. If my belief that c has water in it is true, my thirst will be relieved.

Now suppose c' had been in front of me instead, looking just the same as c did, and c is off to the side and looking empty, just like c' was in the original case. In that case, I would have believed that c' was a certain distance and direction from me, that c' had water in it, and that c did not—same internal states, different propositions believed. Since the internal states are the same, the movement will be the same. But here is where the preestablished harmony kicks in. If a glass is a certain distance and direction from me, is the glass I see, and is the glass that gives rise to my belief state, it will be the glass my belief is about; but if it is that distance and direction from me (and if I am properly attuned to the length of my arms and the relevant gravitational forces and the like), that movement will bring to my lips the very glass I see and formed the belief about. The facts that produce this result are not exactly the same ones that determine which glass my belief is about (hence the difference between F and F' in the conditions), but if the F facts obtain, so will the F' facts. The contents of my beliefs are different in the second case, since they are about c' instead of c. But the results of my action are also different, since I pick up c' instead of c. The attitudes and the states mesh, even though we kept the states fixed while the attitude properties changed with the circumstances.

Here is a twin-earth example. Twin-a is in the same internal cognitive states as a and a pretty similar situation as a, except that he is a zillion miles away on twin-earth looking at glasses d and d'. They have "twater" instead of water on twin-earth (see Putnam, 1975), but they call it "water," since that's the word for it in Twin-English. So, speaking in English, Twin-*a* is in the same state as *a*, but Twin-*a* believes that glass *d* has twater in it, while *a* believes that glass *c* has water in it. Why doesn't that cause a problem? Again, circumstances to the rescue. The reason Twin-*a* is thinking about twater instead of water is that when he grew up, he saw and drank a lot of twater, used it to wash his face, and learned to recognize the difference between twater and tmud, torange-juice, tmilk, and so forth. So he has an idea of twater, an internal state or aspect of an internal state that is *of* twater. This very idea would have been of water if he had been on earth. (The importance of water to our biology and the world in general may make some of these counterfactuals implausible, but I'll press on.) When he learned Twin-English, he associated the word "water" with the subtance he had learned to recognize, drink, wash with, and so forth.

So, if Twin-*a*'s belief is true, given its circumstantially determined content, the glass in front of him will be full of twater. Although the movement his belief and desire cause are the same as those the same states cause in *a*, things still work out. He wants twater to his lips, and that's what he gets if the glass is full of twater.

If condition (5) is met, the causal roles and the contents of the attitudes will mesh. But what exactly does (5) put conditions on? Basically, on the *Y* functions, which assign contents to states, and the causal structure of the part of the world in which these states occur, which is reflected in the *P*-relation.

A naturalistic account of cognitive states and their contents will have to explain how these conditions are met. The hypothesis is that cognitive states evolved as a system of harnessing information to control action and that commonsense psychology is built upon appreciation of this fact.

4. The Reflexive/Circumstantial Structure of Information

I'll call any circumstance, thought of in terms of the information it carries, a "signal." A signal is the fact that *A has* ϕ, for some object *A* and property ϕ. *A* is the *carrier* of information and ϕ is the *indicating property*. Suppose you are at the dentist. The dentist holds an x-ray taken of some of your teeth. He points to a discoloration on a certain tooth. "That shows that you have a cavity," he says. The x-ray is the carrier, the pattern discoloration is the indicating property, having a cavity is the *indicated property,* and the information is the proposition that your tooth has a cavity. Note the circumstantial structure: the signal is a local feature of the x-ray; the information is a proposition about your tooth, in virtue of the circumstance that the x-ray was taken of your tooth.

We get from the signal to the information in two steps. Information is basically what one part or aspect of the universe (the signal) shows about some other part or aspect (the subject matter, in this case, your tooth and the property of having a cavity). This is possible only because events are constrained by laws of nature or, as I prefer, because of its more liberal, commonsense, loose, and nonreductive connotations, by the way the things happen. The information carried by a signal is what *else* things have to be like for the signal to have occurred, given the way things happen. Given the way things happen, an x-ray has a discoloration like that only if the tooth to which the relevant part of the x-ray was exposed has a cavity.

This means that a signal will carry the information that *P* if there is *some* constraint, some principle of how things work, such that given that constraint, *P* has to be the case for the signal to occur. It is useful, however, to have an explicitly relative concept:

> *S* has the informational content that *P* relative to constraint *C* if, given *C*, it has to be the case that *P* for *S* to occur.

One advantage of the concept of informational content is that it allows us to consider false or nonfactual constraints, as well as true ones, which is often useful, as we will see next. That is, we'll think of constraints as states of affairs, some of which are facts (or propositions, some of which are true, if one prefers).

Let's return to our example. Can we say that the spot on the x-ray shows that your tooth has a cavity, relative to a constraint *C*, where *C* incorporates the principles of x-rays and decay relevant to how x-rays work? Not quite. After all, if it were a constraint that every time an x-ray had such a discoloration *your* tooth had a cavity, you would be pretty miserable. The constraint is that every time an x-ray has a spot like that, *the tooth to which it was exposed* has a cavity. All we have so far is

> The spot on the x-ray shows that the tooth to which *the x-ray itself* was exposed has a cavity.

I call this *reflexive* information, because the informational content of the x-ray is about the x-ray *itself.* That is, the proposition *that the tooth to which the x-ray was exposed has a cavity* ascribes a property not to you or your tooth, but to the x-ray—the property of having been exposed to a tooth which has a cavity. With reflexive information, what a signal shows is something about itself; one aspect of the x-ray, the pattern of discoloration, shows something else about the x-ray, something about its history.

To get from reflexive information to information about your tooth, we need to bring in circumstances, namely, the circumstance that your tooth is the very one to which the x-ray was exposed:

> *Given* that the x-ray was exposed to your tooth, the spot on the x-ray shows that your tooth has a cavity.

This is a proposition about your tooth, not one about the x-ray. Our informational content is no longer reflexive. On this concept, the x-ray doesn't show something about itself, but something about the rest of the world. I call this *incremental information:* We've got the x-ray. What *else* does the world have to be like, *given* these circumstances and the state of the x-ray?

We now have three concepts of information to work with:

> A signal S has the reflexive informational content that P relative to constraint C iff according to C, the signal occurs only if it is the case that P.
>
> A signal S has the incremental informational content that P relative to constraint C and given circumstance F iff according to C, given F, the signal occurs only if it is the case that P.
>
> A signal S carries the information that P iff S has the informational content that P relative to some factual constraint C and factual circumstance F.

It would be pleasant to find a direct link from informational content to belief, but things are not so easy. We'll actually need a fourth concept of information, but before getting to that we need to look at the structure of action.

5. The Reflexive/Circumstantial Structure of Action

I'll use "actions" for types of acts; acts are unrepeated events involving an agent executing some movement at some time. As I mentioned, actions come in two basic varieties, executing movements and accomplishing results; we do the latter by doing the former.

Suppose, for example, that I am typing. I move my right forefinger in a certain way; that's executing a movement. By doing that I depress the *j* key; that's an accomplishment. By depressing the *j* key, I bring it about that a "j" appears on the computer screen; that's another accomplishment.

We think of accomplishments as bringing about results, so the canonical form of an action report is

X brought it about that *P.*

This regimentation makes it much easier to see the connection between accomplishments and the propositional attitudes that motivate them.

What I bring about when I execute a movement depends on constraints and circumstances. Moving my finger as I did was a *way of* depressing the *j* key in the circumstance that my finger was poised over the *j* key, according to mechanics and principles about the way fingers and computer keyboards work.

> An action *A* by *a* at *t* is a *way of* bringing it about that *P* in circumstance *F* relative to constraint *C* iff according to *C*, *a* performs *A* in *F* at *t* implies that *P.*
>
> An agent *a* performs *A* at *t* iff *A* is movement *M* and *a* executes *M* at *t* or *A* is the accomplishment *bring it about that P* and *a* brings it about that *P.*

The term "accomplishment" usually suggests that one has done what one wanted to do. It doesn't have that sense within this theory. One might say it includes the somewhat ironical sense: By tripping over the books on the floor of my office, I spill the coffee I was holding on a report on my desk that I just printed out. A colleague says, "My, look what you've accomplished, and it's only 9 A.M." On our usage, ruining the report is an accomplishment of mine: a result brought about by something I did, however unintended.

An act is *successful* or *unsuccessful* relative to a goal or, if one wants to sound more scientific, a chosen end state. The act is successful relative to the goal if the goal is one of the things the act brings about. An action *A* can be assigned success conditions relative to a goal and a constraint. The success conditions will be those circumstances in which the action will be a way of bringing about the goal according to the constraint. For example, suppose I want to mail a letter. According to the way the post office works, walking up to a metal box on a street corner and dropping a stamped letter in the box is a way of mailing a letter *if* the metal box is an official mail depository box. So, that is the success condition of my action, relative to the goal of mailing a letter and the constraints arising from the way the post office does things.

6. Harnessing Information

Intelligent design often means designing something so that information guides action in a way that produces the result one wants. A mousetrap is a relatively simple device that illustrates this. Old-fashioned mouse-traps really weren't traps, but mouse killers. Now one can purchase a more humane device. There is a little tunnel with an opening at one end. The tunnel is mounted off-center on a little fulcrum, so the whole thing acts like a teeter-totter. If nothing is in the tunnel except a little peanut butter (the recommended bait), the open end will be on the floor, and the closed end, where you put the peanut butter, will be about $3/8$ of an inch above the floor. The open end has a door that swings shut from above. When the open end is on the floor, the door stays open, perched above the opening, its center of gravity just slightly to one side of directly above the hinge. When the open end rises even a little bit, the center of gravity of the door passes over the hinge and the door swings shut. When a mouse enters and goes down the tunnel to get the peanut butter, as it passes above the fulcrum the weight shifts, the closed end goes to the floor, the open end goes up in the air, and the door shuts. The mouse is trapped but unharmed and can be released humanely in the neighbor's yard.

Here is how one can look at this as an information-using device. The change of weight as the mouse passes the fulcrum is a signal. It contains the information that there is a mouse in the tunnel, relative to the constraint that only mice will enter the tunnel. It is the job of the user to put the mousetrap in some place where this constraint will hold. The closing of the door is an action that will be successful if there is a mouse in the tunnel, relative to the goal of trapping a mouse and the constraints about mice and plastic, for example, that mice cannot walk through plastic doors or open them, at least not those of this kind. The device is constructed so that the very event that carries the information that certain circumstances obtain (the change of weight) is also a cause of an action that will be successful in just those circumstances. This gives us a new concept of content, which I'll call "pragmatic content." The pragmatic content of a state is the success conditions of the actions it causes. Pragmatic content is relative to architecture, circumstance, and goal. One wants the informational content carried by a state to guarantee the pragmatic content of the state. Then the actions the state causes will be successful. It is pragmatic content, rather than informational content, that is our model for the content of beliefs.

The information that the door will close is what we call *architectural* information. It is incremental information rather than reflexive, in that it is not information about the carrier itself. But it is information about something that is part of the same device, as opposed to something that is outside the device. The architecture is the key to harnessing information; the design creates the information by creating causal connections.

The sort of scales found in some doctor's offices provides another example of architectural information. You step on the scale, and the doctor moves some little weights on a little bar; the position of the weights when the bar balances shows your weight. The doctor lowers another bar to the top of your head. That bar is attached to a vertical bar that slides in a holder which is fastened to the scale just in front of the platform on which you stand to get weighed. An arrow on the vertical bar points to calibrations on the holder, and this shows how tall you are. Let's suppose that you are z and that the pointer points to 6' 3". Then we have:

> The position of the pointer has the reflexive informational content *that the person whose head is stopping its downward movement is 6'3" tall,* according to constraints about metal and human bodies.

> The position of the pointer has the architectural informational content *that the person who is standing on the weight platform is 6'3" tall,* according to constraints about metal and additional constraints about human bodies and the architectural constraints and given the architectural circumstance that it is attached to the scale.

The additional constraint is the way human bodies are built; this is required to establish that the person who stands on a weight platform of the scale will be the person whose head stops the downward movement of the height bar. If humans were built like the Leaning Tower of Pisa, this might not be so; the height bar might stop at the head of the person standing on the next scale. Finally,

> The position of the pointer has the incremental informational content *that z is 6'3" tall,* according to constraints about metal and human bodies, given the circumstance that z is the person who is standing on the scale.

Architectural information is very important in understanding how human technology works, for technology often depends on vast systems of signals that contain information about one another according to a myriad of different constraints. Particularly important are technologies that allow for the *flow of incremental information.* Consider, for example, the pattern of pixels on my television on the day of the 1980 National Football Conference (NFC) playoff game, which carried the information that Dwight Clark had caught a pass from Joe Montana, defeating Dallas and sending San Francisco to the Super Bowl for the first time. The process started at Candlestick Park where Clark caught the ball. The camera that was focused on him—call it c—went into an internal state ϕ that carried the reflexive information that the person on whom *it* was focused had caught a football, relative to constraints about people, footballs, light, cameras, and so forth. It carried the incremental information that Dwight Clark had done so, relative to those constraints and given the fact the camera was focused on him. Slightly simplifying, the camera caused a satellite s to go into state γ, which had the reflexive information that the camera sending signals to *it* was in state ϕ, relative to constraints about cameras, wireless transmission, and satellites. Satellite s being in γ carried the architectural information that c was in state ϕ, relative to the (architectural) circumstance that c was the camera sending signals to it. It also carried the architectural information that the person on whom c was focused had caught a football, relative to all the constraints listed so far. Relative to all those constraints and given that c was focused on Dwight Clark, it carried the information that he had caught the ball. Finally, in our very simple system, the satellite s caused a pattern of pixels on my television screen, which carried the reflexive information that the satellite that transmitted the pattern to *it* was in state γ, relative to constraints about satellites, wireless transmission, cables, televisions sets, and the like. The pattern of pixels carried the architectural information s was in state γ, given the architectural fact that s sends signals to my screen.

The pattern of pixels inherits the architectural information that the fact that *s* was in state γ carried, that the person on whom *c* was focused caught a football, relative to the constraints so far plus those relevant to the step from *c* to *s*. And, finally, the pattern of pixels on my screen carries the incremental information that Dwight Clark caught the ball, relative to all the constraints listed so far, given the architecture of the system and given the fact that *c* was focused on Clark.

A flow-of-information system such as this is designed to preserve incremental information. The form in which it is preserved is important in the last step; the display of pixels carries the information in a way that I, the person who pays for the satellite hookup and buys the advertised beer, can recognize. I don't care much about the system that lies between my set and the field. A cable, rather than a satellite, or a transmitter and antenna system would be equally satisfactory from my point of view if the picture were as good. The connections and constraints contain all sorts of information relative to all sorts of constraints, but it is the flow of incremental information at which the whole system is aimed. I'm not interested in the state of the satellite or of the camera; I'm interested in Dwight Clark and the 49ers.

7. Indirect Classification and Attunement

The statement

> Signal *s* shows that Dwight Clark caught the ball.

can be given a relational analysis; one thing, the signal, has a certain relation, showing (carrying the information) to another; the proposition that Dwight Clark caught the ball. There is another way of looking at it, however, which I call "indirect classification." The picture is that we are really not classifying a pair of objects by a relationship that holds between them, but classifying one object, the signal, by the state that it is in, identified in a very roundabout way. It is a bit like

> My car is the color of that ripe tomato.

We can look at this as classifying a pair of things, my car and the tomato, as having the same color. Or we can look on "the color of that ripe tomato" as a somewhat roundabout way of identifying a color, which is being predicated of my car, the tomato really just serving as an aid to identifying the color. This possibility of looking at the same statement in two ways will prove crucial in seeing how propositional attitudes can do the work they do.

Suppose, having seen the pattern of pixels on my television, I say, "Dwight Clark caught the ball." What is my evidence? I saw it on TV. That is, the picture, or pattern of pixels, on my television screen shows that Dwight Clark caught the ball. The pattern of pixels is a local event, one that could be described without any mention of Dwight Clark. It seems a rather roundabout way of describing the state of my screen, to bring in the activities of some individual forty miles away connected with my television by a hunk of metal in space.[1] I am indirectly classifying the screen in terms of what it shows, relative to the constraints and connections that I pay my monthly Dish TV bill to be able to exploit. The reason I do this is a part of an explanation of why I believe that Dwight Clark caught the ball. The incremental information, in terms of which I describe the picture on my television, is the very same proposition that I come to believe by watching it. It is a bit of a miracle if one thinks about it like that.

In this example, I am *attuned* to two things. First, I know how to interpret pictures on a television screen; I know what they depict. If the pattern of pixels had been like that but I had been watching a movie, I wouldn't have taken it to show anything about what happened at Candlestick Park, but I would have taken it to depict a man catching a football. Second, I am attuned to the way television broadcasting systems work. If I know that a game is being televised live, I take the event depicted on the screen to have happened; I take the pixels on the screen to carry information about the events that a camera, or something like it, is trained on at the site of the game.

To say that I am attuned to the way the television broadcasting systems work is not to say that I could list or state or understand the nature of the constraints and connections involved. I might not even know whether the television I'm watching uses cable, satellite, or

---

[1] To tell the truth, neither dish satellite nor even cable were available in Palo Alto in 1980, where I saw a pattern of pixels on my neighbor's television that showed that Dwight Clark caught the ball in the NFC playoff game with Dallas, an event known, at least in the Bay Area, as "The Catch." The dish satellite story seems to me one of the more amazing cases of the flow of information, and the catch is one of the few historic events almost universally regarded as pleasant that I have watched on TV, so I decided to combine them ahistorically.

antenna. To say I am attuned is to say that my beliefs track the information carried by the events on my screen, given the connections and according to the constraints that are part of the system. This attunement is necessary to *use* the system, although of course it would not suffice to repair it or to build it in the first place. The common-sense concept that handles this is *know-how.* When one knows how to drink a glass of water, ride a bike, or get the news on TV, one is able to do things to achieve goals that depend on all sorts of connections and constraints that one doesn't have the concepts or the need to explicitly believe. One has a positive doxastic attitude, included under our wide use of "belief" in section 2 of this essay, but not the sort of thing one ordinarily calls beliefs.

My being attuned to the system is a bit like my becoming part of the system. Each link in the system, the camera, the satellite, and my television, are set up to carry the same incremental information, depending on different constraints and connections. So am I, just like another link. The pattern of pixels causes me to believe that Dwight Clark caught the ball and to say so. What I believe and what I say are just the very incremental information carried by the camera, the satellite, and the TV screen. Here the relational point of view helps; we think of the incremental information as a proposition to which each of these events is related in different ways.

Let's return for a moment to the mousetrap. A mouse crawls in the trap and the door shuts. Why did the door close? We might say, "Because the trap knew a mouse had crawled inside." This is clearly metaphorical. Can we more carefully say, "Because the trap was in a state that showed that a mouse had crawled inside?" What sort of explanation would that be? It seems to me that we have the same sort of dual-aspect explanation that we saw is typical of attitude explanations. We have given both a reason and a cause. To see the reason, we look at the statement as telling us the success condition for the door closing. We assume the goal of catching mice. The proposition shown, that a mouse had crawled inside, is the success condition for the door closing, given that goal. We can, on the other hand, look at the statement as giving us the cause of the door closing, for the very state that shows the success condition to be met causes the door to close. We are giving an explanation in the context of an understanding of the goal of the trap and the assumption that it embodies an information-harnessing design. We give both a reason and a cause, and they mesh.

8. Information, Action, and Intentionality

Our concept of "carrying the information that" is factive: if s carries the information that P, then it's true that P. It doesn't provide a very promising candidate for a helpful analysis of belief, our paradigm propositional attitude, which is quite non-factive.

Our concept of "having the informational content that" is a bit more promising. The constraints relative to which a signal has informational content need not be true, so even if an actual signal s has the informational content that P, it might be false that P. For example, it might be that every so often a glitch in the network makes pixels appear depicting a football player catching a ball when he didn't. The ball actually hit something out of bounds, ending the play, and then bounced back into the player's outstretched hands while he still hung in the air. Cosmic rays caused by sunspot activity erase the part of the signal the camera sends to the satellite registering the bounce. It's very rare. It would cost a lot to fix. So the system gets by with informational content rather than information.

Birds of various species became attuned, over centuries or millennia, to the constraint that the path to any clearly visible object is unobstructed. This hasn't been true since humans started making transparent windows; a certain number of birds fly into the windows and die, because all their visual states has is informational content rather than information. Still, most birds do well in spite of being attuned to mere informational content.

I became attuned to the information contained in broadcasts of football games over many decades before the problem with cosmic rays showed up. Even though no cosmic rays were involved on the NFC playoff day, all I really had available from my TV was the informational content that Dwight Clark caught the ball. I was attuned to a false constraint, because the broadcasting system had been designed in terms of one.

If we regard beliefs as states that have informational content, rather than carry information, we can allow for false beliefs, in virtue of attunement to constraints that may be quite reliable but are not exceptionless. This is a start, but it doesn't seem to provide much leverage. Lots of false and fallible beliefs seem to arise in ways that don't have much to do with attunement to false constraints.

Things get more promising if we look at how fallible informational content can be in the context of our concept of success conditions. Consider our mousetrap. There are really a lot of ways that the trap can be moved so that the door shuts other than a mouse crawling in. It usually happens several times just setting the trap in place. A cat might rest its paw on top of the trap. There might be an earthquake. A marble might roll in the trap. A mouse might crawl across the top of the trap on his way to the floor from the pasta shelf, and so on. The constraint that whenever the center of gravity shifts across the fulcrum there is a mouse in the tunnel of the trap isn't even close to being true. Still, it doesn't have to be true for the mousetrap to be a pretty good one. No great harm is done if the door shuts for some other reason. Even the old-fashioned mouse-killing mouse "traps," with the blade that snaps when a cheese pedal wiggles, are still a successful product, even though the results of a "false positive" can lead to a crushed toe or finger or paw. We can imagine attunement to a myriad of overlapping, not all that reliable, constraints, as long as the benefits of success are high and the costs of failure low.

Designing mechanisms to act on the basis of constraints that are not true, invariable connections among types of events but merely somewhat probable, even in the most favorable conditions, can be a good strategy. Another simple example is the automatic pencil sharpener. You can trigger these things with all sorts of lead-pencil-shaped objects, including automatic pencils, ballpoint pens, pencils stuck in with the eraser first, and so on. It's not an entirely unpleasant way to kill time. Even in a well-designed office, an absentminded academic can be counted on to falsify the constraint a couple of times a month. Still, it's a good product for somewhat lazy and somewhat responsible people.

Let's call devices that are attuned to constraints that are only sometimes right "information-content harnessing devices." My philosophical hypothesis is that (i) human beings are naturally occurring information-content harnessing devices; (ii) our system of using propositional attitude reports as explanations of actions (including internal acts such as theoretical and practical inferences) is a system of dual-purpose indirect classification, which involves attunement to the way humans work as information-content harnessing devices; and (iii) our concept of persons and personal identity reflects this attunement.

(I also think this whole system has gone somewhat berserk as a scheme for survival of the species or anyone's genes, yet much of what we value in human life is a product of this craziness. I won't defend or expand on these deep thoughts in this essay.)

This hypothesis obviously needs to be worked out in considerably more detail; perhaps it even deserves to be. However, for the purposes of this essay, I will simply consider one rather weighty objection to the whole.

9. Pains, Pleasures, and Original Intentionality

One can object to this idea as follows. The broadcasting system, the mousetrap, and the pencil sharpener may well be describable in terms of informational content and success conditions. Dennett (1987) has shown how we can take the "design stance" and the "intentional stance" towards lots of artifacts and naturally occurring processes, and these applications of the "informational stance" are in the same boat; perhaps the informational stance is a species of the intentional stance. But, as Searle (1992) has emphasized, humans don't merely have this sort of "attributed" intentionality; our beliefs and desires and hopes and fears really have content. When we take the intentional stance, the content ultimately comes from *us,* users of the artifacts or observers as he processes. We are describing the operations of the network, the mousetrap, and the pencil sharpener in terms of what we use them for. If our goal were to ruin ballpoint pens, the success conditions of the automatic pencil sharpener's beginning to spin would not be that a pencil has been inserted, but that a ballpoint pen had. It's just up to the interests of the describer. That isn't the case with the beliefs and desires of humans.

The problem is that pragmatic content, unlike information or informational content, is relative to goals. Our attribution of success conditions to the mousetrap door closing, or the pencil sharpener beginning to spin, are clearly based on our goals for creating and using the mousetraps and pencil sharpeners, not the goals of the mousetraps and pencil sharpeners themselves. What sense can we make of the attribution to systems of goals that are intrinsic to the system, rather than coming from the outside to a system? We cannot start with desires in attempting to show that our system of propositional attitudes can be seen naturalistically. We need to build a bridge from goals that can be attributed to an organism on the basis of its own situation to our ordinary concept of desire.

Evolution teaches us that the fittest survive and pass on their genes. So there is something naturalistic about the goal of surviving.

Actions are successful if they promote the goal of survival. So the success conditions attributed to our actions ought to be relative to that natural goal.

This seems to work fairly well for some animals. The chicken sees a bit of grain and pecks. The success condition of the act was that an edible was at the end of the arc of the peck, so that's the relevant informational content of the visual/brain state caused by the pattern of light reflected from the grain on the ground.

But we can't carry this too far. In the first place, modern biology seems to emphasize that the evolutionary importance of our fitness is for the survival of our genes, which seems one step further removed from our desires than our own survival. The goal of dispersing our genes doesn't seem to be a very good candidate for directly anchoring our propositional attitudes. My present motion towards the jar of chocolate chip cookies seems to be motivated by a desire to have the taste of a chocolate chip cookie flood the tastebuds in my mouth.

A more promising strategy is to ground our desires in the natural goals of avoiding pain and pursuing pleasure. Avoiding pains and pursuing pleasures are as natural as goals get. We might think of these as natural goals further grounded in promoting propagation of our genes. For some animals, there are states it is like something to be in; some of these are pleasurable, some painful. Animals try to avoid getting into, or try to remove themselves from, painful situations and try to get themselves into, or stay in, pleasurable ones. At one time, we may speculate this natural tendency served the goal of gene dispersal well enough; there was a close correlation between actions that promoted the dispersal of our genes and pleasures and between actions that didn't promote them and pains. Eating is more fun than starving or being eaten. Procreating is fun, while having the urge to procreate with no possibility of doing so isn't. This is probably why pleasures and pains were originally exploited by evolution. They evolved as internal signs of what would help the genes and what might not.

The hypothesis, then, is that pains and pleasures provide the intrinsic goals that can naturalistically ground the concept of success for our actions and hence the concept of pragmatic content and hence the concept of doxastic states. In virtue of basic architecture, doxastic states have informational content and, together with desires, cause actions, originally in the service of the natural desires of avoiding pain and attaining pleasure. These desires are natural in two senses; pains are unpleasant, and we want to avoid them, and we do the opposite for pleasures. And during a long period of evolution, avoiding pains and pursuing pleasures was a good strategy for dispersing one's genes.

The link between painful and pleasurable activities and activities that promote or don't promote the survival of our genes has largely been broken by civilization. Most of what we eat is bad for us. Successful acts of procreation mostly hasten the end of the world through overpopulation, so they really don't serve anyone's genes.

If we are well brought up, our desires don't center on our pains and pleasures. Some ability to forgo pleasure or endure pain in certain circumstances evolved in the service of gene propagation, for example, when one's offspring are at stake or when a little pain now means a lot of pleasure in the future or vice versa. Human invention, knowledge, culture, superstition, and the rest have taken charge of this mechanism. I struggle to produce a philosophical essay when I could be eating a cookie. Stanford's Provost, John Etchemendy, chairs meetings trying to find a way to balance Stanford Medical School's budget when he could be writing a philosophical essay—or eating a cookie—or both, for that matter.

10. Conclusion

The speculations of the prior section may seem quite naive to the biologist or ecologist, but I'm satisfied if naiveté is the only big problem. The point is to come up with a picture, even if it's a bit of a cartoon, that suggests how humans can have goals that can be naturalistically explained as intrinsic to them and not just attributed to them by designers, theorists, and the like. We need goals to have success; we need success to have success conditions; we need success conditions to have pragmatic content; and pragmatic content is my candidate for seeing that doxastic states both have informational content and, in conjunction with desires, cause actions that, if the content is true, will succeed. And, I claim, seeing doxastic states and desires in this way is the key to solving the meshing problem naturalistically.

III. THE SELF

10

The Self, Self-Knowledge, and Self-Notions

1. "Self" and the Self

The English expression "self" is a modest one; in its normal use, it is not even quite a word, but something that makes an ordinary object pronoun into a reflexive one: "her" into "herself," "him" into "himself," and "it" into "itself." The reflexive pronoun is used when the object of an action or attitude is the same as the subject of that action or attitude. If I say Mark Twain shot *himself* in the foot, I describe Mark Twain not only as the shooter but as the person shot; if I say Mark Twain admired *himself,* I describe him not only as the admirer but as the admired. In this sense, "the self" is just the person doing the action or holding the attitude that is somehow in question. "Self" is also used as a prefix for names of activities and attitudes, identifying the special case where the object is the same as the agent: self-love, self-hatred, self-abuse, self-promotion, and self-knowledge. When we say "the same" and "identity" in these contexts, we mean that there is *only one thing.* The way I use "A and B are identical," it means there is just one thing that both *is* A and *is* B. Mark Twain and Samuel Clemens are identical because there is just one fellow that was Mark Twain and was Samuel Clemens. When I use the word "identity" in some other way, I'll put it in scare-quotes.

Given the meaning of "self," one might expect the phrase "the self" to be simply an alternative way of saying "the person," and sometimes it is used this way. In fact, the term is often appropriated for various inner agents or principles that are thought on various

---

"The Self, Self-Knowledge, and Self-Notions" was written for this volume but borrows examples and ideas from "Self-Notions," *Logos* (1990): 17–31; and 'Myself and I" in *Philosophie in Synthetisher Absicht* (A festschrift for Dieter Heinrich), edited by Marcelo Stamm. Stuttgart: Klett-Cotta, 1998), 83–103.

philosophical and religious views to be necessary for consciousness, knowledge, freedom, or personal identity. The phrase is also often used to refer to the most central parts of the concept a person has of himself or herself.

In different disciplines, somewhat different things are regarded as most central. In psychology, "the self" is often used for that set of attributes a person attaches to himself or herself most firmly, the attributes the person finds it difficult or disturbing to imagine himself or herself without. The term "identity" is also used in this sense. Typically, one's gender is a part of one's self or one's "identity"; one's profession or nationality may or may not be.

In philosophy, the self is the person considered as agent, knower, subject of desires, and conscious subject of experience. These are philosophically the most central parts of a person's self-concept: I am the person doing this, knowing this, wanting this, and having these sensations and thoughts. It is this concept of ourselves that is extended through memory and anticipation and forms the basis of personal identity. I am the person who *did* this and *will* do that; I am the person who *had* this experience and wants to have it again. If the present thought of future reward or punishments is to encourage or deter me from some course of action, I must be thinking of the person rewarded as me, as myself, as the same person who is now going to experience the hardships of righteousness or not experience the pleasures of sin to gain this reward.

Given the meaning of the particle "self" and the nature of our self-concept, a reasonable hypothesis is that *the* self, in the philosophical sense, is simply *the* person who is the knower, agent, subject of desires, and possessor of thoughts and sensations. It seems this same self, the knower, agent, and conscious subject, comes up in many quite mundane transactions and turns out to be the person. If I pick up the cake and shove it in this mouth rather than that one, isn't it because I think it is *my* mouth and so it will be me, the very same person who picks up the cake, who will have the pleasure of tasting it? Isn't identity of the metaphysical agent, the ultimate locus of reward and punishment, simply being the same person, simply identity? Isn't what I worry about, when I worry about going to prison or going to Hell, simply that the person to be punished and I are one and the same—identical, without scare-quotes? If so, this self, the identity of which is at the bottom of every action and involved in every bit of knowledge, the self of the philosophers, is simply the person who does the action and has the knowledge—not anything more, or less, mysterious.

A straightforward view of the self, then, is that the self is just the person and that a person is a physical system with the unity physical systems can possess, not a unity based on some other inner agent and perceiver or mysterious principle. This view has been challenged on (at least) two fronts. First, the nature of freedom and consciousness has convinced many philosophers that there is a fundamentally non-physical aspect of persons. I'm not going to talk about these issues. As to freedom, the problem is large and complex, the issues are familiar to most philosophers, and I don't have anything new to say about it—although I do have hopes of some day having a good idea. The arguments in favor of immateriality of the mind or self do not have as strong a hold on the philosophical community as they once did. While there are many philosophers who think that mental properties cannot be fully reduced to physical or material properties, most such philosophers would allow that these are properties of a physical system, rather than an immaterial self. I've considered at length the issue of whether the nature of subjective experience shows that not all of our properties are physical in *Knowledge, Possibility, and Consciousness* (2001).

The second challenge stems from puzzling aspects of self-knowledge. The knowledge we have of ourselves seems very unlike the knowledge we have of other objects in several ways, and this has led some philosophers to rather startling conclusions about the self. In his *Tractatus,* Ludwig Wittgenstein tells us that "I am my world" and that "the world is my world" (1921/1961, 5.63, 5.641). This should lead us to the rather surprising conclusion that I am the world or that at least Wittgenstein was. He draws at least one conclusion that would follow from this; he says, "[A]t death the world does not alter, but comes to an end."

The contemporary philosopher Tom Nagel has been led to a possibly less radical but still quite dramatic view. According to Nagel (1983), when he says "I am Tom Nagel," at least in certain philosophical moods, the "I" refers to the "objective self," which is not identical with, but merely contingently related to, the person Tom Nagel. This self could just as well view the world from the perspective of someone else other than him. I discuss Nagel's view at length in essay 11. Here we will examine puzzling features of self-knowledge that give rise to such views.

2. Self-Knowledge

"Self-knowledge" seems to have a straightforward meaning: cases of knowledge in which the knower and the known are identical. But this doesn't seem sufficient. In a footnote to his book *The Analysis of Sensations* (Mach 1914, p. 4n.), the philosopher Ernst Mach tells of getting on the end of a bus and seeing a scruffy, unkempt bookish looking sort of person at the other end. He thought to himself:

(1) That man is a shabby pedagogue.

In fact, Mach was seeing himself in a large mirror at the far end of the bus, of the sort conductors used to use to help keep track of things. He eventually realized this and thought to himself:

(2) I am that man.
(3) I am a shabby pedagogue.

Now consider Mach at the earlier time. Did Mach have self-knowledge? In our straightforward sense, it seems that he did. After all, he knew that a certain person was a shabby pedagogue. Furthermore, that person was, in fact, him. The knower and the person known about were the same. But this case isn't really what we have in mind when we talk about self-knowledge. Self-knowledge is something Mach really only had when he got to step (3), when he would have used the word "I" to express what he knew.

Self-knowledge in this restricted sense seems peculiar. First, it seems "essentially indexical." Statement (3) expresses self-knowledge because of the word "I"; it is hard to see how Mach could have expressed self-knowledge without using the first-person. If he said, "Mach is a shabby pedagogue," he would be only claiming to know what everyone else may have known—something he could have learned by reading the papers, even if he had amnesia and didn't know who he was or that he was a shabby pedagogue. It doesn't seem that there is any objective characterization D of Mach, such that knowing that *he* is a shabby pedagogue amounts to knowing that D is a shabby pedagogue (Castañeda 1966; 1968; Perry 2000, 2001b).

Second, we seem immune to certain sorts of misidentification with respect to self-knowledge. If we learn, in certain ways, that someone is in pain, then we cannot miss the fact that it is we who are in pain. That is, if Mach discovers that he has a headache in the ordinary way that a person discovers a headache, he can scarcely be wrong about *who* has the headache if the range of choices is "I/you/that man, etc." Of course he can be wrong if the range of choices is "Mach/Freud/Wittgenstein," etc., for he might not realize which of those people he is if he has amnesia.

Third, self-knowledge seems to play a unique cognitive role. If Mach desires that *he* do so and so and believes *he* can do so and so by executing such and such a movement, then he will execute that movement without further ado (Perry 1990b).

While (3) expresses self-knowledge, (1) does not. And yet (1) is, in a perfectly clear sense, a case of Mach believing something about himself. Mach *implies* that he was, in fact, a shabby pedagogue. It is because he was a shabby pedagogue that we take the belief expressed by (1) to be true. If it is Mach's being a shabby pedagogue that makes (1) true, then (1) was about Mach and expressed a belief about him. Nevertheless, (1), unlike (3), is not an expression of self-knowledge.

I shall sometimes use the term "self-belief" rather than "self-knowledge." Although "self-knowledge" is more familiar, it is somewhat misleading since the distinction between knowledge and mere belief is orthogonal to the issues I discuss. I take beliefs to be complex cognitive particulars that come into existence as a result of perceptions, inferences, and other events and influence the occurrence and nature of other beliefs and actions. I assume that two beliefs are involved here, one that Mach acquired when he stepped on the bus and one that he acquired a bit later when he figured out that he was looking at himself. I want to understand the difference between those beliefs. It is not sufficient, for this purpose, to note that (3) contains the word "I" where (1) contains the words "that man." This is why (3) is an expression of self-belief and (1) is not. But I want to know why the belief thus expressed is a self-belief.

3. Beliefs

My account will presuppose a fairly commonsense view of beliefs. The mind has ideas of things, properties, and relations. I'll call ideas of things "notions." A belief is a complex in which an idea of a property or relation is associated with the appropriate number of notions of things. The content of a belief is that the things the notions represent stand in the relation that the idea represents. A number of beliefs with a common notion is a "file."

The function of beliefs is to retain information picked up through perception, to formulate hypotheses, to allow for the combination and comparison of beliefs and the formation of new beliefs through inference, and to motivate actions that will promote one's desires if the beliefs are correct. The object an idea represents depends on its role in a psychological system within which beliefs play their role and on the way that system is set into the wider world. When Mach stepped on the bus, he formed a notion of the man he saw stepping on the bus. The fact that this was a notion—an idea of a thing—and not some other kind of idea depends on the way it functions internally; the fact that it was of a certain man (Mach, as it turned out) depends on external circumstances. If Mach had been looking at some other man, the very same idea would have been a notion of that other man.

We have unlinked notions of the same thing when the external factors that determine which thing the notions represent happen to make them represent the same thing, although there is nothing in the notions themselves, or the ideas associated with them, that reflects this identity. The beliefs involving those different notions of the same thing can function independently. They can arise at different times and can affect actions in quite different ways. A student who hears of Tully from a classics professor and Cicero from a philosophy professor may believe that Cicero was a philosopher but not be sure whether Tully was. Cases of this type have been examined extensively in the philosophy of language, usually known as "morning star/evening star" cases in honor of the alleged ignorance of the Babylonians that the same heavenly object (namely, Venus) was both (Barwise and Perry 1999; Crimmins and Perry 1989; Crimmins 1992).

It doesn't take long-dead philosophers or distant planets to generate such cases. I easily could have two unlinked notions of you, one formed as a result of reading articles by you and one formed as a result of seeing you in the library of my university, where you happen to be visiting without my previously knowing it. When I read your latest article, the first notion will become associated with new ideas based on what I read. When I see you in the library, the second notion will become associated with new ideas based on what I observe. I have two clusters of beliefs, or files, about you, each consisting of all the ideas associated with one of the two notions. It is theoretically possible for there to be two unlinked notions of the same object, which are associated with the very same ideas, so that a person has two exactly corresponding files for one object. But this seems unlikely. To have two unlinked notions of the same thing, we must have interacted with it in different ways or circumstances, or at least at different times, and some of the associated ideas are likely to reflect these differences.

Beliefs and files of the same object may motivate quite different actions. When I interact with you, my behavior will be guided by one file or the other, depending on the situation. I know how to write to you, as the author of the articles I have read, for they include your name and a department where you can be reached. Perhaps I write you a letter praising you for your kindness, sensitivity, and clarity of thought. I know how to speak to you as the person I have seen in the library, for the file corresponding to my first notion contains information about where you hang out and what you look like. Perhaps, based on my observations of you around campus, where I have seen you go out of your way to be kind, I also think you are sensitive. This leads me to associate the campus-based notion with the idea of sensitivity. This doesn't lead me to write you a letter. There is no information in the campus-based file about your name or address. I just walk up to you one day and compliment you on your kindness and sensitivity. As long as the files remain unlinked, the information in one will not affect the actions guided by the other. For example, I won't call you by your name when I see you, and I won't mention seeing you on campus if I write you.

In this example, I have two beliefs with the same content: that you are kind. The beliefs have quite different causal roles. This is explained by the different notions involved in the beliefs and the other different ideas with which those notions are associated. While the two beliefs have the same content, the files of which they are a part do not. What unifies files, and makes two beliefs about the same person relevant to each other, is not that they are about the same person, but that they contain the same notion or linked notions. One can have a file made up of a lot of information about different individuals mistakenly associated with a single notion, just as one can have two notions where there is only one object.

The phenomenon of having two unlinked notions of one individual is very common and doesn't require unusual circumstances or unusually confused people. I see my friend Al limping towards me but cannot yet recognize him; I form a notion of this person. At that moment I have two unlinked notions of Al. Certain of my beliefs about Al I have twice over, such as that he is a man. Others I have in one file but not in the other, such as that he has a limp. I accumulate information about him as he gets nearer; finally, I recognize him as Al. At that point the notions become linked; the newly acquired perceptual information combines with the old information, and I say, "Why are you limping, Al?" If the identification is tentative, the notions may retain their identity; if not, they may merge and become one.

4. Self-Ideas and Self-Notions

Mach's confusion is a special case of this sort, where the person he comes to recognize is himself. At the beginning of the episode, Mach had two notions of Mach. One he acquired when he stepped on the bus and saw what he took to be a man at the other end. The other is a *self-notion,* the sort of notion usually involved in his beliefs about himself. Beliefs involving one's self-notion have a special role in one's cognitive life, and we usually reserve the term "self-knowledge" for knowledge involving beliefs of this sort. But we need to say more about this special role.

The natural place to look is the ideas with which self-notions are associated. Consider the self-idea, the idea we would express as "being me." The notion involved in Mach's first belief isn't associated with this idea, while the one involved in his latter belief is. But what idea is this? We cannot identify the idea by the property it represents. Mach has two ideas of the property of being Mach, one which he would express with "being me" and one which he would express, directing his attention towards the man he sees, with "being him." The former is the self-idea but why? What makes one of the ideas that represents the property of being identical with Mach his self-idea and not the other? We might suppose that the self-idea is a complex idea, composed of the idea of identity in association with the self-notion. This seems plausible, but now we have just gone around in a circle: what is special about the self-notion is that it is associated with the self-idea; what is special about the self-idea is that it has the self-notion as a constituent.

Another approach is to characterize self-notions semantically. We can think of a self-notion on the analogy of the indexical "I." Just as utterances of "I" stand for their utterers, these special self-notions would be of the thinkers to whom they belong. All such notions, and any other notions linked to them, would be self-notions. Beliefs with self-notions as constituents would be self-beliefs. The notion Mach acquires when he looks at the fellow in the mirror is not a self-notion at the beginning of the episode, but becomes one when he recognizes himself and links his "that man" notion to his self-notion. This characterization leaves a question unanswered, however. After stepping on the bus, Mach had two unlinked notions of himself. Which of these should be characterized as a self-notion? They both represent Mach, so that can't be the difference between them.

An analogous question about language would be why we take "Ernst Mach" to be a name of Mach and the German "ich" to be the first person pronoun in Mach's idiolect. They both stand for Mach, so that isn't the difference between them. The answer to this question lies in the different ways Mach uses these terms in communication, both as speaker and as listener. He takes every utterance containing "Ernst Mach" to be about him, while he takes utterances containing "ich" to be about their speaker.[1] This is suggestive but doesn't quite get at the difference between Mach's two notions of himself. These notions are not devices for communication. They are not public; Mach does not produce them as an aid to securing recognition by others of his communicative intentions. Rather, they are parts of a system for the pickup, retention, analysis, discovery, and utilization of information by an individual. To explain what we mean by self-notions and how Mach's two beliefs differ, we need to explain the role of these notions and beliefs in this informational system.

5. Epistemic/Pragmatic Relations and R-Notions

Just as there is a special way of thinking about the person you are, there is a special way of thinking about the place you happen to be in, the way you think of the place you call "here."[2] Without realizing it, I could be in, say, Grand Island, Nebraska, at the same time I was

---

[1] I am ignoring the complication provided by other people named "Ernst Mach."

[2] I am ignoring the complication that "here" isn't usually a name or pronoun referring to a place but an adverb of place.

watching a video of Grand Island scenes. When I thought, "That city looks like a fun place to visit" as I watched the screen, I was thinking about Grand Island, but not as the place I was at, not as "here." Thinking for a bit about what is involved in thinking about a place as "here" will be helpful in seeing what is involved in thinking about a person as "I."

Suppose you are traveling and wake up in a hotel room in Grand Island. You look out the window and see rain. So you grab your umbrella before departing from the hotel. Here is a simple case of using information acquired perceptually to guide action. When you look out the window, you get information about the weather in Grand Island. And when you depart from the hotel, your decision to take an umbrella is vindicated because of the weather in Grand Island. The fact that the place whose weather you learned about when you looked out the window is the place whose weather determines whether you need an umbrella is crucial to the success of your use of the information. How do you have to think about Grand Island to facilitate this use of information to guide action?

One possibility is that you think about Grand Island via its relation to you—as the occupant of an agent-relative role. You think, "It is raining here" or "It is raining in this city." A second is that you think about Grand Island via some attribute that is independent of its relation to you, such as its name. The appropriate expression of your thought is "It is raining in Grand Island." These different ways of thinking correspond to different beliefs you might hold independently of one another. You look out the window and see rain: it's raining here. You watch TV and hear the reporter on the Lincoln station say "It is cloudy in Omaha, sunny in Lincoln, and raining in Grand Island": it's raining in Grand Island. You could acquire either belief without the other if you had forgotten that you were in Grand Island.

Let's imagine that you have a very poor memory and keep track of information by using three-by-five-inch cards. You have a number of these for the various cities you frequent, including one for Grand Island. When you hear the news report, you take out this card and jot "rain" on it. Then later we suppose you have forgotten where you are. When you look outside and see rain, you don't know which of the city-cards to write "rain" on. So you take out your "here" card and write "rain" on it. Call this card the "here-buffer." Information accumulates on this card: Grand Island Chevrolet and Isuzu is on the corner (here). The Grand Island Hotel is across the street (from here).

The Grand Island Rotary meets (here) for lunch every Wednesday. At last you figure out that you are in Grand Island. When you do, you transfer the information from the here-buffer to the Grand Island card, which already has "rain" on it. At that point the two cards would not only in fact contain information about the same place, but be recognized by you as doing so. Perhaps you put a rubber band around them to help you remember which city you are in. The cards are linked. They not only refer to the same place, but this coreference is reflected in the way you have them organized.

As time passes, you have to update your cards in various ways. But the relatively permanent features you have noted on your Grand Island card, such as "on Interstate 80" and "has an interesting museum," do not need to be changed just because you move on to Kearney or North Platte. This card is of Grand Island whether you happen to be there or not. Your "here-buffer," however, should be erased and unlinked from your Grand Island card.

Switching back to our little model of the mind, let's suppose there is a notion permanently associated as a self-notion and the idea of being at: the place "I'm at." This is the here-buffer. For the person who doesn't know where he or she is, the only here-notion will be a here-buffer. If the person has this buffer linked to a permanent notion for a place, that notion will be a here-notion as long as the link is in place.

Note that when the information that it was raining was only in your here-buffer, not linked to your Grand Island notion, you decided to take an umbrella: "If it's raining *here* I need an umbrella," no matter where "here" is. What you need to know to determine whether rain in a given city provides a reason for taking an umbrella is whether that city is the city you are in. On one hand, you know that the city you see out your window is the one you are in without knowing which city it is. On the other hand, having the information that it is raining in Grand Island from the radio, so it is associated with your Grand Island notion but not your here-buffer, will not motivate you to take an umbrella.

There are ways of getting information about the city you are in quite independently of which city it is. And there are actions the success of which depends on the conditions prevailing in the city you are in quite independently of which city it is. You can be motivated by information picked up in these ways to perform these sorts of actions without knowing where you are. Looking outside your window is a way of finding out what the weather is like in the city you are in, whichever city that happens to be. And taking an umbrella is an action that will be a good idea if it is raining in the city you are in, whatever city it happens to be. I shall say that there are "normally here-informative" ways of getting information and "normally here-dependent, here-directed, and here-effecting" ways of acting. It will be reasonable for normally here-informative ways of getting information about cities to motivate normally here-dependent actions whose success depend on that information. That's a theory-laden way of saying that reasonable people take umbrellas when they see rain out the window, even if they don't know which city they are in.

Taking an umbrella is a "here-dependent" action because its success depends on how things are here. It's successful if it is raining; if not, it's an unnecesary burden. It is "here-directed" because it is your situation here that your are going to change by doing it. And it is here-effecting because it is your situation here that it will effect. Sometimes one of these words is more appropriate than others, so I won't always repeat the whole phrase in what follows.

I shall call relations between an agent and another object—including places, material objects, and other persons—that support such special ways of knowing and acting "epistemic/pragmatic relations." The relation of *being at,* that holds between people and places, is an epistemic/pragmatic relation. There are many others. There are special ways to know about the material objects and people *in front of* one (open your eyes and look, reach out and touch) and special ways of dealing with them. There are special ways to know what a person is saying when *on the phone* (listen to the sounds coming out of the ear piece) and special ways of saying things to them (speak into the mouthpiece). Where R is an epistemic/pragmatic relation, we may speak of "normally R-informative ways of perceiving" and "normally R-directed/dependent/effecting ways of acting."

We are all masters of hundreds of such ways of gaining information about things and dealing with things. They allow us to gain information about and deal with things without having any way of identifying them independently of their relation to us. They allow us to interact with individuals we know about once we determine or bring it about that they stand in an epistemic/pragmatic relation to us. When you call, I use such methods to accumulate information about who is talking to me until I figure out it is you. Once I realize it is you, I link my "on the phone" buffer and my permanent notion for you and combine the information in them. I know you want to know what Elwood said last night, and I know I can tell you by talking into the mouthpiece, so I do.

The informational role of an *R*-notion is to serve as the normal repository for information gained in normally *R*-informative ways and as the normal motivator for normally *R*-effecting and *R*-dependent actions. The information I pick up by looking around me will, normally, become associated with my here-notions. The beliefs involving these notions will motivate actions such as taking an umbrella, whose success depends on the weather around me. The information that motivates a normally here-dependent action need not have been obtained in a normally here-informative way. If you know you are in Grand Island, you may take an umbrella because you heard on the radio that it was raining there. The action motivated by information gained in a normally here-dependent way may motivate actions whose success is not normally here-dependent. Seeing that it is raining, you may tell someone on the phone that it is raining in Grand Island, a statement that would be as true if you said it standing in Valentine or Ainsworth.

"Not knowing who someone is" usually amounts to having an *R*-buffer and a permanent file that are unlinked. There are two sorts of cases. In the earlier example about my friend Al, I had the buffer and need to pick the right file. But suppose instead that Al is a philosopher I have read and written to; he is in a room full of philosophers, and I want to talk to him but don't know what he looks like. I've got the file but need to pick the right buffer. A calendar entry, with a date and some appointments by it, is like a permanent file. It doesn't help if you don't know what day it is—if you don't know whether to think of the day as "today" or "tomorrow" or what. But it would be equally frustrating to be in the position the cartoon character Ziggy was once depicted as being in: he rips off one page on his calendar and reads "the next day" on the next page. We want calendars to give us objective representations of days so that we can use them to organize information objectively.

We might think of our notions as forming a multileveled system. At the top level are notions that are completely, or at least maximally, independent of relationships to us. These are "objective" representations. The lower levels contain buffers for various relationships to us, associated with various epistemic/pragmatic relations, of increasing specificity. These are the buffers. We pass information up the levels as we gather information about objects in epistemic/pragmatic relations to us, recognize them, and store the information in ways that are more independent of our relationships. We pass information down the levels when we recognize an object and act on it in ways that depend not just on its present relation to us, but other properties about which we have gathered information in the past.

When we think of beliefs, we are usually thinking about information stored at the relatively high levels. In fact, it is difficult to describe links between levels if we confine ourselves to "believes" and its cognates, as any philosopher who has dealt with the puzzles from the philosophy of language is aware. We have an additional vocabulary, including "recognizes," "takes to be," and "identifies," to describe linking. For objects and persons with which we are familiar, we have relatively rich permanent files, and it is the contents of these files that primarily count as our beliefs about the thing or person in question. Such beliefs provide the extra or incremental information we have to bring to bear on our interactions with these objects and persons, in addition to what we perceive about them at the time of a given interaction.

6. Self-Notions as R-Notions

I believe what is special about self-notions is that they are the normal repository of normally self-informative ways of perceiving and the normal motivator of normally self-dependent ways of acting. Identity is an epistemic/pragmatic relation.

We might call the example about Mach a "Castañeda example," after Hector-Neri Castañeda, who introduced a number of examples of this sort, and insightfully analyzed them (1966; 1967; 1968; see also Perry 1983/2000). They typically involve perceptual states that are not normally self-informative in the sense I am using the term, but nevertheless carry information about the person who is in the state. A person writes a biography of a war hero who was missing in action after a certain battle; in fact the person is the war hero but doesn't know it because of amnesia sustained in the battle. A philosopher asks friends about the new editor of *Soul,* not realizing he has been named the new editor. The state Mach was in, when he saw the man in the mirror, was the sort of state one is usually in when one sees that someone else, standing at some distance, is shabbily dressed, not when one sees oneself as shabbily dressed. (Or perhaps he realized that the person he was seeing was reflected in a mirror. Seeing someone in a mirror a short distance in front of one is a normally self-informative way of seeing, but seeing someone in a mirror at the end of a streetcar is not.)

Contrast with such cases what we might call "Shoemaker cases." Sydney Shoemaker has emphasized that we often find things out about ourselves in ways that are "immune to misidentification" (1963; 1970a; see also Evans 1982, especially sections 6.6 and 7.2). Suppose you are at a party. You bend over to pick something up and hear the ripping sound characteristic of trousers splitting. Then you feel a hot flush in your face. You are aware you are blushing. Now, who is it, of whose blushing are you aware? We are almost inclined to say that the question makes no sense. It is, of course, your own blushing of which you are aware. It's not that you cannot be aware of the blushing of others. You can see them blush. But you can't feel them blush; you can't come to know someone else is blushing in the way that you typically come to know you are.

Shoemaker emphasizes that immunity to misidentification should not be confused with incorrigibility or even privileged access, although they often go together. Compare blushing with being embarrassed. It seems that there is a way of knowing that one is embarrassed, the normal way, which is immune from misidentification, privileged, and at least close to incorrigible. In the pants-splitting episode, I can't be wrong that I am the one embarrassed (immunity); I know this in a way that is more direct and error free than anyone else can (privilege), and perhaps I can't be wrong about it (incorrigibility). But I can be wrong about whether I am blushing. I may know that I am embarrassed but be mistaken in thinking that I am blushing. I may not be in as good a position to tell if I am blushing as someone else who can see my face redden. So my judgment that I am blushing is neither incorrigible nor privileged. But one way this judgment cannot turn out wrong is this: the person I take to be blushing is blushing but is not me. Feeling one's face flush is a corrigible way of finding out that one is blushing; but it cannot be used to find out whether someone else is blushing, so if there is a mistake, it won't be about *who* is blushing, but only *whether* that person is blushing.

It is the way of finding out, not what is found out, that is immune to misidentification. One could look in a mirror and think that one saw oneself blushing, although it was someone else. I could believe

204 / THE SELF

that I am blushing, and believe it on the basis of observing someone blush, but be wrong about who it is.

These ways of knowing that are immune from misidentification are, I suggest, just a special case of "normally R-informative ways of knowing." A perceptual state S is a normally self-informative way of knowing that one is ϕ if the fact that a person is in state S normally carries the information that the person in state S is ϕ and normally does not carry the information that any other person is ϕ. Identity is an epistemic/pragmatic relation. Feeling one's face flush is a way of registering the information that the person identical with the feeler is blushing. Feeling hunger is normally a way of detecting that one's own stomach could use some filling. The feeling of needing to urinate is normally a way of knowing that one's own bladder is full. In each case, someone else can determine the same thing using a different technique. Perhaps you can see me blush even when I am not aware that I am blushing. Perhaps you know that my stomach is full, having noticed what I have put into it, while I am still in that charming interval between being full and feeling full. Parents often are better judges of how full children's bladders are than the children themselves are. But you cannot (normally) know that I am blushing or full or need to urinate in the way that I do.

Why do I say normally? There are some cases where this qualification is clearly required. Think about watching your hands as you type or play the piano. There is a characteristic way of seeing one's own hands and limbs and torso, a way in which one hardly ever sees anyone else's hands or limbs or torso. Yet when our teacher shows us how to play the piano, his hands could conceivably be mistaken for our own; one sees them in the same way as one sees one's own hands. Of course one would quickly spot the mistake, since however similar one's teacher's hands are to one's own, one cannot move them like one moves one's own.

Suppose that a way is developed to repair spinal column injuries by using an external shunt, which connects the column below the injury to the brain stem. One can imagine the shunt having an external connection for some reason. One could go on to imagine that there was enough similarity among people that one person's shunt could be plugged into another person's brain stem receptor so that coherent signals would arrive at the latter's brain about the bodily conditions of the former. (In fact, although this seems a possibility, I don't think we have any reason to suppose it is a very likely one.) When a fly landed on the first person's leg, the second person would feel the sensation and perhaps slap his own leg. The second person would be perceiving that there was a fly on someone's leg in the way that one normally perceives that there is a fly on one's own leg. Because of possibilities like this, I add the qualification "normally."

Paralleling normally self-informative ways of knowing are normally self-dependent/directed/effecting ways of acting. Towards the end of the movie *Spellbound,* we see Leo G. Carroll point his gun at Ingrid Bergman as she walks out the door. Holding the gun in this way and pulling the trigger is a way, in the circumstance in which there is a person in front of the agent, of killing that person. As the movie continues, we see Bergman continue to walk away, toward the door of Carroll's office, from his perspective. Slowly, we see the hand holding the gun turn, until the barrel of the gun is all that is visible on the screen. Then it fires. We know what Carroll has done and to whom. He has killed someone, and the someone is him. The way Carroll held and fired the gun was a normally self-effecting way of killing someone. Of course, if Carroll had a head shaped like a donut, he could have shot someone behind him. But normal people normally kill themselves when they shoot like that.

This is only a particularly dramatic case of a whole class of actions. Imagine George W. and Laura Bush seated across from each other at a boring dinner. Both know that the president is thirsty. Both may desire that he get a drink. The appropriate action for the president to take is the familiar one of reaching out and bringing the glass of water towards his lips. That is an action that will succeed if the agent is thirsty. It is a normally self-dependent/directed/effecting action. It won't do any good for the First Lady to perform it. At least, it won't help relieve the president's thirst. She should pick up the water and offer it to him. That is a way of relieving (or helping to relieve) the thirst of someone sitting across from you.

I suggest, then, that self-notions are those that have the special role of being the repository for information gained in normally self-informative ways and the motivator for actions done in normally self-effecting ways. This does not imply that there won't be a lot of information associated with the self-notion that is gained in other ways or that the beliefs and desires involving the notion don't motivate actions done in ways that are not normally self-effecting. Hume sent a rather favorable (anonymous) review of his *Treatise* to a journal; this was a normally other-affecting way of acting but was motivated by his desire for literary fame *for himself.* When he read reviews by others, he was picking up information about other people's view of the book he himself wrote. But most of the reviews he read in journals were about other people; reading a review is not a normally self-informative way of picking up information, just a way that occasionally provides information about oneself.

Recall that in our discussion about Grand Island and the "here-notion," we noticed that one could see it to be raining where one is and decide to take an umbrella without knowing which city one is in. The "here"-informative nature of the perception of rain, and the "here"-effecting nature of the action of taking an umbrella, guarantees that the information is relevant to the action. Similarly, one can gain information about oneself and apply it without knowing who one is, as long as the informaton is gained in self-informative ways and applied in self-effecting ways. A thirsty amnesiac, who doesn't know who he is, can still drink glasses of water, eat when hungry, and the like. Normally self-informative perceptions can trigger normally self-dependent actions without needing to be linked to any self-independent notion of oneself.

7. What's Special about the Self

There is one big difference between identity and most other epistemic/pragmatic relations, and this difference makes the self-notion virtually unique. With most of the other epistemic/pragmatic relations, a given agent will stand in relation to different objects at different times. The place one is at, the person to whom one speaks, the food in front of one—these things change all the time. This means that one cannot use a buffer tied to one of these relations to accumulate information about a given object. But one is always identical with the same person. My self-notion can be both tied to an epistemic/pragmatic relation and also serve as my permanent file for myself.

If one did not move from city to city, one could also use one's "here-buffer" as a permanent file for the city in which one happened to live. As a matter of fact, almost no one leaves the earth, so for most of us "this planet" will always refer to it; our "this planet" buffer can serve as a permanent notion for the earth. That's why I said, "virtually unique."

Suppose one not only did not move from city to city, but did not have anything to do with other cities. One never acquired information about them or performed actions whose success depended on them. Imagine a child who has no knowledge that there are other cities. Such a child would not even need a here-buffer. She needs no notions of cities (or "places one lives") at all.

We often talk about the weather as if rain and snow and sleet were states of times rather than states of places at times. We say, "It is snowing," rather than "It is snowing here." In effect, we handle relational phenomena with a one-place predicate. This works fine so long as we can take it for granted that we are all talking about the weather in the place where we are talking. We can also *think* about the weather in this way. So long as the place in which we pick up information about the weather and the place to which we apply that information are fixed as the same by factors outside of thought, we don't need to keep track, as the example about Grand Island showed. We can have a one-place idea for a relational phenomenon (see Perry 1986).

Consider, for example, the way we think about time before we learn about time zones. When we look at the kitchen clock or our watches, we learn about what time it is in the time zone we are in. Looking at one's watch is a normally time-zone-one-is-in-informative way of learning the time of day. If one had very long arms and very acute vision, or lived right where the time-zone boundary is, one might have to be careful. But it's pretty secure. Most of the actions we use our kitchen clocks and watches to guide are normally time-zone-one-is-in-dependent ways of acting. This is because many of the things we do, such as getting up, eating, going to school, going to bed, and the like, are things that people try to do when it is a certain time of day in the time zone they are in. As long as our dealings with time amount to using information gained in normally time-zone-one-is-in-informative ways to guide actions that are time-zone-one-is-in-dependent for their success, we have no reason to even be aware of the fact that the time of day is relative to time zones.

We need to be aware of this relativity when this condition is broken. A child may learn how things can go wrong when she speaks to her grandmother long distance or takes a trip that crosses time zones. Her watch still tells time accurately enough, but it is the time at home, not the time at the place the child is visiting. It is the time in the place the child is visiting that determines when lunch is served, when the good television programs come on, and when one is expected to go to bed.

Similar remarks apply to self-notions. For many purposes we don't need notions of ourselves at all. Consider the simple act of seeing a glass of water in front of one and drinking from it. The perceptual state corresponds to a relation between an agent and a glass of water. It is the state an agent is typically in when there is a glass of water in front of that agent. The perceptual state is then not only normally object-in-front-of-one-informative, but one-who-is-in-the-state-informative. The coordinated motion of hand, arm, and lips by which the agent gets a drink is not only normally object-in-front-of-one-effecting, but also agent-who-does-the-action-effecting. The identity between the perceiver and the agent is (normally) guaranteed outside of thought, by the "architectural" relations between the eyes and arms. One need not keep track of it in thought.

Another somewhat Tractarian (Wittgenstein 1921/1961, secs. 5.62ff; see also Moore 1962, pp. 302–3) or Carnapian (Carnap 1967, sec. 163) way of making this point is to say that the world as we perceive it does not include ourselves, but has ourselves as sort of a point of origin. Suppose I tell you that one point is at (4,5) and another point is at (5,4). As long as you can assume that the points have been given relative to the same point of origin, you know that to get from the first to the second you take one step away from the y-axis and one step towards the x-axis. But if they are given relative to different origins, you will not know what the relation between them is. Similarly, if I show you how things look through a certain pair of eyes focused on a table with a cup on it, you will know what an arm will have to do to intersect with the cup. You will, that is, if the arm is connected to the body to which the eyes belong, in the normal way. But you would have no idea how any arbitrary arm might have to move to perform that operation on the seen cup.

The self really comes in twice over when one notes that one is hungry or that one's hands are dirty, as both the perceiver and the object perceived. And when one eats or washes one's hands, one is both the agent and the object effected. The success of sticking one's hands under the faucet, as a response to the sight of one's own dirty hands, depends on a number of identities that are usually architecturally guaranteed. When one sees dirty hands in a certain way, it is the perceiver's hands that are dirty. When one washes hands in a certain way, it is the agent's hands that get clean. And when a perception of the first sort causes an action of the second sort in a more-or-less direct way, the subject of the perception is the agent of the action. We don't really need a self-notion to handle any of this. We will need one when we start to get information about ourselves in ways that are not normally self-informative.

In a world like ours, with mirrors, newspapers, lists of people who are supposed to be in various places and the like, we all have many ways of knowing about ourselves that are not normally self-informative. They are just the same ways we have for knowing about others. I can look at my ticket and see when I am to leave; you can look at my ticket and see when I am to leave. The ticket gives the same information in the same way to anyone who looks at it: John Perry is to leave at a certain time on a certain day. I need an objective notion of myself to pick up the information and a self-notion to put it to use. Unless I already have or acquire a notion of John Perry as John Perry, I won't have any place to store the information I get from the ticket. Unless this is or is linked to a self-notion, I won't end up performing the normally self-effecting actions that I need to perform (like getting out of bed) in order to get to the airport on time.

We have seen, then, that there are three kinds of knowledge about oneself. First of all, there is knowledge that doesn't require a self-notion: knowledge that is picked up in normally self-informative ways, is not combined with other sorts of information, and guides actions performed in nomally self-effecting ways. This is the sort of self-knowledge required to drink a glass of water or feed oneself. I'll call this "agent-relative" knowledge. It is knowledge represented in agent-relative ways.

The second kind of knowledge I'll call "self-attached" knowledge. This is knowledge of oneself, however obtained, that has been added to one's self-concept or self-file by being attached to the self-notion. This is the knowledge we express with the word "I."

The third kind of knowledge about oneself really doesn't strike us as self-knowledge at all. It is knowledge a person has about himself or herself that is not attached to the self-notion. This is the sort of knowledge that we have in the Castañeda cases. The biography writer knows that the war hero saved many lives but doesn't know that *he* saved many lives, even though he is the war hero. I'll call this "knowledge merely about the person one happens to be." If we remove the "merely," we get a sort of knowledge that we all have a lot of. I acquire a lot of knowledge about John Perry in the same way that others do; I look up the times of my classes in the *Time Schedule,* my phone number in the phone book, and so forth. This is knowledge of the person I happen to be. But normally I associate this with my self-notion. When I don't, so that I am a little like Castañeda's biography writer, it is knowledge *merely* about the person I happen to be.

8. Back to Mach

When he looks to the far end of the bus, Mach gets information about himself in a way that is not normally self-informative, but normally "person-I-am-looking-at" informative. This information doesn't pass into his self-notion; it is not combined with information gotten in normally self-informative ways. And it doesn't motivate normally self-dependent actions. Mach has knowledge about Mach, but it is not attached to his self-notion; it is knowledge merely about the person he happens to be.

Suppose Mach looks down at his own vest and sees a big piece of lint. (Mach himself provides us with a picture of the way one's front characteristically looks to oneself.) This is a normally self-informative way of knowing that a person has lint on his vest. If he had seen the lint in this way, he would have associated the idea of having a large piece of lint on one's vest with his self-notion. That's what I mean by saying that the self-notion is the repository of normally self-informative perception. Now, if Mach had desired not to have large pieces of lint on himself, he would have reached out and removed it in a way that works when the piece of lint is on one's own vest—sort of a downward brush with the side of the hand often works. If he has the desire to be lint-free associated with his self-notion and the idea of having lint on the vest is associated with his self-notion, we would expect him to take such a normally self-directed and self-dependent action. That's what I mean by saying that the self-notion is the motivator of normally self-dependent/directed/effecting actions.

But when Mach sees a piece of lint on the vest of the person in the mirror he does not act in this way. The information is not gotten in the normally self-informative way. It is not combined with the other information in the self-notion and doesn't lead to the action that works to remove lint from oneself.

At the beginning of the episode, Mach formed a notion for the person he saw, whom he took to be getting on the other end of the bus. This was a notion of himself but not a self-notion. We assume Mach knew who he was, and so he had a notion of Ernst Mach as having all of the well-known properties of Ernst Mach that was also a self-notion. But even if Mach had been in the middle of a bout of amnesia, he would have had at least a self-buffer, a notion tied to normally self-informative action and ways of knowing. Mach's beliefs change during the episode, in that he comes to link the new notion formed when he got on the bus with the old self-notion or notions that he has. If, after he has made the connection, he notices that the person in the mirror has a piece of lint on his vest, he will pick the lint off his own vest in the normally self-dependent and self-effecting way of picking lint off one's vest.

9. Self-Knowledge Problems Revisited

Now let's return to the issues about self-knowledge that seemed to stand in the way of the simple and straightforward account of the self as the person. These peculiarities of self-knowledge can be explained by taking self-knowledge to be a species of agent-relative knowledge.

These kinds of knowledge are, like self-knowledge, "essentially indexical." We use "now" and "today" to express our knowledge of what time it is and "here" to express our knowledge of where we are. These locutions are not reducible to names or objective descriptions, just as "I" was not. I cannot express what I mean when I say, "The meeting starts right *now*" by saying, "The meeting starts at *D*" for any objective description *D* of the present moment.

We are also immune to certain sorts of misidentification when we use certain methods of knowing. There is a way of finding out what is going on around one, namely opening one's eyes and looking (Evans 1981). Now, when one learns what is going on in this way, one can hardly fail to identify the time at which this is happening as *now* and the place as *here*. And, finally, the forms of thought we express with "now" and "here" seem to have a unique motivational role. If I want to do something *here* and *now*, I will simply do it.

So, to summarize: We cognize things, times, and places not only objectively, but via their present relationship to us—via agent-relative roles. There are ways of knowing and acting that are tied to such roles, and our knowledge exhibits immunity to misidentification relative to such roles. And knowledge via such roles plays a special motivational role. Finally, because different objects play these roles in our lives at different times, it is invalid to accumulate knowledge about them.

"Self" expresses an agent-relative role, that of identity. As with other agent-relative roles, there are special ways of knowing and acting that are associated with identity. If Mach had wished to know, during the interval while he was confused, if the shabby pedagogue he was seeing had lint on his vest, he would have had to walk over to him and look. If Mach had wanted to know if he himself had lint on his vest, he could have simply lowered his head and looked. Had he done this, he would have had no doubt about whom the lint was on. If Mach found lint and wanted to brush it off, he would engage in self-brushing, a quick movement of the hand across one's front that each of us can use to remove lint from our own vest and no one else's.

Unlike most of the other agent-relative roles, identity is permanent. I will have many things in front of me, talk to many people, be in many places, and live through many days in the course of my life. But there is only one person I will ever be identical with, myself. I never have to unlink my self-buffer from my John Perry notion. It can be a self-notion; it can just be my self-buffer. Accumulating information in one's self-buffer for life is valid, unlike accumulating in one's here buffer longer than one stays in one place, in one's today buffer for more than twenty-four hours, or in one's person-talked-to buffer longer than a conversation.

I also won't ever be on another planet, in a position to pick up information about that planet by looking around, and able to refer to the planet as "this planet" with a demonstration towards my feet. I would be relieved if this were necessary, but it is contingent. But my identity with myself is necessary. I do not claim that identity is the only necessarily stable epistemic/pragmatic relation. Perhaps it is necessary that I am in *this* universe. So, identity might not be unique in providing a necessarily stable agent-relative role, a buffer which can be used to accumulate information. But it's pretty special.

Earlier we rejected the straightforward account of self-knowledge as knowledge about a person by that very person. Now we can put forward an alternative. Self-knowledge is knowledge about a person by that very person, with the additional requirement that the person be cognized via the agent-relative role of identity. This agent-relative role is tied to normally self-informative methods of knowing and normally self-effecting ways of acting. When these methods are employed, there will be immunity of misidentification as to whom is known about or whom is acted upon. So, agent-relative knowledge and self-attached knowledge count as self-knowledge on this definition, but we don't need to count knowledge merely about the person one happens to be as self-knowledge.

Being the person known about in self-informative ways, and the person affected by actions done in self-effecting ways, can serve as a person's fundamental concept of himself or herself. In this way our self-conceptions have a different structure than our conceptions of other individuals of importance to us. If we understand the special way in which a person's self-knowledge is structured, we do not need to postulate anything but the person himself or herself for the knowledge to be about.[3]

---

[3] Various versions of the material on which this paper is based have been given in lectures at Stanford University, Notre Dame University, Cornell University, the University of Wisconsin at Madison, the University of California at Davis, Princeton University, and Santa Clara University. I am grateful for the many helpful comments that have been made on each of these occasions; I'd particularly like to thank David Copp and Carol White.

11

The Sense of Identity

1. The Philosophical Self

As I write this, I see a specific hand guide a specific pen across a specific page at a specific time and place. The hand belongs to John Perry—JP for short—one among the billions of persons who exist. I have a rather special relationship to JP, one which I can express by saying "I am JP." He is the only one among all the persons who ever have existed or will exist who happens to be me. It is natural to take this special relationship to be identity; there is just one thing, one entity, one metaphysical unit, that is both the person I call "me" and the person I am calling "JP." We are the same not only in this possible world but in every possible world that one could describe or imagine, for there is only one thing to imaginatively project into different circumstances. So it seems that I am necessarily JP and could be no other person.

But this doesn't seem quite right. In certain moments, there seems to be at least a trace of contingency in this relationship between JP and me. In fact, I see the world from his perspective and interact with the world through his body. But I can imagine being someone else, having the perspective of another person, with a different body, living in a different place, perhaps even during a different period of time. I can imagine being Napoleon exiled on Elba or Bertrand Russell puzzling about "the" or even Tom Nagel writing the article from which these thoughts are drawn (Nagel 1983).

These thoughts, that I am not John Perry, that I am Napoleon or Bertrand Russell or Tom Nagel, are surely false. But they do not seem to be utterly incoherent or even necessarily false. They seem like possibilities. Indeed, they seem to be possibilities of a sort we need to think about. It is important for various projects—in particular, literary

---

"The Sense of Identity" was written for this volume.

and philosophical projects—to imagine being other people, people with different needs, emotions, political views, social roles, incomes, interests, and so forth. What we are doing does not seem to be incoherent. We can first view the world from no point of view and then imagine what it would be like to have different points of view than the one we ended up with almost, as it seems, by accident. We can try to think things through from the new, imagined perspective. It is not like trying to reason from the premise that two plus two equals five, or that there are round squares or some other contradictory starting point. There are limits to what one can figure out by imagining that one is someone else, but they are more like the limits of reasoning from any other counterfactual premise than the roadblock of contradiction.

Ordinarily, I think of the world from my point of view, centered on the here and now. We might call this our "subjective" point of view, but I prefer the term "agent-relative" as being somewhat less encumbered with various alternative and not quite on-target meanings. The agent is the thinker, the speaker, and the doer. An agent-relative role is a role things play in the life of agents, different things for the same agent at different times and for different agents at the same time. What is in front of me is not what is in front of you, what is to my left now is not always what will be there tomorrow, and so forth. When we classify events, places, things, and people by the roles they play in our lives, we are adopting the agent-relative perspective. Events are divided into past, present, and future. Places are spread out in various distances, those that are here, those that are there, those that are near, those that are far, those to the left, those to the right, those above, those below, and so on. As to people, there is me, the person I am; you, the person I am addressing; my family; my neighbors; my generation; and so on.

But I can also think of the world from no point of view, impersonally or objectively. Events are classified by their relations with each other: before, after, or simultaneous with. There is no "now" in this way of thinking, or, rather, there are many; each class of simultaneous events provides a "now," but none of these "nows" is by nature more privileged than any others. Places are organized by their relation to one another or some absolute coordinate system. None of them is a "here" objectively; each is "here" relative to itself, "somewhere else" relative to other places. People are thought of by their names, perhaps, or their position in space and time. The representation, so long as it remains objective, has no "I"; I am in it, but everyone else who is in it is equally an "I" relative to themselves, and I am "someone else" relative to them. I realize that in this objective world, I am nothing special. The evidence of my senses counts for no more than anyone else's in arriving at truth; my interests and desires, and pains and pleasures count for no more than anyone else's in considering what is right.

If we think that facts are objective and the world is some sort of totality of objective facts, then it seems this view from nowhere is a more faithful representation of reality than any agent-relative view. And surely there is nothing it needs to leave out. If all the facts are objective, each can be represented impersonally. It doesn't leave out me; John Perry is in this view of the world, with all of his thoughts and experiences, desires and interests, and pains and pleasures. But what of the fact *I am John Perry*—the fact whose contingency seemed so important? Where is it in the world? How is that fact to be represented? Can I find it in the representation? It seems it cannot be found, for then the impersonal representation would build in a point of view; it would not be a view from nowhere. It would represent my view, accurate relative to me but not relative to you, for the thought "I am John Perry" is true when I think it but false when you do. But . . . *I am John Perry.* This is some sort of fact; if not an objective fact, then what kind of fact is it?

The last thought, the thought that I am one of those people in the objective world, that I am JP, is difficult, perhaps impossible, to express without the first person. It seems (a bit) contingent that I am JP. It does not seem contingent that JP is JP. That JP is JP is clear in the objective representation by the very fact JP is there. But the fact I am JP isn't in the representation; as we saw, if it were, the representation would cease to be objective. There is a problem here, which I'll call the "problem of the philosophical self."

Contemporary semantics ought to help us to understand what I think when I think "I am JP." It would thus provide the sense of identity and illuminate the philosophical self. But it is not clear how it does so. The standard semantics for indexicals and names identifies the propositions expressed by "I am JP" with the necessarily true proposition expressed by "JP is JP"—a thought anyone can think truly (Kaplan 1989). It identifies the proposition I express with "I am Napoleon" with the necessarily false proposition that JP is Napoleon. But that is not the proposition I am thinking when I imagine being Napoleon. Something seems to have been left out, after all. But from what has it been left out? Is there a side of the world left out by thinking that all facts are objective? Or is a part of ourselves left out when we take ourselves to be just flesh-and-blood persons with a perspective on the world? Or could it be something more boring— something left out of the semantics we have for understanding and describing our thought and language?

2. The Objective Self

One approach to this question is to find something special, other than JP, for "I" to refer to, at least in my philosophical moments, something that is, or might reasonably be thought to be, only contingently related to JP. Thomas Nagel, whose thoughts we followed in setting up the problem, advocates this approach in his essay "The Objective Self" (Nagel 1983). For each person who has a conception of an objective or centerless world, there is an objective self. This self perceives the world through the person's sensory systems and affects the world through the person's motor systems. But an objective self should not be identified with the person to whom it has this contingent connection. When the word "I" occurs in the expression of a philosophical thought of the sort described earlier, it does not refer to the person who expresses the thought. It refers to that person's objective self. When I thought, in this philosophical mood, "I am John Perry," the "I" referred to the objective self, the "John Perry" to an occupant of the world whose perspective the objective self has.

So Nagel gives the word "I," as used to express the philosophical thought, a new reference: the objective self, rather than the person. He also gives it a new sense, that is, a condition that identifies the reference: "the subject of this impersonal conception (1983, p. 229)."[1] In my impersonal conception of the world, there is a representation of John Perry, a rather full and robust one, since I know a lot about him or at least have many opinions. But its status, within the impersonal representation, is on a par with my representations of everyone else. Usually I have another rather intrusive representation of myself, one I

---

[1] I do not think Nagel intends to use "sense" as a theoretical term within a Fregean account of meaning, but simply as the way one is thinking of oneself when one uses "I" in this philosophical setting. At any rate, that's how I use it here.

might retain even if I forgot who I was, based on the contemporary information I can pick up about myself through feelings and perception and tied to the word "I." But in this philosophical mood this representation is attenuated; I bracket off most of this information, and I focus on the impersonal conception. But I cannot fully sever the connection; while what is conceived may be objective and impersonal, the mental conception itself belongs to only one of those people represented in it. That person has a special way of attending to it, which allows him to think of it as *this*. Whatever else I may be at the moment of objective philosophical thought, when all that can be has been bracketed and put aside, *I* am the subject of *this* impersonal conception.

I like Nagel's suggested sense for philosophical uses of "I," but not his suggestion of a new reference. I think of myself as saving Nagel's insight from his metaphysics.[2]

3. Nagel's Problem

Nagel asks, "How can a particular person be me?" and he immediately glosses this question as follows:

> Given a complete description of the world, from no particular view, including all of the people in it, one of whom is Thomas Nagel, it seems on the one hand that something has been left out, something remains to be specified, namely, which of them I am. But on the other hand there seems no room in such an objectively described world for such a further fact . . . everything true of TN is already in it. (1983, pp. 211–12)

This "further fact" is also described as "The fact that one of these persons, TN, is the locus of my consciousness, the point of view from which I observe and act on the world" (p. 213).

It will be worthwhile to pause for a moment to get more of a feel

---

[2] Nagel (1983) sets up a problem in his section 1 and 2. He outlines his solution in sections 6 and 7, and there he introduces the "objective self." These sections are the core of his paper, insofar as we want to understand his positive view, and they are all I try to deal with. Sections 3 and 4 are a critique of attempts to solve his problem without postulating an objective self. Sections 8 and 9 qualify his views in subtle ways, and if I dwell on them I find I have only a vague idea what is going on, so I am ignoring them. The version of this essay that appears as a chapter of Nagel's book *The View from Nowhere* (1986) has a number of changes.

of this problem. Let's imagine that Tom Nagel is standing next to an ordinary, if somewhat large, physical representation of a very large part of the world. I don't think we need to suppose that this is a representation of the whole world, for that is clearly a requirement that might bring large problems with it. It is just a representation of a lot of stuff, let's suppose. We can imagine a huge illustrated *Who's Who* with a photograph of Nagel, a listing of important events from his life and his accomplishments, and the same for a billion or so other people.

This is an objective representation in that it contains no indexicals or demonstratives, the linguistic expressions of the agent-relative way of classifying things. That is, the content of the representation doesn't depend on who wrote it, when, and where; we don't need to know this information to understand what is said. An objective representation has the same content, no matter who created it or uses it.

To appreciate the difference, consider telephone books, great objective repositories of useful information. Here is a typical entry from one:

    Chung, Dae-Hyun. 312–4312

There is no indexicality, no context sensitivity. There might be more than one Dae-Hyun Chung in the world, but this is an issue of ambiguity or something like it (see Perry 2001b), or perhaps even different words (see Kaplan 1990) and not indexicality. Once the words and meanings are clear, there is no part of the entry that directs us to context, the way "I" and "you" and "here" do.

We could have a telephone book that used indexicals. I could make such a book and give it to Dae-Hyun, with entries such as

    You. 312–4312
    Me 372–5191

Imagine that a philosophy department, as a sort of experiment or perhaps as a protest against realism and objectivism, puts out a nonobjective phone book with entries such as

    Me 41275
    Her. 45682
    That guy over there 73298

It probably wouldn't work very well. It would put a large cognitive burden on the user. To use it, one would have to learn and keep in mind facts about the creator at the time of creation of the phone book. Who was he—the "me" of the phone book? Who was he referring to with "her"? Who was he looking at when he wrote "that guy over there"? And so forth. Once one found out these answers, one would naturally *annotate* the phone book with names. Perhaps mine would look like

Her (Debra). 45682
That guy over there (Bratman) 73298

This seems to suggest that objective representations are truly useful.

But consider this old joke. Dae-Hyun is talking to a woman he has met at a party. "We've had a nice chat," he says. "I'd like to see you again. Can I have your phone number?" "It's in the book," she replies. "And what is your name?" Dae-Hyun goes on. "It's in the book, too," she replies.

Now suppose that Dae-Hyun has an ordinary phone book with him. You can even suppose he has memorized it. All the facts about people in the town and their names and phone numbers are in his possession. They are objectively represented—no indexicals, no demonstratives. This won't do him much good. It seems objective representations aren't always what we need, either. If the woman was making a joke and not brushing Dae-Hyun off completely, she might agree to annotate his phone book by writing "me" next to one of the numbers or pointing to a name and saying, "That's me." Then Dae-Hyun would have the information he needs. It's beginning to look like there is something really useful about the interaction of the two kinds of representations, as happens with these annotations. We'll return to this point later.

Back to Nagel. Let's suppose he is looking at the page from *Who's Who* and he recognizes himself as he reads the entry. He points to the entry and says, "That's me" or "I am (that) Thomas Nagel" or, for short, "I am TN." Now he has said something that expresses his discovery. Perhaps he annotates the objective representation. But *what* did he discover? It seems like it is a fact, but which fact? None of the ones listed in the entry, it seems, for he was able to grasp them without making the crucial discovery.

The point is not that there is some philosophical difficulty about how recognition happens. We can imagine there is a sort of pattern-matching with attributes of the newly presented objects and objects about which one already has information. When there are enough important matches, the two are identified. The problem is rather with what recognition means: the sense of identity and, in particular, the sense of self, of identity with the person doing the identifying. What possible worlds does this identification exclude? What fact about the world does it represent? What fact is it, the grasping of which constitutes recognition?

Let's try to supplement the entry to see if we can find the fact. Suppose Nagel was reading copy 5 of *Who's Who* in the Princeton Library on August 20, 1983, at 3 P.M. So, we add to the Tom Nagel entry, "Read, August 20, 1983, 3 P.M., *Who's Who*, copy 5, Princeton Library." This is an objective fact in the requisite sense. Have we added the fact the grasping of which amounts to Nagel's recognition that TN was him?

It seems we have not. For, again, Nagel could read that entry and not be sure. Then, if he figured it out, he would say, "Oh, I am TN." Maybe he even looks at his watch and at the spine of the volume where it says "copy 5." Still, there seems to be a gap between his reading and believing this additional fact about TN and the realization he expresses with "I am TN."

Let p be Nagel's current perception of the TN entry. We add to the entry, "Has perception p on August 20, 1983." So now Nagel learns from the entry that TN has p, which is the very perception he is having. How can he believe that and not believe he is TN? But of course he can, for he may not realize that the perception referred to by "p" is the very one he is having. This presents the same problem again. He could already know that p is the perception TN is having without realizing that p is his perception, and he is TN.

The pattern is clear; any fact, an objective representation of which we might add, seems not be to the fact in question. Nagel's grasping that fact, via the objective representation, will not constitute his realization that he is the TN whose representation he studies, for that fact could always be added to the objective representation and grasped by Nagel without his having that realization.

4. Against the Objective Self

Can the objective self rescue us? According to Nagel, for each person there is an objective self, which is contingently related to that person. So for TN there is an objective self; we can call it "OSTN." And for me there is one; we can call it "OSJP." These objective selves have no specific location in space and time, but they do have a special though contingent relationship to the body of the person whose objective self they are. When one has the philosophical thought "I am TN" or "I am JP," the "I" has the sense "the subject of this objective representation" and stands for one's objective self.

It is very difficult to see how the postulation of objective selves provides any solution whatsoever to the original problem. Part of that problem was to find what to add to our objective representation of the world to correspond to the fact that TN discovers when he discovers he is TN. Now we can add our objective selves to the representation, and it doesn't seem to help at all.

When TN looks at this representation, he gets the information that OSTN belongs to TN and, if he looks in the right place, that OSJP belongs to JP. He can know this and still remain confused about whether he is JP or TN. When he realizes he is TN and thinks, "I am TN," he is realizing something new that he didn't realize already, even though he did realize that TN was the one with OSTN. So it is very difficult to see how the postulation of objective selves helps at all with our problem. There is nothing in Nagel's explanation of objective selves to explain why TN's having an appropriate contingent relation to one objective self (OSTN) rather than another (OSJP, say) isn't an objective fact that can be represented in an objective way.[3] But, as we noted, anytime a fact is a candidate for being what Nagel grasps when he grasps he is TN, it turns out not to work. We add an objective representation of the fact to the objective representation Nagel is studying; he can in theory grasp the fact without grasping he is TN. This argument seems to disqualify the relation between TN and OSTN from being what Nagel grasps, as surely as it disqualified all of the other candidates we have considered.

5. The Subject of the Impersonal Conception

The new reference for "I" doesn't help. How about the new sense: "the subject of this impersonal conception of the world." Nagel says, having introduced objective selves:

---

[3] Sometimes it seems that there is meant to be only one objective self, rather than one to a person. This clearly won't help the present difficulty.

I believe this accounts for the content of the philosophical thought we have been trying to track down. It is qua subject of this impersonal conception of the world that I refer to myself as "I" in thinking the philosophical thought, "I am TN." Though the "I" is still essentially indexical, the content of the thought is that this impersonal conception of the world is attached to the perspective of TN and is developed from that perspective. . . . while it does not translate the thought into one about the world objectively conceived, it does identify an objective fact corresponding to the thought (1983, pp. 228–29).

The content for the missing thought seems to be

The subject of this impersonal conception is TN.

Let's acknowledge that when we have the philosophical thought, we are indeed thinking of ourselves in this way. So when I have my thought, I have an objective conception of the world. Now we are not thinking of a huge phone book or some other public representation, but my own internal objective, impersonal representation of the world. It is my conception; I am the subject of it. And so I think of myself in this way, and when I think "I am JP," I am thinking "the subject of this conception of the world is JP." Still, how does this solve the first problem?

It doesn't seem to solve it at all. My impersonal conception of the world can be added to the objective picture. We can add representations of a variety of impersonal conceptions; TN and JP are both subjects of impersonal conceptions, and we can represent those conceptions and their relation to TN and JP in the picture. And either TN's or JP's conception or both might conform to our picture. I might be thinking, "So the world has TN in it, and he has an impersonal conception of the world; call it 'ICTN.' It has JP in it, and he has an impersonal conception of the world; call it 'ICJP.'" Now, my use of "this impersonal conception" to refer to my own conception of the world, and of "ICJP" to refer to JP's, both refer to the same impersonal conception, mine. I can grasp that JP has ICJP and still wonder: am I JP?

But we must remember that Nagel said that when I have the experience of the philosophical self, I am thinking "the subject of *this* impersonal conception is JP," not "the subject of ICJP is JP." Do these two thoughts correspond to the same fact or not? If they do, then the fact that the subject of ICJP is JP can no more be the one I grasp when I realize that I am JP than any of the other facts we have considered.

Nagel said the thought was "essentially indexical," meaning that the "this" was crucial. Are there, then, somehow different facts corresponding to the two formulations "the subject of ICJP is JP" and "the subject of *this* impersonal conception is JP"?

There are. But to find them and put Nagel's insight into a place where we can say why it works, we need to get less profound for a while.

6. Information Games

I want now to go back to those annotated representations that we found so useful when we were thinking about phone books a couple of sections back. Let's shift to a slightly more lofty example, business cards.

Suppose I am trying to raise money for Stanford and I am to meet a potential donor. First I come into the room and see a well-dressed person in front of me. Remembering my coaching from the Development Office, I smile, walk over, and extend my hand and say, "Hello, I am John Perry."

What happened here? There was an object in front of me. I have a technique for finding out about objects in front of me: I open my eyes, look straight ahead, and notice things about them. I used this technique and discovered that there was a nicely dressed, important-looking person in front of me.

I also have techniques for doing things to persons who are in front of me. I can introduce myself by looking at them while I say, "I am John Perry." I can offer to shake hands by moving towards them and extending my hand. These are appropriate if there is a person in front of me—but not if there is an apple or a wall or a hungry bear in front of me. There are different things I know how to do with apples in front of me. I can take a bite out of them by executing a certain complex movement: extending my arm, grabbing them, moving them to my mouth, etc. The same movement probably would be a way of irritating a hungry bear.

"Being in front of" is what I called an *agent-relative role;* it is a role an object can play in someone's life. With it are associated *epistemic* and *pragmatic* methods—methods for finding out about the object and methods for doing things to the object (more accurately, doing things the success of which depends on facts about the object). I will speak of picking up information *via* a role and acting *via* a role.

When I introduced myself and extended my hand, I was applying information I picked up *via* the *being-in-front* role to guide an action I performed via that very same role. This is a very basic *information game.* I'll call it the "straight-through" game.

But now let's return to my story: the potential donor gives me her business card. This card is full of objective representations: her name, Sarah Toorich, let's say; her company; her position in it; and so forth. There is nothing on the card indicating her relation to me.

When she leaves, I put the card in my shirt pocket. For the rest of the day, I carry around this objective representation—objective in the sense given; there is nothing in the card that makes its content depend on who created it. It does not contain words like "I" and "here" and "you."

In the beginning, the information I had about Sarah Toorich, the way she looked and where she was in relation to me, was drawn from my perception of her as the person in front of me. When she gave me her business card, I had objectively represented information but it remained *attached* to that perception. Attached information is like what I called annotated information earlier, except that there is no bit of language serving as an annotation. Instead of having the annotation "that person over there" attached to the business card, I simply have it connected with my perception of Toorich.

When I left the room, I retained the objective representation, the business card, but it was detached from any perception. It was no longer tied to a perception of Sarah Toorich. What possible use can such detached information—objectively represented information—be to me? It can be useful to me if I am later in a position to interact with Sarah and can recognize her. Once I have done that, I reattach the objective representation to a perception and use it to guide my action.

Later on I run into this same person and I say, glancing at the card, "Hello, Ms. Toorich. How are things going at the old Megabux.com today?" In this case I apply information I got in one situation, via one role, in a new situation. I will call this the "detach and recognize" information game. I use "detach" because I detached the information about Ms. Toorich from any agent-relative role. I use "recognize" because I had to encounter her again and to recognize her in order to reattach and use that information already "on file" to guide my action.

The detach-and-recognize information game is very much a part of human life. It works because we live in a world with certain very general characteristics—a "Strawsonian" world, we might say, remembering some of the themes of Peter Strawson's *Individuals* (1959). The success of our actions often depends on the relatively enduring properties of objects. We are often in a position to gather information about objects that will be relevant to the success of actions we may want to take when we encounter them in other situations. And we are often able to recognize objects we encounter more than once. Put these characteristics together, and we have a world in which the detach-and-recognize information game is a very useful technique.

The detach-and-recognize information game also fits into a more complex information game, involving communication. What we want to communicate in many cases is detached information that each party to the communication game can use to recognize and attach to the particular perceptions they have of the object the information is about.

This detach-and-recognize picture should help us put objective representations in their proper place. They are basically *supplements* to agent-relative ways of thinking and acting. They give us information that helps us get ourselves into position for such thought and action. Some of the information helps us recognize who we are interacting with, such as my memory of what Sarah Toorich looks like and the aids to recognition I jotted on the back of the card. Other information helps us decide what to do once we are interacting: she is a wealthy but pensive businesswoman, so ask for a contribution to the accounting and philosophy joint major.

Although the world is objective, all perception is by agents at certain times and all actions are performed by agents at certain times. An objective representation with no possibility of being reattached to its source via some agent-relative role that supports pragmatic techniques is quite useless. If I can't recognize Sarah Toorich, for example, the bits of information about her I have stored in my shirt pocket, or my palm pilot or in the little mental three-by-five-inch note card that I like to think comprises my internal objective conception of her, will be of no practical value.

Philosophers often think of beliefs as relations to propositions, which are objectively true or false, not true from one perspective and false from another. In describing the belief, we may identify the constituent of the proposition indexically, but that doesn't mean we think that those indexicals play a role in the belief. If I say, walking in Manhattan, "Nagel believes this city is exciting," I am saying what Nagel believes but not how he is thinking of it. He might be in London as I speak, unable to think of New York City as "this city." But what I say is true, for he has an objective way of thinking of New York City and associates the property of being exciting with it. This part of the picture of belief, as relations to propositions, is at the heart of the ordinary philosophical way of thinking of belief as a "propositional attitude."

This picture gets at only part of the story—the detached, objective, and impersonal part. It can't handle the derivation of and reapplication of detached beliefs. The problem that Nagel finds, that leads to the postulation of the objective self, is just the problem of this missing element in the philosophical picture of belief merely as a propositional attitude. This is the point I'll now try to make vivid and plausible, going back to our exciting example.

Suppose I am in a meeting with Toorich and four or five other businesspersons around a big table. I have been very organized, and I have all of their business cards in front of me. Unfortunately, I don't know who is who. I jotted down some "aids to recognition" on the back of the cards when I received them, but I have momentarily forgotten that I did so. Unless I can *orient* myself, the information is useless. That is, I need to reattach my objective information, my business cards, to the agent-relative roles that are occupied. That is my theory-laden way of saying I need to recognize the people in front of me.

Now suppose the person across from me is Sarah Toorich. Echoing Nagel, in what objective fact does this consist? When I recognize *her* as Toorich, what fact do I grasp?

This question has a false assumption, namely, that recognition *ever* consists in grasping an objective fact or, rather, consists in that *and nothing more*. This is simply not so. Recognition is quite a different concept than belief in a proposition. Recognition consists of attaching objectively represented information to some perception, readying the information for use. Recognition will occur *because of* the beliefs one has; one compares the attributes of the objects one perceived with the attributes of the objects one has on file. But recognition does not *consist in* having those beliefs. I recognize Sarah Toorich as the person in front of me or as the person on the phone or as the person I see in the distance. Recognition is a prelude to action that is then partly guided by belief, a prelude to the application of detached information (or misinformation, for that matter).

7. Self-Recognition

I too have business cards, which say on them that my name is "John Perry" and that I am a professor of philosophy at Stanford and give my phone number, e-mail, etc.

Suppose, now, that on my way to work one morning I fall off my bike and hit my head and get temporary amnesia. I'm sitting on the curb wondering who I am. I reach in my pocket and pull out the business cards I have there, searching for a clue. Here is a card that says, "Sarah Toorich, Megabux.com." Could that be me?

I think people with amnesia don't forget whether they are male or female. I'm not sure. Suppose that in this case I have. I can check to see if I am a male, say, by feeling the beard on my face. This is an agent-relative way of finding this out, quite different than how I would check to see if you were a male, which I could usually do just by looking. I am wondering if I am Sarah Toorich. I eliminate this possibility since "Sarah" is usually a woman's name.

Next I pull out one of my own cards, "John Perry." That is a bit more plausible—but who knows?

I want to analyze this situation much like I did the situation where I was sitting with the businesspeople around a table. I had plenty of objectively represented information about the people in various positions relative to me but wasn't able to apply it, since I didn't recognize them. That is, I couldn't attach the detached representations I had to the agent-relative roles they occupied and thereby make some use of the information on the cards.

I claim that identity is an epistemic/pragmatic relation and self is an agent-relative role consisting of identity with the agent. This is elaborated in essay 10, so I'll be brief. Identity is a relation that brings with it certain epistemic and pragmatic techniques. There are special ways of getting information about the person one has the relation of identity to—one's self—and special ways of acting so as to have effects on that person. We are happy when children learn to recognize when they need to go the bathroom. We are happy when they learn to feed themselves. It's quite a different ability than feeding other people, which we usually discourage children from doing too much of.

To get back to me in the example, we left me sitting on the curb after a bike accident wondering who I am and staring at my own business card. In the argument, I am comparing this situation with that earlier one, where I had objectively represented information about several people around a table but couldn't apply it.

I have just finished making my first point about that, which is that *self* is an agent-relative role, being identical with the agent, that is associated with special epistemic and pragmatic methods—just as *being in front, being on the phone,* and other agent-relative roles are.

My second point is that in our own case, as in the case of others, objective representations of facts are useless in and of themselves and don't ever explain any action. Their importance is as potential parts of attached representations.

This is just the situation I am in as I sit on the curb. My business card gives information about me. Lots of people have this card. For each of us, it is of interest as a potential component of applied information. Toorich has my card. Next time she sees me, if she recognizes me, she can apply this information to me, greet me with my name, make some wisecracks about the philosophy business, and so forth.

I have here in my hand this same objective information, this same potentially attachable information. It would be very useful for me to know my name, etc. But before I can use the information, I need to recognize myself, to associate the information with my self-notion. Luckily, being a man of very orderly habits, I jotted down a few salient facts about the appearance of each person on the back of these business cards to help me recognize them, and I even did this in my own case. So I know that John Perry has gray hair and a gray beard and wears glasses. I use self-informative techniques for getting information in this case, just as I use persons-around-the-table techniques in the other. For example, I can see a little bit of my moustache just by looking down towards the floor, and I can see that it is gray. I can also see the rims of my glasses. So I figure out who I am, call home, find out what kind of health insurance I have, and check into the hospital until my amnesia clears up. When I check in, I will consult my business card and say, "I am John Perry. I teach philosophy. My phone number is 372–5191." These remarks will be guided by the card, because I have attached it to my self-notion, my repository for information acquired in normally self-informative ways, and other information gotten in more neutral ways, such as business cards, that I have determined to be about me (see essay 10).

8. The Missing Facts

Let's review the bidding. We've got the philosophical uses of "I," and we want to know what their content is, what I grasp when I think, in the right Nagel-inspired mood, "I am JP." The strategy is to see this as a special case of self-recognition, and self-recognition as a special case of recognition, and recognition as involving an interplay of the objective and the agent-relative. I've developed a certain picture of recognition and applied it back as far as the ordinary cases of self-recognition. But I haven't really said what the missing facts were.

As I sit on the curb before recognition, looking at my business card, I am in a situation in many ways analogous to Nagel's problem situation. I'm looking at an objective representation of me, my business card with my name and some essential information about me. As I stare at it, I learn all of these facts about JP. He is a philosophy teacher at Stanford, has a nifty e-mail address, and the like. Then I realize I am JP. What does this knowledge consist in?

Here is where modern semantics seem a bit unhelpful.[4] Since the 1970s we have been told that names and indexicals are "directly referential" or "rigid designators." That means that "I," as said or thought by me, and "JP," as a name that stands for me, contribute exactly the same thing to the propositions in which they occur, namely me. Suppose you say "John Perry was born in Nebraska." What does the world have to be like for what you say to be true? Do I have to be named "John Perry"? It seems not. After all, it was true that I was born in Nebraska before I was named John Perry. I would have been born in Nebraska even if I had been named "Elwood Perry" or something like that. Although you exploit that I was in fact named "John Perry" and not "Elwood Perry" when you say "John Perry was born in Nebraska," it is not part of what you say. What you say seems to be just that a certain person, who in fact is named "John Perry," was born in Nebraska.

Now suppose I say, "I was born in Nebraska." What does the world have to be like for what I say to be true? Well, it would have been true even if I hadn't said it. My saying it didn't have any effect on where I was born. The word "I" stands for me because I used it, but that isn't part of what I said. What I said would have been true if I

---

[4] With some exceptions, of course; I particularly recommend my *Reference and Reflexivity* (2001b).

hadn't said anything; what I said was true because a certain person was born in Nebraska, period. But, then, what I said with my utterance of "I was born in Nebraska" was just what you said with your utterance of "John Perry was born in Nebraska." The truth conditions are just that a certain person, me, was born in Nebraska—the same for both statements. That's more-or-less what philosophers mean by saying that both names and indexicals contribute the thing they stand for (in this case, me) to the propositions they express.

But then

(1) JP is JP.
(2) I am I.
(3) I am JP.

all seem to say the same thing, to express exactly the same proposition, the trivial and necessary proposition that John Perry is John Perry. But only (3) expresses recognition.

Here is where I think modern semantics needs some supplementing, which is relevant to our problem. The basic point is a distinction, or, rather, a pair of them, one for language and one for thought:

what is said by a statement, versus the truth conditions of the statement

what is believed in virtue of having a belief, versus the truth conditions of the belief

Let's go back to your utterance of "John Perry was born in Nebraska." We agreed that it is not part of what you said that I, or anyone, is named "John Perry." You are talking about people and states, not names. Still, your actual utterance would not have been true if I hadn't had that name. Actually, an enormous number of things have to be the case for your utterance to be true. We just don't count most of them as part of what is said. What we are *usually* interested in is the conditions put on the subject matter—the things the names and indexicals stand for. That's what we count as "what is said." But the other truth conditions are very relevant to understanding how communication works.

Suppose, for example, that a drunk in a bar says something scurrilous about Nebraska and then asks in a loud voice, "Is anybody here from Nebraska?" Trying to be helpful, you say "John Perry is from Nebraska." The drunk will learn that someone from Nebraska is named "John Perry." That wasn't what you *said,* but it was something that had to be true for your statement to be true—not for *what you said* to be true, but for the *statement you actually made,* your utterance, to be true.

Still things aren't too bad. He knows that someone from Nebraska is named "John Perry," but he doesn't know that I am. However, if I, trying to be helpful, had said, "I am from Nebraska," even though I would have said the same thing, things would have been a lot worse. He would have learned that someone right in front of him, who he could reach out and hit, was from Nebraska. That wouldn't have been part of what I said. But he knows that for my utterance to be true, the person "I" refers to must be from Nebraska, and he knows that "I" refers to the person who uses it, and he saw that I used it. I would have been in trouble.

Here we have two ways of saying the same thing, and yet they have different *total* content. The facts that explain the difference are part of the truth conditions but not part of the *subject-matter* truth conditions. They are conditions on the things we take for granted in getting to the subject matter, namely, the words themselves. For this reason, I call them "*reflexive* truth conditions" or "*reflexive* content."

This same distinction carries over to thoughts. In essay 10 I discussed self-notions. Notions are ideas we have of things, and self-notions are ones that are tied to the epistemic and pragmatic methods tied to identity. The self-notion is the repository of information picked up in self-informative ways and the motivator of self-effecting actions. I said that my self-knowledge involves my self-notion and is to be distinguished from mere knowledge of the person I happen to be. When I was sitting on the curb reading John Perry's business card, I had knowledge about John Perry, the person I happened to be. Self-recognition consisted of linking that idea of John Perry with my self-notion; I came to believe not only that John Perry worked at Stanford, but that I did. Before the episode of self-recognition, I believed the proposition that John Perry worked at Stanford, and this is what I believed after the episode. But I believed it in a different way. Call my self-notion "*self*$_{JP}$." My later belief can be true only if *self*$_{JP}$ belongs to someone who works at Stanford. That is the reflexive content of my belief, and it is this that changed when I recognized who I was.

Now let's turn to more-or-less normal cases of self-recognition. Suppose I am watching a home movie made in the late 1940s by my uncle Art. It is a movie of some kind of family reunion, and there are a lot of kids in the movie—my cousins. At one point I recognize a certain small child as myself. "That's me," I exclaim to the generally uninterested audience.

Let's suppose the child in the movie is wearing a cowboy costume and playing with guns. Suppose further that I don't remember playing with guns and didn't even realize that I ever had played with guns. Because I recognized the five year old playing with guns as me, I added to the information associated with my self-notion that I used to play with guns. This addition is what motivates my saying, "I used to play with toy guns!" Note that that the word "I" gives us a self-directed way of asserting things; the sentence I used is a way for any speaker to assert of himself that he used to play with toy guns.

In essay 10 I discussed knowledge that is acquired in normally self-informative ways, such as one's current state of hunger or the nature of the scene before one. It is the job of the self-notion to handle such things. As a result of recognizing that I am the five year old in the movie, I include a bit of information gotten in a way that is not normally self-informative with information that is. The person who I know in a special way to be hungry and tired I also know to have once played cowboys and shot toy guns wildly at his cousins.

To get at what I learned, we again need to appeal to the reflexive level of the content of my thoughts. Before the recognition occurred, I had two beliefs which we can describe structurally:

The idea of being tired and hungry was associated with n_{SELF}.
The idea of playing with guns was associated with $n_{kid\ in\ movie}$.

The subject-matter contents of these beliefs imply that a single person was tired, hungry, and played with guns. This is because the two notions are of the same person, me. But this identity is not reflected in the structure of my beliefs and so cannot affect my behavior. In particular, I won't say, "I played with guns as a child." Once recognition has occurred, the information is associated with my self-notion,

The idea of playing with guns is associated with n_{SELF}.

and I will say, if asked, that I played with guns as a child.

What, then, is the sense of identity, of self, in this kind of situation? It is the complex of epistemic and pragmatic relationships that are most closely and firmly tied to the self-buffer. "The child playing with guns is me" is true if the person whose present perspective is *this one,* whose present sensations are *these,* whose present thoughts are *these,* and the like.

The core of our self-concepts, our sense of identity, our sense for "I," is as the knower of facts about objects that are playing agent-relative roles with respect to us and as the agent of actions that are done in agent-relative ways. I am the possessor and controller of these hands; the subject of these sensations; the maker of these movements; the sufferer of these pains; and so forth. Since only we can attend to our own inner sensations and thoughts and only we can see our bodies and things around us from our perspective, it is natural to use the demonstrative "this" to express the aspects of our self-concept.

Russell once held a "hidden description" theory of the self, with similarities to the view being put forward here (1956). "I" was a "hidden description" for "the person with *this* sensation," where the "this" signifies an act of internal attention. (Russell also held a hidden-description theory of proper names; a sophisticated version of this genre of theory was developed by Searle, a "cluster theory." No *one* description corresponds to a proper name but a cluster of weighted descriptions [1958].)

My view of our self-concepts is something like a cluster version of Russell's hidden-description theory of the self, in that I think we have a cluster of things in our self-concept, which are weighted in their importance to us. The most important and inseparable from us are the things in our own mental life that we can attend to and think of with an internally directed "this." In spite of this similarity with hidden-description and cluster theories, however, my view is quite different on the crucial matters of reference and truth. My self-notion is a notion *of* me because it is *my* self-notion; that is, (i) it is a self-notion, one whose informational role is as the repository of information gotten in normally self-informative ways and that motivates normally self-directed actions; and (ii) it is mine. It is *of* me even if it is full of false stuff. My self-concept or self-file, the notion together with the ideas associated with it, is *of* me because the notion is of me, not because I am uniquely denoted, or denoted at all, by the combination of ideas.

It seems to me quite likely that I am in fact denoted by some weighted combination of the properties that seem to me to be most certainly mine. Such properties are the core of our self-concept, because these properties are very hard to separate from ourselves. The degree of difficulty is not uniform, however. We can easily imagine cases in which certain hands are not mine, even though I see them in the peculiar way that people normally see their own hands. We can even imagine cases in which the stomach, the state of which I learn about through my feelings of hunger, is not mine. These cases are not likely to occur, and perhaps only a philosopher would have the curiosity and patience to think (however superficially and incompletely) about the rewiring of nerves and the like that could produce these results. These are open only to philosophical doubt.

The separability of my own sensations and thoughts is at least an order of magnitude more difficult. Can we imagine any circumstances in which the sensations I can attend to are not mine? where the thoughts that run through my head are not mine? John McTaggart Ellis McTaggart (1927, vol. 2, p. 67) criticized Russell on the grounds that the hidden description "this sensation" may be "improper," like "the senator from Nebraska," which doesn't denote anyone, since there are two senators from that state. I may be certain that I am one of the people with *this* sensation, but how do I know that I am the *only* person with this sensation? McTaggart asksed. On Russell's own theory of descriptions, "The person with this sensation is John McTaggart Ellis McTaggart" would be false if more than one person had the sensation in question. How can he know for sure, McTaggart asked, that no one else has the sensations he can attend to?

This isn't a problem for my account for two reasons. First, unlike Russell, I'm not trying to build up a hierarchical account of our knowledge with self-knowledge somewhere near the bottom. I'm as sure that I am the only person having my sensations as I am that I am the only person with my body and brain. Moreover, even if someone else could also have my sensations and thoughts, it wouldn't be a problem, since I don't need to salvage a proper description from my self-concept to have it be a self-concept of *me*. My self-beliefs are a cluster, but it is not the denotative properties of this cluster that make the beliefs about me. So even if against all odds I am not the unique person with these sensations and thoughts or even the best fit for the weighted sum of the most central parts of my self-concept, it would still be a concept of me.

Suppose, for example, that David Chalmers is right about qualia, and so I am wrong (see Chalmers 1996; Perry 2001a). When I think, "I am a philosopher who is right about qualia," I think something false; the indefinite description fits Chalmers, not me, even though this is a very important part of my self-concept. Suppose further that as a result of his research on the mind, he has learned how to share his thoughts and sensations with others when he wants, so his thoughts are accessible to them in just the way their own thoughts are and seem like their own thoughts. He often picks on me, transmitting thoughts via my mouthful of gold fillings, confusing and embarassing me in various ways with the thoughts and sensations of a younger man. Perhaps on Thursday I am thinking about myself, and the central-most part of my self-concept is as a person who is right about qualia and has *these* thoughts and *these* sensations. But in fact this is a moment when most of the sensations and thoughts are Chalmers's; they are either not mine at all or not mine uniquely and at least are more his than mine, since the sensations are caused by his bodily states in the normal way, and he controls the thoughts. So, just considering the sensations and thoughts, my self-concept fits him better than it fits me. When we add that he is a philosopher who is right about qualia—an important part of my self-concept—he is clearly a better fit. Still, my self-concept is a very confused concept of me, not an accurate one of him.

This is, of course, in several ways a very fanciful example, certainly implausible and perhaps utterly incoherent. I do not claim to have a clear idea of the difference between Chalmers's causing me to share *his* sensations and Chalmers's causing me to have sensations and thoughts that are mine but are like his; I suspect there is no difference in what is conceived, and the latter is the correct way to describe it. But I'm not completely certain. Perhaps someday I'll have a clear conception of the difference or a clear idea of why the first option makes no sense. The bottom line is that even if it does make sense the way I described it and my self-concept fits Chalmers better than it does me, it is still a concept of me, and I am thinking about myself when I use it. On my view there need be no metaphysical necessity connecting me with some aspects of my self-concept, nor do I even have to be the one it fits best, for my self-concept to be of me. If there are such metaphysical necessities and a good fit, that's fine. But it is not what makes my self-concept of me.

9. Content and Cause

My account has two sides, and it is not yet clear how they fit together. On the one hand, I have said that objective knowledge is incomplete; it is made to supplement agent-relative knowledge. Nagel's problem is trying to find an objective proposition, belief in which would give him the requisite self-knowledge, but this cannot be done. On the other hand, I seem to have offered a proposition that does exactly that. I said that the difference between the thought expressed by, say,

(4) JP teaches philosophy.

and that expressed by

(5) I teach philosophy.

is that the belief expressed by (5) has the truth condition.

(6) The owner of n_{SELF} teaches philosophy.

where n_{SELF} is my self-notion. But (6) is an impersonal representation of an objective fact that could be added to the impersonal representation. What is going on?

The point that must be kept in mind is that (6) is not an additional belief that I gain. Most people don't have any *beliefs* about their self-notions. They don't have the requisite concepts to have these beliefs. One doesn't need to have beliefs about one's self-notion in order to have beliefs whose truth imposes requirements on it.

Another fanciful example will perhaps make this clear. Suppose I am giving a lecture about this theory to a group of students who accept everything I say as very plausible, if not absolute gospel. I give my own self-notion a name, "n_{SELF}," and write on the board

(7) The owner of the self-notion n_{SELF} is from Nebraska.

I believe (7); I have the requisite concepts to have such an odd belief. But believing (7) is not the same as believing that *I* am a philosopher. Each of the credulous students in the class will believe (7), but they won't thereby believe that they are from Nebraska.

The picture is this. There is a certain way of believing things that involves the self-notion. It is a species of attached beliefs, beliefs that involve the kinds of notions I call buffers, that are tied to epistemic/pragmatic relations. What is special about these notions, and the beliefs that contain them, is the way they work, the way they are connected to our perceptual and motor systems. So, the beliefs that involve these notions will have subject-matter content, but also they will have a different information-handling role, and hence a different causal role, than other beliefs with the same content.

But their content and their causal role need to mesh. The subject matter of a belief involving a self-notion will be the person that owns the notion; that is who such beliefs are about. It will be true if that person has the requisite property. I have a belief that involves the association of the idea of being from Nebraska with my self-notion. The subject-matter truth conditions of this belief is that John Perry is from Nebraska, because John Perry is the owner of the belief. That content does not guarantee that it is a self-belief, however.

What guarantees this is the self-notion. Because it involves a self-notion, its truth puts conditions on that notion. The truth of a belief always puts conditions on the ideas that make it up, just as the truth of an assertion puts conditions on the words that make it up. These conditions are not *what is believed* or *what is asserted*. But they are features of a belief's truth conditions that tie into its structure. The level of reflexive content is where content and causal role meet.

Now consider (7). Belief in (7) will never explain much of anything. But having a belief with (7) as its reflexive content will explain a lot. Anyone can believe (7), but only I can have a belief with (7) as its reflexive content, because only I can have a belief with my notions as components. The fact that being from Nebraska is associated with my self-notion explains why I say, "I am from Nebraska" when asked where I am from. That sentence provides a self-directed way of saying that someone is from Nebraska. If someone opens a booth giving $100 to Nebraska natives (not a very likely occurrence), I would rush over and claim my money. All of the Nebraskans lined up at the booth will have a belief with a reflexive content like (7) but involving their self-notion instead of mine. In every case, it's not what they believe that explains their lining up, but how they believe it: via their self-notion. But if they believe that they are from Nebraska, via their self-notion, their belief cannot be true unless their self-notion belongs to someone from Nebraska.

Let's return to Nagel and the giant illustrated *Who's Who*. We add to the TN entry,

(8)   TN is the owner of $n_{SELF\text{-}TOM\ NAGEL}$.

This obviously wouldn't help. Nagel could believe (8) without believing *he* was TN. What he could not do is have a belief with (8) as its reflexive content without realizing he was TN.

On this theory, then, there is no need for any kind of facts other than objective facts, no need for true propositions that are "subjective" or agent-relative. The facts that make it the case that Tom Nagel realizes he is TN are all objective facts. But the propositions that need to be true for him to realize this are not all ones he needs to believe, and the propositions he believes when he realizes this need not include all of those that need to be true for him to do so. The reflexive content of his belief needs to be true, but he need not believe it.

As far as I can see, all facts are objective; I'm not very clear what would make a fact not objective. The proper place for the term "objective" to draw a contrast seems to be in the context of belief, knowledge, and representation. I do not think that all knowledge is objective or impersonal or should be or could be. If knowledge is to be useful, the objective knowledge must be supplemented by agent-relative knowledge.

10. The Objective Self

Nagel in his philosophical mood attends to a certain feature of his inner life, an impersonal conception of the world, which includes an impersonal representation of TN with as many impersonal representations of facts about him as one may want. The inner conception labelled "TN" is a notion of Nagel, but not Nagel's self-notion. That is, Nagel does not apply the information associated with TN to his own situation, and he does not add information gotten via self-informative ways of knowing to the concept of TN. What makes the TN notion a notion of Nagel is not that it plays the self-notion role in Nagel's life, but that it is in fact used as a repository for information about Nagel gotten in other ways. In this way, Nagel's TN notion is like his notions of other people in the world. His knowledge of TN via his objective representation, before the moment of recognition that he is TN, is what we called "knowledge merely of the person he happens to be" in essay 10.

At this moment, Nagel's situation is formally analogous to mine of sitting on the street corner after my bike accident. I have a sheaf of business cards. It seems to make perfectly good sense to hope that I am this fellow, hope I am not this other fellow, and wish I were this third fellow, although I'm sure I'm not. Similarly, it seems that Nagel, because of philosophy, has severed the connection between his self-buffer and his Nagel notion. It makes sense for him to imagine being various people, to be glad or unhappy he turns out who he turns out to be.

In this mood, one wants to say that there are many people I might be, who I might have been, and who I might turn out to be. There is a sense of contingency in Nagel's being Nagel and me being John Perry. The saying "There but for the grace of God go I" can just mean that John Perry could have had a lot of bad luck and wound up as a pauper or a tax lawyer, rather than having the privilege of earning a living as a philosopher. But it might also have a different meaning, that John Perry might be just as fortunate as he is, but *I* might not be; I might be someone else doing something else, even tax law.

For familiar reasons, these thoughts are hard to make sense of. Since I am John Perry, there is just one person, one thing, one metaphysical being, who is both John Perry and I. When I take John Perry and myself to another possible world, I take only one thing. So I can't very well manage to find a possible world in which I am there and he is not or I am there and he is there but I am not he. Identity is a necessary relation; if A and B are one in any world, they are not two in any world. So what possibilities can correspond to these various thoughts we have been considering; what can we make of the felt sense of contingency we have in these philosophical moods?

11. Searching for Contingency

For a contingent connection, we need two things. Here we have Tom Nagel attending to his own impersonal conception of himself, which we label "TN." There is not a contingent connection between Tom Nagel and TN, because there is just one thing that is both Tom Nagel and TN. There is no room for subject-matter contingency.

How about the issue of how the thought fits into the world? Can we find that kind of contingency? That gives us two more things to deal with; one is the thought "I," which has the sense, in this situation, of "the subject of *this* objective conception," since everything else in Nagel's self-buffer has been bracketed off. This is an agent-relative role that Nagel in fact plays; he is the owner of both the objective conception and the thought directed at the objective conception, which is the sense expressed by the word "I" in this case. Can we find a world in which we have that very thought, that in fact is Nagel's, but Nagel is not the owner of the thought and hence not the subject of the conception attended to? I don't think so.

That leaves us with one thing to work with, the link between Nagel's impersonal conception of himself and Nagel. It is a conception of Nagel. But does it have to be a conception of Nagel? Is there a possible situation in which this very conception, the very one Nagel attends to, is *not* a conception of him, but of someone else?

What makes it a conception of him? There are basically two routes from the conception to Nagel. One is the route of *fit*. If Nagel's TN file includes enough detailed true stuff about Nagel and nothing very important that is false, then he is probably, if not the unique object denoted, at least the best overall fit for the conception. Is there a possible situation in which we have Nagel with his conception and his thought but the conception doesn't "pick out" Nagel—he is not the best fit? This seems fairly straightforward. We just have to imagine a world in which Nagel is very different than he in fact is and someone else is very much like Nagel in fact is. Of course, Nagel's objective conception of TN may include some necessary truths; perhaps the objective conception includes who TN's parents are and what his DNA is. But it seems like enough repeated applications of finding alternative denotations should eventually lead us to the desired situation, although it's hard to be sure. However, I don't think *fit* is what makes the conception a conception of Nagel in the first place. It might be a conception of Nagel even if it not only might not fit him, but did not fit him.

The other route from the conception back to Nagel is from the conception to its *origin*. Nagel's impersonal conception, his TN notion in my language, belongs to a network of such notions. The network began when Nagel was born or perhaps a bit before. His parents saw him at birth; they formed notions of him. They showed him to relatives and friends and neighbors who formed notions of him. They sent telegrams and wrote letters to distant friends and relatives, perhaps enclosing photographs. They named him, creating a convention whereby people could use the name "Tom Nagel" to refer to him. A network of notions, in different people's minds but linked to others by the purposeful exchange of information aimed at affecting one another's notion of the same person, was set in motion. It continues. I'm part of it, and so are you, since we are talking about Nagel in this essay. And so is he. Normally, he would be the one and only person whose self-buffer was also a part of this network, because normally one can use one's self-buffer as one's permanent notion of oneself. But that's not the notion he is using. Conception has gone temporarily impersonal, so his TN notion is not his self-buffer.

Now suppose Nagel thought he was Gil Harman, to pick what one assumes is a somewhat unlikely example. Don't worry about how this happened. Nagel has a notion of Gil Harman, part of the Gil Harman network, started by Gil Harman's parents. For some reason Nagel has mistakenly come to think that he is Gil Harman. So he has linked his self-buffer with his Gil Harman notion. Asked his name, he says, "I'm Gil Harman." Asked his opinion about cognitive science, he says, "I think it is just terrific," and so forth. Now, the point is, he would be wrong. When he said or thought, "I am Gil Harman," the "I" would refer to Tom Nagel and the "Gil Harman" would refer to Gil Harman. They wouldn't refer to the same thing, even though they were guided by the same internal notion.

Now, what of his thought, the one he expresses with "I am Gil Harman"? We *might* have here what I have elsewhere called a mess (Perry 2001b). That is, we have one notion which is of two different people, with the information thoroughly mixed together. It is the same sort of thing that happens when you think you recognize someone as someone you have met before, but you are wrong, and it takes you a long time to figure it out. However, let's assume we don't have a mess. Although Nagel has gone a bit crazy, he is a little worried and keeps his identification with Harman tentative—the way I might have kept my identification of myself as John Perry tentative in the example until I had called my wife and checked that she recognized me. Think of a link between the self-buffer and the Harman notion, rather than an outright merger.

Even though it is tentative, his identification is false. What would it have taken for it to be true? At the subject-matter level, there is no way it could have been true. Nagel is Nagel, Harman is Harman, and there is no possible world in which two things are one. But what possibility did Nagel confusedly have in mind? He thought that his impersonal conception of Gil Harman was of him, that is, that he was the origin of the network of which his impersonal conception of Gil Harman was a node. And that, I think, is a possibility. We can imagine worlds in which the very network that started with Gil Harman's birth started with Nagel's instead. We can imagine worlds in which the Sherlock Holmes network does not start with Arthur Conan

Doyle at his study, but with the birth of a child destined to be a detective on Baker Street.

Given this exercise, it seems clear what we ought to say about Nagel's philosophical thought "I might not be TN." The kernel of this, "I am not TN," is not a subject-matter possibility. But it is a conceptual possibility, a possibility for how our thoughts fit into the world. What is at issue here is one of the alternative contents, what I elsewhere have called "network content." (2001b)

At this point one may protest that this is certainly *not* what Nagel is supposing when he supposes he is not TN; he is not supposing something about the network that ties his and other notions of him to past talk about him and eventually his parents' decision to call him "Tom." But I agree that he is not supposing that. What Nagel is supposing is that he is not TN; he is supposing something impossible. What I am finding is a contingency that is not *what* he is supposing, but is a contingently false thing, such that if it were true his supposition would be true. What he actually supposes would not be true, but if this contingent falsity were true, his supposing would be a supposing of something else which would be true. This contingent falsity is the condition that his impersonal TN conception does not have Nagel as its origin. That falsity is one of the contents of Nagel's thought "I am not TN," and its contingency accounts for the phenomenology of the philosophical moment, the moment when the connection Nagel has with TN seems a matter of contingency, accident, and, I would have thought, in terms of choosing a philosopher one might want to be, good luck.

References

Where collections in which articles have been reprinted are listed, page references will be to the collections.

Alston, William, and Jonathan Bennett. 1984. Identity and Cardinality: Geach and Frege. *The Philosophical Review* 93: 553–67.

Barwise, Jon, and John Perry. 1999. *Situations and Attitudes.* Stanford: CSLI Publications.

Bennett, Jonathan. 1967. The Simplicity of the Soul. *Journal of Philosophy* 64: 648–60.

Bergson, Henri. 1912. *Matter and Memory.* London: Allen and Unwin.

Blanchette, Patricia. 1999. Relative Identity and Cardinality. *Canadian Journal of Philosophy* (June): 205–23.

Brandt, Richard. 1969–70. Rational Desires. *Proceedings and Addresses of the American Philosophical Association* 43: 43–64.

Butler, Joseph. 1736/1975. Of Personal Identity. Dissertation 1 of *The Analogy of Religion, Natural and Revealed, to the Constitution and Course of Nature (with Dissertations).* London. Reprinted in Perry (1975), 99–105.

Care, Norman S., and Robert H. Grimm, eds. 1969. *Perception and Personal Identity.* Cleveland: The Press of Case Western Reserve University.

Carnap, Rudolf. 1958. *Introduction to Symbolic Logic and Its Applications.* New York: Dover.

———. 1967. *The Logical Structure of the World.* Berkeley: University of California Press.

Castañeda, Hector-Neri. 1966. He: A Study in the Logic of Self-Consciousness. *Ratio* 8: 130–57.

————. 1967. Indicators and Quasi-Indicators. *American Philosophical Quarterly* 4: 85–100.

————. 1968. On the Logic of Attributions of Self-Knowledge to Others. *Journal of Philosophy* 65: 439–56.

Chalmers, David. 1996. *The Conscious Mind*. New York: Oxford University Press.

Chisholm, Roderick. 1969. The Loose and Popular and Strict and Philosophical Senses of Identity. In Care and Grimm (1969): 82–106.

————. 1976. *Person and Object*. La Salle, IL: Open Court.

Clarke, Samuel, and Antony Collins. 1736. *Clarke-Collins Correspondence*. London.

Coburn, Robert C. 1960. Bodily Continuity and Personal Identity. *Analysis,* 117–20.

Cohnitz, Daniel. Forthcoming. The Science of Fiction: Thought Experiments and Modal Epistemology. *The Vienna Circle Institute Yearbook 2002*. Dordrecht: Kluwer.

Crimmins, Mark, 1992. *Talk about Beliefs*. Cambridge: MIT-Bradford Books.

Crimmins, Mark, and John Perry. 1989. The Prince and the Phone Booth: Reporting Puzzling Beliefs. *The Journal of Philosophy* 86: 685–711.

Dennett, Daniel C. 1978. Where Am I? In Dennett, *Brainstorms*. Cambridge: MIT-Bradford Books, 310–23.

————. 1987. *The Intentional Stance*. Cambridge: MIT-Bradford Books.

Dummett, Michael. 1973. *Frege*. London: Duckworth.

Evans, Gareth. 1981. Understanding Demonstratives. *Meaning and* ———— ——— ———— Parret and Jacques Bouveresse. Berlin and New York: Walter de Gruyter, 280–302.

————. 1982. *The Varieties of Reference*. Oxford: Oxford University Press.

Feldman, Fred. 1969. Geach and Relative Identity. *Review of Metaphysics* (March): 547–55.

Flew, Anthony. 1951. Locke and the Problem of Personal Identity. *Philosophy* (January): 53–68.

Frege, Gottlob. 1884/1960. *Grundlagen der Arithmetik.* Breslau, 1884. *The Foundations of Arithmetic,* 2nd ed. Translated by J. L. Austin. New York: Northwestern University Press, 1960.

Gale, Richard. 1969. A Note on Personal Identity and Bodily Continuity. *Analysis* 29: 193–95.

Geach, Peter. 1957. *Mental Acts.* New York: Routledge.

————. 1962. *Reference and Generality.* Ithaca: Cornell University Press.

————. 1967. Identity. *Review of Metaphysics* 21, no. 1: 3–12.

————. 1969. A Reply. *Review of Metaphysics* 22, no. 3: 556–59 .

————. 1972. *Logic Matters.* Berkeley: University of California Press.

Grice, H. P. 1941. Personal Identity. *Mind* 50. Reprinted in Perry (1975), 73–95.

Hall, Lisa. 1993. *Individualism, Mental Content, and Cognitive Science.* Doctoral dissertation, Stanford University Philosophy Department.

Hume, David. 1741/1968. *Treatise of Human Nature.* Edited by L. A. Selby-Bigge. Oxford: Oxford University Press. (Originally published 1739–1741. London: John Noon).

————. 1741/1975. Of Personal Identity. Part 4, section 6, of Hume (1968). Reprinted in Perry (1975), 161–72.

Israel, David, and John Perry. 1990. What is Information? In *Information, Language and Cognition.* Edited by Phillip Hanson. Vancouver: University of British Columbia Press, 1–19.

————. 1991. Information and Architecture. *Situation Theory and Its Applications,* vol. 2. Edited by Jon Barwise, Jean Mark Gawron, Gordon Plotkin, and Syun Tutiya. Stanford University: CSLI Publications, 147–60.

————. 1996. Where Monsters Dwell. *Logic, Language, and Computation.* Edited by Jerry Seligman and Dag Westerstahl. Stanford: CSLI Publications, 303–16.

Israel, David, John Perry, and Syun Tutiya, 1993. Executions, Motivations and Accomplishments. *The Philosophical Review* 102 (October), 515–40.

Kaplan, David. 1989. Demonstratives. *Themes From Kaplan.* Edited by Joseph Almog, John Perry, and Howard Wettstein. New York: Oxford University Press, 481–563.

———. 1990. Words. *Proceedings of the Aristotelian Society, sup. vol.* 64: 93–119.

Leichti, Terrence. 1975. *Fission and Identity.* Doctoral dissertation, University of California, Los Angeles.

Lewis, David. 1976. Survival and Identity. In Rorty (1976), 17–40.

Locke, John. 1694. *Essay concerning Human Understanding,* 2nd ed. London.

———. 1694/1975. Of Identity and Diversity. Book 2, chap. 27, of Locke (1694). Reprinted in Perry (1975), 33–52.

Mach, Ernst. 1914. *The Analysis of Sensations.* Translated by C. M. Williams and Sydney Waterlow. Chicago and London: Open Court.

McTaggart, John McTaggart Ellis. 1927. *The Nature of Existence.* Cambridge: Cambridge University Press.

Marks, Charles E. 1980. *Commissurotomy, Consciousness, and Unity of Mind.* Montgomery, VT: Bradford Books.

Martin, C. B., and Max Deutscher. 1966. Remembering. *Philosophical Review* 75: 161–96.

Moore, G. E. 1962. *Philosophical Papers.* New York: Collier Books.

Nagel, Tomas. 1971/1975. Brain Bisection and the Unity of Consciousness. *Synthese* 22. Reprinted in Perry (1975), 227–45.

———. 1983. The Objective Self. *Knowledge and Mind.* Edited by Carl Ginet and Sydney Shoemaker. Oxford: Oxford University Press, 211–32.

———. 1986. *The View from Nowhere.* Oxford: Oxford University Press.

Nelson, Jack. 1970. Relative Identity. *Noûs* (September): 241–60.

Nozick, Robert. 1981. *Philosophical Explanations.* Cambridge: Harvard University Press.

Nunnberg, Geoff. 1993. Indexicality and Deixis. *Linguistics and Philosophy* 16: 1–43.

Parfit, Derek. 1971/1975. Personal Identity. *Philosophical Review* 80. Reprinted in Perry (1975), 199–223.

———. 1973. Later Selves and Moral Principles. *Philosophy and Personal Relations.* Edited by Alan Montefiore. London: Routledge and Kegan Paul.

Peirce, Charles S. 1935. *Collected Papers, Volume V.* Cambridge: Harvard University Press.

Penelhum, Terrence. 1970. *Survival and Disembodied Existence.* London: Routledge and Kegan Paul.

Penelhum, Terrence, and J. J. MacIntosh, eds. 1969. *The First Critique.* Belmont, CA: Wadsworth.

Perry, John. 1970a. The Same F. *Philosophical Review* 79. Reprinted as essay 1 in this volume.

———. 1970b. Review of Wiggins's *Identity and Spatio-Temporal Continuity. Journal of Symbolic Logic* 39, no. 3 (September): 447–48.

———. 1972. Can the Self Divide? *Journal of Philosophy* 69 (September): 463–88. Reprinted as essay 3 in this volume.

———, (ed.). 1975. *Personal Identity.* Berkeley and Los Angeles: University of California Press.

———. 1975a. Personal Identity, Memory, and the Problem of Circularity. In Perry (1975), 135–55. Reprinted as essay 5 in this volume.

———. 1976. The Importance of Being Identical. In Rorty (1976), 67–90. Reprinted as essay 8 in this volume.

———. 1976a. Review of Williams's Problems of Self (1973). *Journal of Philosophy* 73 (July): 416–28.

———. 1983/2000. Castañeda on He and I. *Agent, Language, and World.* Edited by James E. Tomberlin. Indianapolis: Hackett, 15–41. Reprinted in Perry (2000), 77–100.

———. 1986. Thought without Representation. *Proceedings of the Aristotelian Society,* sup. vol. 60: 263–83.

———. 1990a/2000. Individuals in Informational and Intentional Content. *Information, Semantics and Epistemology.* Edited by Enrique Villaneueva. Cambridge: Basil Blackwell, 72–189. Reprinted in Perry (2000), 233–51.

———. 1990b. Self-Notions. *Logos* 11: 17–31.

———. 1994. Intentionality. *A Companion to the Philosophy of Mind.* Edited by Samuel Guttenplan. Oxford: Basil Blackwell, 386–95.

———. 1998. Myself and I. *Philosophie in Synthetisher Absicht* (A Festschrift for Dieter Heinrich. Edited by Marcelo Stamm. Stuttgart: Klett-Cotta, 83–103.

———. 2000. *The Problem of the Essential Indexical and Other Essays,* expanded edition. Stanford: CSLI Publications.

———. 2001a. *Knowledge, Possibility, and Consciousness.* Cambridge: MIT-Bradford.

———. 2001b. *Reference and Reflexivity.* Stanford: CSLI Publications.

Prior, Arthur. 1957. Opposite Number. *Review of Metaphysics,* 196–201.

———. 1966. Time, Existence, and Identity. *Proceedings of the Aristotelian Society,* 183–92.

Putnam, Hilary. 1975. The Meaning of "Meaning." *Mind, Language, and Reality,* Philosophical Papers, vol. 2. Cambridge: Cambridge University Press, 215–71.

Quine, W. V. 1953. *From a Logical Point of View.* Cambridge, MA: Harvard.

———. 1953a. Identity, Ostension, and Hypostasis. In Quine (1953), 65–79.

———. 1973. *Roots of Reference.* La Salle, IL: Open Court.

———. 1981. *Theories and Things.* Cambridge: Harvard University Press.

Quinton, A. 1962/1975. The Soul. *Journal of Philosophy* 59. Reprinted in Perry (1975), 53–72.

Reid, Thomas. 1785/1975. *Essays on the Intellectual Powers of Man,* chapters 5 and 6 of the essay of memory. Reprinted in Perry (1975), 107–18.

Rorty, Amélie, ed. 1976. *The Identities of Persons.* Berkeley and Los Angeles: University of California Press.

Russell, Bertrand, 1921. *An Analysis of Mind.* London: Allen and Unwin.

———. 1929. *Mysticism and Logic.* New York: W. W. Norton and Co., Inc., Pub.

———. 1956. On the Nature of Acquaintance. *Logic and Knowledge.* Edited by R. C. March. London: George Allen and Unwin, 125–74.

Searle, John. 1958. Proper Names. *Mind* 67. 166–73.

———. 1992. *The Rediscovery of the Mind.* Cambridge, MA: MIT Press.

Shoemaker, Sydney. 1963. *Self-Knowledge and Self-Identity*. Ithaca: Cornell University Press.

———. 1969. Comments on Chisholm. In Care and Grimm (1969), 107–27.

———. 1970a. Persons and Their Pasts. *American Philosophical Quarterly*, 269–85.

———. 1970b. Wiggins on Identity. *Philosophical Review* 79. 529–44.

Sidgwick, Henry. 1907. *Methods of Ethics*. London: Macmillan and Co., Ltd.

Smart, J. J. C. 1959. Sensations and Brain Processes. *Philosophical Review* (April): 141–56.

Strawson, P. F. 1959. *Individuals*. London: Methuen.

Swineburne, Richard G. 1974. Personal Identity. *Proceedings of the Aristotelian Society 1973–74*. Oxford: Blackwell, 231–47.

Unger, Peter. 1990. *Identity, Consciousness, and Value*. New York: Oxford University Press.

Vesey, G. 1974. *Personal Identity: A Philosophical Analysis*. Ithaca: Cornell University Press.

Wiggins, David. 1967. *Identity and Spatio-Temporal Continuity*. Oxford: Blackwells.

Williams, Bernard. 1957/1973. Personal Identity and Individuation. *Proceedings of the Aristotelian Society*. Reprinted in Williams (1973), 1–18

———. 1960/1973. Bodily Continuity and Personal Identity. *Analysis*. Reprinted in Williams (1973), 19–25.

———. 1966/1973. Imagination and the Self. *Proceedings of the British Academy*. Reprinted in Williams (1973), 26–45, 118ff.

———. 1970/1973a. Are Persons Bodies? *The Philosophy of the Body*. Edited by Stuart F. Spicker. Chicago: Quadraut Books, 137–56. Reprinted in Williams (1973), 64–81.

———. 1970/1973b. The Self and the Future. *Philosophical Review* 79. Reprinted in Williams (1973), 46–63.

———. 1973. *Problems of the Self*. Cambridge: Cambridge University Press.

Wilkes, Kathleen. 1988. *Real People: Personal Identity without Thought Experiments*. New York: Oxford University Press.

Wittgenstein, Ludwig. 1921/1961. Tractatus Logico-Philosophicus. *Annalen der Naturphilosophie.* Translated by D. F. Pears and B. F. McGuinness. *Tractatus Logico-Philosophicus.* London: Routledge & Kegan Paul, 1961.

———. 1953. *Philosophical Investigations.* Translated by G. E. M. Anscombe. New York: MacMillan.

Glossary

There is a quite a bit of redundancy in the eleven essays that comprise this collection. I haven't done much to eliminate it, for it seemed likely that most readers will focus on one essay at any given time, and would prefer them to be relatively self-contained. In this spirit, I've added a little more redundancy with this glossary, which covers several points that come up in various essays, but are not always explained completely. In some cases trying to write an item for this glossary has led me beyond what I said in the essays.

Criteria of Identity This term is used in three related ways in discussions of personal identity. First, it has a straightforward meaning based on the way the component expressions are used in ordinary speech. "Criteria" are indications we rely on to establish something; good criteria are indications that have some kind of blessing from science, tradition, or official policies. In this sense, criteria of identity for X may or may not have anything to do with the nature of X's, or the meanings of the terms we usually use to talk about X's. For example, fingerprints are criteria for identity for persons. The accuracy of fingerprint evidence for personal identity has been established scientifically and is admitted in courts of law. However, the reliability of the fingerprint test for personal identity doesn't need to be grasped in order to know what persons are, or to understand the term "person". Sameness of fingerprints is neither necessary nor sufficient for personal identity on *conceptual grounds* alone. We can conceive of worlds in which a person's fingerprints regularly change, so sameness of fingerprints is not necessary for personal identity. And we can conceive of worlds in which different people with the same fingerprints are found, so sameness of fingerprints is not a sufficient condition for personal identity.

The second use stems from Austin's translation of Frege's *Grundlagen der Arithmetik*. Austin uses "criterion of identity" for Frege's

"Kennzeichen für die Gleichheit" (1884/1960, pp. 73, 73e). It is clear that Frege's identity criteria are related to different categories or kinds of objects, and that understanding criteria of identity is closely related to understanding the objects in question and the terms that refer to them. I think it is this use of the term "criterion of identity" that Geach picks up in describing his doctrine of the relativity of identity, which he takes to be a criticism of Frege's position, but one made from within an approach broadly sympathetic to Frege:

> I maintain it makes no sense to judge whether x and y are "the same" or whether x remains "the same" unless we add or understand some general term—the same F. That in accordance with which we thus judge as to the identity, I call a criterion of identity. (Geach 1962, p. 39)

The third use stems from Wittgenstein's use of the term "criterion" in his *Philosophical Investigations;* it is Anscombe's translation of Wittgenstein's "Kriterium" (1953, §56 and passim). The most famous use of the term is perhaps Wittgenstein's dictum that an internal process stands in need of an outward criterion (§ 580). The idea here is that, in order to understand what pain is and the way we use terms for pain, one needs to understand how people usually express their pain in different situations, and perhaps the typical causes of pain as well. Wittgenstein thought that describing the criteria we use to apply words was a more profitable philosophical occupation than looking for necessary and sufficient conditions. Criteria for X in this sense are connected with the nature of X and the meanings of the terms we use to talk about X's.

In his book, *Self-Knowledge and Self-Identity* (1963), Shoemaker's philosophical project is in many ways inspired by Wittgenstein's later work, especially his *Philosophical Investigations* (1953). Shoemaker explores the criteria for personal identity, rather than trying to come up with a definite list of conceptually necessary and sufficient conditions for it. Shoemaker explains criteria for X as evidence for X that could not fail to be good evidence for X; it's good evidence for X in any possible world.

From a more traditional point of view, the distinction between the factors that make something the case and those that constitute evidence for it is crucial. If something is "conceptually guaranteed" evidence for X, this should be explained in terms of the conditions that constitute of case of X. The use of the term "criteria of identity" can obscure this important distinction. But with either understanding, it seems clear that the criteria of identity are relative to the kind of item in question. If we confuse our criteria of identity (in either sense) with the relation of identity, the doctrine of relative identity will follow straightaway.

Bernard Williams's claim that criteria of identity must be logically one-one relations appears to rest on one or the other of these confusions. He says,

> [N]o principle can be a criterion of identity for things of type T if it relies only what is logically a one-many relation between things of type T (1957/1970 p. 21).

Using, for example, Shoemaker's explanation of the term in *Self-Knowledge and Self-Identity*, a criterion for personal identity would be a relation that could not possibly fail to be good evidence for personal identity. All that seems to be required of such a relation is that, in each possible world, it is good evidence for personal identity; all this seems to require is that, in each possible world, the relation in question be one-one with but a few exceptions.

I distinguish between identity, unity relations for various kinds of things K, and criteria of K-identity. Identity is the transitive, reflexive, and symmetrical relation that holds between any object and itself: if x is identical with y, then there is only one thing that is both x and y. The unity relation for K's is the relation that must hold between occurrences or stages or instances of K's for these to be occurrences, stages, or instances of a single K. Criteria of K-identity are relations between K occurrences, stages, or instances of K's that are evidence for being occurrences, stages, or instances of the same K; in a philosophical context, this usually implies criteria that are typically learned along with the vocabulary for talking about K's.

Identification, anticipation and identity In essay 8, I introduce a concept of identification that is intended to capture the bundle of attitudes we typically take towards our own futures and pasts, but which, I claim, we can also have to the futures and pasts of others. I return to some of these themes in essay 11, but the connection is not very clear. I will try to explain it here more fully, although, I must admit, with no great sense of finality.

In essay 8, I said that a person identifies with the participant in any event—past, future, or imaginary—when he imagines perceiving the event from the perspective of the participant. That is, the person must imagine seeing, hearing, smelling, tasting, feeling, thinking, remembering, etc., what the agent or the person to whom the happened event did (or will or might) see, hear, smell, taste, feel, think, remember, etc., as the event occured. And I said that this does not require taking oneself to be the agent or person to whom the event happened. This sounds rather phenomenological, and this was intended. Let's call this phenomenological identification.

There is another, more logical, sense of identification we need to consider too. Note the difference between "X remembers going to the store," and "X remembers X going to the store." For the first sentence to be true, X must take himself to be the person who had gone to the store. The second sentence may be true even if he does not take himself to be that person. The phenomenon of "subject-deletion under identity" exhibited by the first sentence seems to carry with it the implication that the rememberer identifies himself as the agent in the remembered event. I'll call this logical identification. When the subject is repeated but not deleted, as in the second case, this identification is suggested, but not logically implied. It would be rather strange for X to remember X, say, falling down a staircase without remembering having fallen down the staircase. But suppose X was quite drunk at the time, and the staircase was mirrored. X was watching someone, who just happened to be him, fall down the staircase as he fell down the staircase. But he was quite unaware that, as we might put it, he *himself* was falling down the staircase. We would use the second form to report such a "Castañeda case," in which the rememberer doesn't identify himself as the agent of the remembered act. We wouldn't use the first form.

The same distinction applies to forward-looking attitudes such as intention. If Elwood intends to attend a party, then he logically identifies with the person he plans to have attend the party. But it might be true that Elwood plans for Elwood to attend the party, without intending to attend. The reader can construct a case with mirrors or other such devices. Perhaps it would be philosophically convenient if the way that one logically identifies were also to phenomenologically identify, so the two amounted to the same thing. However, this doesn't seem to be the case.

When I remember marching at high school graduation, I don't imagine from the perspective I actually had—where all I could see was a wide swath of black between the shoulders of my vertically and alphabetically advantaged friend Henry Pangbourn—but from a perspective no one had, up above the entire ceremony. We have logical identification without phenomenological identification.

My claim in essay 8 is that we can have phenomenological identification without logical identification. I can phenomenologically identify with Napoleon at Waterloo, or my daughter in her championship basketball game, without logically identifying. I can imagine what it must have been like to be Napoleon in the battle at Waterloo, or Sarah at the moment of taking the crucial shot. I can imagine having the experiences they had, without imagining that I am either of them.

There seems to be a problem, and the claim needs to be qualified. My daughter makes a crucial shot towards the end of the game. Later I remember the shot. I identify phenomenologically with her as she takes it. I imagine taking the very shot I remember her taking. But then it seems I imagine taking the shot. So we have subject deletion, and logical identification. I must take myself to be the shooter. But I don't, do I?

I think the right thing to say is that in a sense I do, and in a sense I don't. In essays 9, 10, and 11, I talk about self-notions. Our self-notions are the normal repositories for information acquired in normally self-informative ways, and the normal motivators of normally self-effecting ways of acting. When I imagine taking the shot, the things I remember about the shot—the distance from the basket, the imposing size of the person guarding my daughter, the roar of the crowd, the pressure—are imagined as from the perspective of the shooter. My self-notion is a part of the representation. I am imagining the shouts as directed at me, the shot as initiated by me, and so forth. I imagine my muscles tensing, my arms straightening, the ball leaving my hands. Since my self-notion is involved, I am imagining myself to be the agent of the remembered action.

My self-notion is in fact linked to, and perhaps serves as, my John Perry notion, for I believe that I am John Perry. Now, maybe I am not. Maybe I am someone who stumbled across John Perry's computer, pretended to be him, and, lost in the thrill of this pretense, slowly forgot who he really was, and came to wrongly believe he was John Perry, and has by now sunk completely into this fantasy, beyond recovery. This seems rather unlikely, however. For one thing, it's not quite that thrilling to be John Perry, to be completely honest, so it's a little hard to see why someone would fall into this particular fantasy. For another, why wouldn't the real John Perry have shown up by now and kicked me off his computer?

For the moment or two I managed to imagine not being John Perry, the objective and subjective parts of my self-notion came apart, in a way that is explored in essay 11. Something like this occurs in cases in which we have phenomenological identification without logical identification. I am imagining that I am shooting Sarah's basket. My self-notion is engaged; my self-notion is of me, so I am a constituent of the content of the fantasy. On the other hand, my self-notion, for the duration of the imagining, is unlinked from my John Perry notion; the objective parts of my self-concept are bracketed off. I imagine being Sarah Perry taking the shot, in the sense that the information I use to construct the imagining comes from my memory of her shot. I imagine myself taking the shot, for it is my self-notion that is involved in the representation.

But I do not imagine John Perry taking the shot. There are a lot of variations of this sort of imagining. I may be a nervous sort of guy, but imagine taking the shot with Sarah's coolness and confidence. Or I may imagine taking it with my nervousness and my memories of previous athletic disasters.

In this sort of situation, our ordinary method of getting at the contents of our mental activities in terms of the conditions they impose on their subject matter is not quite satisfactory. It is more helpful to retreat to various kinds of what I call "reflexive content." An actual situation corresponding to my imagining would be one in which *this* imagining and the remembered shooting were done by the same person. It doesn't require that the actual shooter, Sarah, be doing the imagining, or that the actual imaginer, me, have done the shooting. Depending on exactly how I am imagining, it may require that this person be cool and calm, like Sarah was, or nervous and full of a sense of imminent failure, as I would have been. What connects the imagined proposition to me is not that I am a constituent of it, but that my imagining is a constituent of it, and what connects it to Sarah is not that she is a constituent of it, but that her shot is.

The story, then, is that phenomenological identification involves logical identification: since to imagine something from the perspective of the agent is to imagine that thing happening to or being done by oneself, one's self-notion is involved in the imagining. However, this does not require that one's objective concept of oneself be involved in the imagining, and typically it is not. As in "Cicero-Tully" type cases, describing the content of the attitude in terms of the proposition with the imaginer as a constituent is really too coarse to be illuminating. The problem is not that the imaginer is ignorant of who he is, but that for the purposes of the imagining, this knowledge is, to a lesser or greater extent, bracketed off.

Meaning and Content; the reflexive-referential theory Consider two utterances of "This book is boring." The first is uttered by a reader of the present book. The second is uttered by a reader of Nabokov's *Lolita*. The way I use the term "content," the two utterances have different contents. They say different things. The first is, I'm afraid, very plausible. The second is surely false. On the other hand, the two utterances involve the same sentence type, in the same language with the same meaning, as I use the word "meaning". The meaning of "This book is boring" is roughly that the book the utterer is attending to and calling others' attention to as they utter "this" typically causes boredom in those who attempt to read it.

Both meaning and content (in my sense) are closely related to truth-conditions. We gave the rough meaning of our sentence by saying under what conditions a statement of it is true.

If we take the meaning of a sentence, and fix an utterance of it, we obtain what I call the *reflexive* content. Let's call our two utterances u_I and u_L. The meaning above gives us two different truth-conditions for the two different utterances:

> The utterance u_I is true iff the book to which the speaker of u_I is attending typically causes boredom in those who attempt to read it.
>
> The utterance u_L is true iff the book to which the speaker of u_L is attending typically causes boredom in those who attempt to read it.

The two propositions on the right of the "iff" are quite different and independent. The first could be true and second false, or vice versa.

If we add the facts about reference to what is given, we obtain what I call the *referential content*. The facts about reference, as we are imagining them, are:

> The book to which the speaker of u_I is attending = *Identity, Personal Identity, and the Self*
>
> The book to which the speaker of u_L is attending = *Lolita*.

The referential contents are then:

> The utterance u_I is true iff *Identity, Personal Identity, and the Self* typically causes boredom in those who attempt to read it.

The utterance u_L is true iff *Lolita* typically causes boredom in those who attempt to read it.

I also call these the *subject matter* contents of the utterances. Usually philosophers have the subject-matter contents in mind when they think about the contents of utterances. I argue in *Knowledge, Possibility, and Consciousness* that this can lead to a bad philosophical mistake, which I call "the subject matter fallacy." In *Reference and Reflexivity* I develop what I call the "reflexive-referential" theory of meaning and content and show how it solves a number of problems about reference.

Relativity of identity; relativity of individuation I use the term "relativity of individuation" for a phenomenon to which Peter Geach called the attention of many philosophers in his books *Mental Acts* and *Reference and Generality*. As I construe it, the relativity of individuation is the fact that many phenomena can be individuated in different ways, depending on what we choose as the *unity relation*. Frege, whose writings influenced Geach, provides the example of a pack of cards. We can think of the pack as a single deck, or as four suits. The way I am thinking of it, decks are one thing, suits another, but they are both comprised of cards in a pack. The suit determined by the two of diamonds, for example, is comprised of all of the cards in the pack that share the diamond pattern with it.

Geach's own explanation of the relativity of individuation is a doctrine that he calls "the relativity of identity," and which he takes to be a departure from Frege, something Frege missed. I argue against this explanation in essays 1–3.

Unity Relations The unity relation for a kind of thing K is the relation that must obtain between two K-parts, K-occurrences, K-stages, or K-instances for them to be parts, occurrences, stages, or instances of a single K. When convenient, I use "occurrence" as a portmanteau phrase for these various relationships. When philosophers discuss personal identity, they are usually interested in the temporal unity relation for occurrences or stages of persons.

One can say that a K is *comprised of* a set of occurrences, all of which have R to one another. The K of which a is an occurrence is the K comprised of all and only the occurrences that have R to a. We can also call this *the K determined by a*. (More generally, *the K determined by a set X of R-related occurrences is comprised of all and only the occurrences that have R to all members of X.)

Let's use R_K for the unity relation for K's, and $=_K$ for K-identity. At a first pass, the connection between R_K and $=_K$ is this: If a and b are (temporal or spatial) K-occurrences, then

$R_K(a,b)$ iff the K of which a is a part $=_K$ the K of which b is a part

This isn't quite right, however, given the way we have set things up. There might not be a unique K of which a (or b) is a part. This situation is very familiar in the case of spatial unity. A stretch of a road might be a common part of more than one highway. When you drive across the Golden Gate Bridge, you are driving on both U. S. Highway 101 and California Highway 1. That stretch of road is a part of two highways, but it doesn't determine either of them in the sense of the last paragraph. It is less familiar in the case of temporal unity. If people split, as they are supposed to in a number of philosophical examples, one way to describe it would be that an earlier person-stage was a common temporal part of two persons, but didn't determine either of them. All we can say for sure is

If A and B are K's, and a determines A and b determines B, then $R_K(a,b)$ iff $A =_K B$

The logical properties of the unity relation for K's are not quite the same as the logical properties of K-identity. K-identity will be transitive, symmetrical, and weakly reflexive—anything that is K-identical with something is K-identical with itself. These properties assure that K-identity can be conceived as a restriction, to the domain of K's, of a universal relation of identity.

Any relation R that is transitive, symmetrical, and weakly reflexive is an *equivalence relation*. Equivalence relations break up their domain into mutually exclusive equivalence classes. Perhaps ideally the relation of K-unity should be an equivalence relation on K-occurrences. But this usually is not a matter of necessity, even when it is true. A relation can serve as a unity relation for a very practical and important kind of object even when it isn't an equivalence relation. Even though highways sometimes have common parts, for example, the units comprised by stretches of road that all connect with each other without doubling back (a sort of first-pass candidate for highway-unity) have interesting properties.

In a possible world in which R_K fails to be an equivalence relation, won't $=_K$ also fail? No; as we saw in the case of the Golden Gate

Bridge, failure of reference acts as a sort of fuse that prevents the exceptions to transitivity and symmetry from flowing from unity to identity.

A number of arguments in the personal identity literature seem to turn on not distinguishing the unity relation for identity. In essay 1, I argue that this is true of Geach's doctrine of relative identity, and in essays 3 and 6, I argue it is true of Williams's duplication arguments against memory accounts of personal identity.

Index